MAYOR OF MISSION

From the Cotton Patch to City Hall

A Story of Surrender, Service, and Survival

Lambert C. Mims
Former Mayor — Mobile, Alabama

An Autobiography

Llumina Press

ISBN: 1-59526-492-2

Printed in the United States of America by Llumina Press

Library of Congress Control Number: 2005934597

Dedication

This autobiography is dedicated to Lindsay and Katie Mims, my beautiful granddaughters, who have brought great joy to their "Big Daddy."

Table of Contents

Author's Preface
Plowboy, Peddler, Politician, Prisoner

It is my sincere hope that this book will inspire all who read it to never give up on their dreams. If they should, for whatever reason, along the way fail, try again until success is accomplished.

Plowboy

I have intentionally included a great deal about my upbringing on the farm to acquaint young people with the realities of rural life when I was young. Since the majority of young people today are brought up in urban areas, they don't have a clue as to what was involved in life on a farm in the early part of the twentieth century. There is a real danger of losing an important part of American life that taught millions to work hard and never give up.

Peddler

I went into business at an early age, was unprepared and didn't have my priorities in order, which led to failure. I hope that my story will challenge all who read it to keep their eyes on their dreams, and never give less than one hundred percent to whatever their goal may be.

My conversion experience when I was a traveling salesman, and the dramatic change it brought about in my life, is an example of what God can do in one's life if he or she surrenders to his will. All I have ever accomplished, or ever will accomplish, is because of my Christian experience and dependence upon God.

Politician

After my conversion, many doors opened for me in the church, but the one that set me on the road to where I really felt I belonged was the door to public service. In this section of the book, you will learn how I became involved in politics and organized my campaign to win. You will see some of the challenges I faced and opportunities I enjoyed during my twenty years as mayor and commissioner of the city of Mobile, one of Alabama's largest cities.

Prisoner

The most traumatic experience of my life was being falsely accused, tried, convicted without evidence, and caused to serve time at a federal prison camp. You will get a glimpse of how my family and I depended upon loyal friends and the grace of God to see us through a travesty of justice that could have destroyed families without faith.

You will also get a glimpse of how God used this unpleasant ordeal for his glory as He led me to become a chapel worker and witness in the prison compound. As I endeavored to be a blessing to others, I found myself being blessed the more. I may have touched hundreds of lives, but mine was touched the most, as by God's grace, I became a survivor.

It is my prayer that this book will help all realize that, regardless of the difficulties of the past or the circumstances of the present, God will see us through the storms of life, as he promised.

Lambert C. Mims

Acknowledgements

To all who have influenced my life for good, I am indebted. To my ancestors, my parents, my in-laws, and teachers, I acknowledge the great influence you have had on me.

To my wife and sons, who mean more to me than they could ever know, I am truly grateful to you.

To the many co-workers and employees, whose dedicated efforts made me look better than I could have expected, I am sincerely appreciative.

To Joe Pope, Louis Ferguson, and other Christian men whose witness brought me to know Christ as my Savior, I am eternally grateful.

To my pastors over the years, fellow deacons, the many denominational leaders and laymen whose paths I have crossed, to all who have helped me grow spiritually, I give praise to the Lord for the impact You have had on my life.

To the three ladies from Riverside Baptist who knocked on our door and invited us to church, I am thankful.

To Lisa Boothe, who spent many hours at the computer assisting with this manuscript; and Reecie Mims, my beloved wife, for her tireless editing, I surely owe a debt of gratitude for helping to make this possible.

Finally and most importantly, I acknowledge unashamedly that without the Almighty God, who saved me and set me free, I would be nothing. I am what I am by the grace of God; and to him be all the glory, praise, and honor.

MAYOR ON MISSION

Chapter 1

Born in a Cotton Patch

After my first political victory, a television news reporter asked me if I had anything to say to my parents, who lived on a farm some sixty miles away. Looking straight into the camera, feeling as though I were on a mission I responded "Mama and Daddy, I'm a long way from the cotton patch tonight!" This comment had great significance to me, especially since, thirty-five years prior to this exciting and important event, I was born in a cotton patch.

Fifty feet from the very room where I came into this world, on Easter Sunday, April 20, 1930, was a cotton patch. In fact, there was cotton planted on three sides of the house that my Grandfather built. He built it with lumber sawed from trees that once grew where the house stood. The long, straight rows of tiny, two-leaved cotton plants, just up from the spring-warmed earth, would turn the entire area into a blanket of white by summer's end.

It was near the turn of the century (1890), when my great-grandfather, David Cullen Mims, brought a tiny group of kinfolk and friends from the hills of North Monroe County Alabama, to the piney woods at the county's southern end. Here, they would clear the forest and saw the timbers and planks for their soon-to-be homes. The task of breaking and clearing new ground, uprooting stumps, and plowing ground that had never been disturbed was no easy task.

With lumber sawed by hand and primitive sawmills my grandfather, known as "Daddy Raymond," some of his brothers, and my great-grandfather, known as "Big Pa," constructed their homes. The virgin timber produced the long, wide boards used in period houses, with the large rooms, hallways, and porches that typify southern living. Wooden shingles provided roofing materials, while hand-planed planks were used as flooring. When scrubbed with corn shuck mops, they glistened with beautiful yellow hues.

1

The house where I was born was in sight of Big Pa's house, which was one of the most impressive in that part of the county. As time and many months and even years passed, the wilderness known as the piney woods became some of the most productive farmland in the state. My youngest brother, Bibb, and his son Buddy now farm most of this land, known as the Mims plantation, first cleared over a century ago by folk with a pioneering spirit and a will to work hard.

It was before the days of hospitals, when doctors made house calls, so with the visit of the local country doctor and the aid of a mid-wife, I was ushered into this world. Needless to say, I do not remember the day I was born, but according to my mother, as soon as this big boy was cleaned up, and she was able to admire her fourth son, Bessie, who was like a member of the family, had me in her arms. As the story goes, Bessie carried me to the kitchen and attempted to feed me a southern favorite—sweet potato. When mama asked what she was doing, Bessie replied, "This boy is hungry, and I'm giving him some sweet potato." Whether she actually fed me the sweet potato, or whether I could even take it that soon after being born, I don't know, but I do know that I love sweet potatoes in any form, whether baked, fried, pie, or casserole—to this day. The story goes that mama shouted to Bessie, "You are gonna kill that boy."

Well, it didn't kill me, but that's just indicative of the constitutions of both sides of my family. Down through the centuries, the Mims and Lamberts have had the pioneering spirit, producing civic leaders, successful farmers, merchants, traders, accomplished musicians, teachers, doctors, and politicians.

It was in 1657 that Thomas Mims, my ancestor, first set foot on this soil, arriving from England and landing at Flowerdieu Hundred, Lancaster County, Virginia, near Jamestown. There was another Thomas Mims, who served in the First Assembly of Virginia, held on July 30, 1623. I am not sure what the connection is, but these two Thomas's must have been related.

The Mims family made their way from the coastal area of Virginia inland, and after nearly a hundred years, on southward to North Carolina. From there they took the Federal Road, which was mostly a trail chopped out of the woods, to West Florida, which was Spanish territory. In 1784, several families of Mims made their way to Tensaw, Alabama, which was Mississippi territory, then under United States control.

It was there, on August 30, 1813, that Samuel Mims and his brother David lost their lives in the massacre at Fort Mims, where Creek Indians, led by William Weatherford, better known as "Red Eagle," slaughtered five hundred and fifty-five men, women, and children (Indians, whites, and blacks).

Peter Joe Hamilton wrote in his book, *Colonial Mobile*, "It was the blood of gray-headed Sam Mims crying from the ground and his spirit that opened the interior of Alabama to civilization."

Albert Jones Pickett, in his book, *History of Alabama*, wrote, "The honorable David Mims, attempting to pass to the half finished bastion, received a large ball in the neck…A cruel warrior cut around his head and then waved his hairy scalp exultantly." I am a descendant of David Mims, of Fort Mims' fame. From the ashes of this massacre, the worst in the nation's history, the Mims and the other few survivors scattered. My folks ended up in North Monroe County, near Indian Springs, where many of them were buried.

Someone traced the Lamberts, my mother's family, back to Oliver Cromwell where Sir John Lambert was a general, and one of Cromwell's top men in 1647, and even centuries beyond, to Ralph de Lamber, one of the nobles from Falaise, France, who defeated the Saxon King Harold of England, at the Battle of Hastings in 1066. Lambert roots go even further back to Charlemagne, Emperor of the West, born in 742, and to Clovis, Frankish King of Cologne in 420.

The first Lambert to come to America is a mystery. The earliest Lamberts I can trace my lineage to were Andrew and James, who settled in the colony of North Carolina in 1750. By the fall of 1756, Andrew and James had relocated to Indian country in Georgia.

Tuesday, May 17, 1791, was a red-letter day for the Lambert family. According to George Washington's diary, he dined at the Lambert home. He went on to record the number of mileposts carved on the trees along the trail from Savannah, which corresponds with the location of James Lambert's place.

In 1818, Andrew Lambert, Robert Lambert, and Isaac Lambert—brothers—and a total of sixteen adults and children made the long journey from Georgia to Claiborne, located on the banks of the Alabama River, in Monroe County, Alabama. There were an equal number of slaves on the journey, belonging mainly to the elder brother, Andrew.

At the time, Claiborne was a bustling river town, where all kinds of commodities were shipped to and from the area by steamboat; with Montgomery to the north, Mobile and the Gulf of Mexico to the south, Claiborne was well situated. The Lamberts bought land, became farmers on a large scale, and got involved in community affairs, as well as the Baptist Church.

It is said that my great-grandfather, Joseph Franklin Lambert, born in 1827, fought for the Confederates in the Civil War, and upon returning home, fell off his horse at his front gate, and died. My grandfather, Joseph Franklin Lambert Jr., born in March of 1858, married his second cousin, Ruth Jane Lambert, in 1888. "Mr. Frank," as he was known, purchased land from a Native American family named Dees. President James Buchanan had granted the land to them in 1858. The house where my grandparents brought up their ten children, including my mother, Carrye, stands today across the road from Poplar Springs Baptist Church, which was built on land donated by my grandfather. My brother Bibb and his son also own this farmstead, known as the Lambert Plantation.

Mr. Frank was a farmer, timber man, and community leader, actively involved in the church, the Masons, and other organizations most of his life. He was well known for his fishing skill, and people from far and near vied for his time to go fishing with him. It was said, "Mr. Frank knows where they are, and if he can't catch them, no one can." I suppose my sons, Dale and Danny, received some of those fishing genes from their great-grandfather, because both of them love fishing.

"I am a long way from the cotton patch," was my response to a television news reporter, on the night of my first campaign victory, when asked what I had to say to my parents, who were watching some sixty or seventy miles away.

Thirty-five years had passed since the day I was born beside the cotton patch, on land that had been cleared by my grandfather and great-grandfather. I had come a long way. I was soon to assume the position of mayor and commissioner of Mobile, the second largest city in the state, founded in 1702, long before Alabama became a state.

Yes, I was a long way from the cotton patch.

Chapter 2

Big Mama's Cookies, Mama's Churn, Daddy's Belt

It has been a blessing to be able to recall events from early childhood. I remember going to Big Ma's big house, just down the road from where we were living in Daddy Raymond's house, the house where I was born, when I was no more than two years old.

I don't remember much about my great-grandmother, except she was old and very kind. The thing I remember most was her cookie jar. It's amazing I remember this, because she died in 1932, and I couldn't have been more than two and a half years old. Vividly embedded in my mind is how she would go to the big, brown, ceramic jar and re-move some of the nicest, most delicious, fresh-baked cookies one could ever wish for. Of course, this left an indelible impression upon my young mind; I suppose that is why I still love cookies. Cookies of any variety I love, but especially those baked on the order of Big Ma's de-lectable sugar cookies.

One of my earliest memories of Mama was of her sitting by the fireplace, with the churn on the hearth, churning butter. A fire warmed the room on winter days. There she was, sitting as close as she could to keep warm, just a-churning.

The dasher moved up and down through the wooden top of the ceramic urn at Mama's command. Her hand and arm hard at work, the buttermilk splashing, this is the picture stenciled in my mind—Mama churning by the fireplace, in milk-splattered shoes.

I have never forgotten one of my uncle's new cars, either. I was about three years old; it was before we moved to the McKenzie place, where I grew up, which was about a mile to the west of Big Pa's house. Most cars at the time were either black or dark blue, but on this occasion, one of Daddy's brothers drove up in a bright red coupe. It had big chrome headlights, a bright chrome radiator grill, sweeping front fenders, and a rumble seat. As I grew older, I realized it must have been a Chrysler or Desoto, but my recollection of my perspective at the age of three is that this was the most beautiful car I had ever seen.

I remember how much fun it was for me to climb up on the step plates and get into the rumble seat, a seat located in the trunk on early automobiles. It opened up from the front into a compact, but comfortable, seat for two, which was fun to occupy, except during rains and extremely cold weather.

In 1934, my father purchased the old McKenzie place, a 140-acre farm, located west of Big Pa and Big Ma's house, which we always called "the Big House." There were fields as far as you could see on both sides of the graveled road, known as Alabama Highway 59.

My daddy always had a good car or pick-up truck, which was a sign of prosperity during the Great Depression in the early thirties. We were not rich, nor were we poor. Poor people had no property, no cars, and lived on other folk's farms, working as sharecroppers and tenant farmers. I remember at least two things about our dark green, four-door Chevrolet: It was a nice car, just a plain-Jane model, but it was new and smelled good, just like all new cars.

Daddy was going somewhere one rainy, dreary day, and I wanted to go with him. Usually, he was good about letting us go with him, but on this day, he said, "No, I have business to take care of; you can't go."

In my little four-year-old mind, I devised a plan. I decided to crawl between the seats and get down low so he would not see me. When we got up the road a-ways, I would jump up and he wouldn't want to turn around to bring me back home. Good plan, I thought.

I made my move and worked my plan. I heard daddy get into the car, place his foot on the starter, throw it in gear, and away we went. The plan is going great, I thought. After a few minutes, maybe three or four miles up the road, I jumped up. Immediately, my plan began to unravel.

"Boy!" my daddy scolded, "What are you doing in this car? I told you that you could not go with me. I'm taking you back to the house, and I'm going to wear you out!"

He turned around, drove to the house, yanked me out of the car, and literally wore me out with his belt. Then he took me to Mama, and said, "Watch this boy 'til I get in the car." Mama wanted to know what happened. I'm not sure how I explained it at the time, but I can tell you I received the whipping of my life. I still remember it today. It was a ride to remember.

Another thing that left an imprint on my mind was the night the barn burned, and I saw my daddy running to get the '34 Chevrolet from under the shed attached to the burning barn. Next to the living quarters, barns were the most important buildings on the farm. They contained the hay and corn for the livestock and the seed for next years' plantings. A barn was a storage area for farm tools and equipment and was surrounded by the compound or lot that held mules or other livestock.

Daddy saved the '34 Chevy and was able to open the gates, allowing the mules to escape, but the barn burned to the ground. The cause was never discovered. It was a time when people would deliberately set fire to others' buildings, just for spit. Fires were sometimes caused by spontaneous combustion brought on by hay and grain that hadn't completely dried before being stored, or by oil rags balled up from repair work. Sometimes rats would find matches and chew on them, starting fires.

The image of the burning barn has stuck with me, despite the security of smoke alarms. Before going to bed, I always do two things: check the doors to make certain they are locked, and sniff for smoke. Both are good habits to get into, whether you live on a farm or in the city.

Back then, steamboats delivered goods to landings all along the Alabama River, not very many miles from our house. Merchants would meet the steamboat to pick up the merchandise they ordered from Mobile, Montgomery, and Selma wholesalers.

There were several small general mercantile stores in our area, mostly located at the main crossroad. Daddy was very good about rewarding us with small packages of candy or, my favorites, ginger snaps or "zu zu" cookies. When he didn't remember to bring us anything, he would say, "Well boys, the steamboat didn't run, no candy or cookies today." I can still hear him.

I remember how it thrilled me, when I was between four and six years old, to try to follow my daddy as he walked through the cotton fields. In the spring, he would check the growth and decide whether the crops needed rain or the grass needed hoeing; in the early summer, he would check the blooms that started close to the ground and moved upward as the summer progressed, with varying colors indicating the age of the plant. Then he checked the bolls that came from the blooms. Soon would appear the weevils that could easily destroy the crops. Then, in late summer, daddy would look in on the opening bolls and silky white cotton that came forth, and by the end of the summer, the fields would be a blanket of white, as far as the eye could see.

As hard as I tried, my short legs could not keep up with daddy, but I did my best to step in the tracks where he had stepped, in the cotton patch back home.

Chapter 3

Bashful Boy's Long Hair
and Wet Pants

I was six years old, and had hair that looked like Shirley Temple's. Men and boys with long hair are nothing new. I received my first haircut the day before I went to school. I do not know why my parents wanted me to have long hair. It could have been that they had already had three boys, and wanted a girl. If that was the case, they never got their wish. The two that followed me were also boys, making a total of six boys in my immediate family.

From early photos, I can admit that the long hair looked nice, and I've been told that everyone commented on how beautiful it was. It must have been a job keeping a boy's hair clean, especially when we played in the dirt, building roads with toy tractors and dump trucks, never mind the rainy days, when we played in mud.

The day before school started, daddy took me to Frisco City. On the town's main street was a barbershop, owned by Mr. Hayes. He gave me my first haircut. Mama had Daddy bring those locks home, where she kept them until her death; I now have them in my possession.

During the thirties, things were turbulent in the south. I can't remember all the details; we were brought up to respect everyone, regardless of color. We were taught to call people Mister and Miss, and treat people as we wanted to be treated.

There were many African-Americans on our place and the adjoining farms. The only playmate I had, other than my next youngest brother, was a black boy my age. Junior Boy Beasley and I enjoyed many a day, playing under the house, where it was cool. Houses were built on pillars at least three to four feet off the ground, which provided an ideal playground. I remember one occasion, when Junior Boy and I got the bright idea that we would build a campfire, of all places, under the house where we played.

I had slipped into the house and got a big box of kitchen matches, the kind that would strike anywhere. I made it out of the house with the matches, but thankfully, Mama caught us, and kept Junior Boy and me from burning our house down. Mama sent Junior Boy home and gave me a thrashing with a switch from the yard broom, one I remember to this day.

Although we lived in a segregated society, there were no racial problems on the Mims farm. However, some whites terrorized blacks and right-thinking white folk. They were called "nightriders." I remember on Saturday evenings, late, how my daddy would call us in from the front yard, away from the highway. He would say, "The nightriders are riding tonight, and I don't want you boys out front." He abhorred their actions, and didn't want us to witness them. He knew who they all were by the vehicles they drove, and they knew that he didn't approve of their cowardly acts.

While he lay on his deathbed, seventy-five years of age, I questioned him as to whether he was ready to meet the Lord, and he responded in the affirmative. I asked my Daddy why he had quit going to church. (Incidentally, he'd had the longest arm of any person I ever knew. When he did still attend church with Mama and us boys, if you didn't "Be still, and sit up straight" during the church service, he would reach way across Mama and pinch a plug out of our legs.) I pressed him hard.

"Why did you quit the church? You made things right with the Lord a long time ago; you accepted Him as your Savior; so why did you quit?"

Well, he never said, specifically, who or what caused it, but the implication was that some of the people leading and participating in the services would be out the night before with the nightriders, terrorizing black people and poor whites. He couldn't stand the blatant hypocrisy, and he wouldn't go back.

Six years old, with my first haircut, I met the school bus that fall. It was a frightening day for me. Even though one brother, who was graduating high school that year, met the bus with me, I was still scared. This was the biggest yellow bus I had ever seen. It looked like it was a mile long. It had bench seats down each side and two benches down the middle. Kids sat facing each other, and the older boys and girls, high schoolers, I learned later, liked to play knees. By the time I was that age, we had modern buses, with the seats facing the front and an isle down the middle.

Being that we were one of the last stops on the route, when I boarded the bus, it was just about full. I had to push my way through all those knees, with the other kids and teens screaming and growling. I was so bashful, and I thought they were all directing their remarks toward me.

Even into my later years, I was so bashful I did not want to be around people I did not know. When strangers came over, I would leave the room or get off the porch and sometimes go behind the house and hide. I do not know why I had such an inferiority complex, but thank God, he helped me overcome it. I will go into my deliverance from timidity later, but for now, let us go back to the first day of school.

We arrived at the school, seven miles up a bumpy, dusty, gravel road from home. The J.U. Blacksher High School at Uriah, although a small County School, housing grades 1-12, was the biggest building I had ever seen. The oil-soaked, splintered wood floors, the long halls, the loud bells, the potbelly stoves, and windows so high off the floor I couldn't see out, made me even more frightened. The first-grade teacher was nice enough, but I had never been in a room with twenty other six-year-olds. I had only played with Junior Boy, my brother Maston, and occasionally a cousin or two, who came to visit us, or who I met on occasion at Granddaddy's house. I was horrified. When recess came, there were all these other kids in the hall. I was more horrified.

I needed to go to the bathroom, but didn't know where the boy's toilet was and was too afraid to ask. I was accustomed to outdoor toilets, or outhouses. I went as long as I could, and you guessed it, I wet my pants. When play period came, I rolled around on the grass, in the sun, and hoped my pants would dry. I was ashamed and embarrassed and timid, and my whole world had changed. My hair was gone — even my looks had changed. I felt inferior to the other kids, and all I wanted was to be back in the cotton patch and not to have to face people. Although I made good grades through all twelve years, this timidity, and that streak of inferiority, was with me all through school, even into young adulthood. I am so grateful that God helped me overcome it.

Chapter 4

Outhouses, Foot Logs, and Rolling Stores

In the thirties, only a few people could afford automobiles, so the majority of folk had to depend on mules and wagons for transportation. Few had horses. Mules were used extensively to do the farm work, but on Saturday afternoons and Sundays, you would see many families riding their wagons to the nearest crossroads store or church.

Many poorer people had no manner of transportation at all, since they could not afford to buy a mule. How were they to get their commodities? A good question! The commodities were brought to them by way of the "rolling store." In the south, during the 30s & 40s, even into the 50s, the rolling stores provided a great service to the rural south. What was a rolling store? It was a truck with a specially built body and rows of shelving that accommodated almost everything you could buy at the grocery store, miles away.

The rolling stores had routes, and on a certain day, you could count on the operator being in front of your house at a certain time. Everything from kerosene for the oil lamps, to sides of bacon and bolts of cloth was available. Underneath the main body, along the frames of the rolling stores, were crates to hold live chickens that had been traded for merchandise. Most country folk would trade eggs, cane syrup, chickens, or even pigs, for salt, baking soda, flour, for whatever they could not produce. The rolling store is long remembered by every young person brought up in the country. One of the highlights of the day the rolling store ran was meeting the store with eggs, to be swapped for candy or cookies. I remember well the people that lined up by the highway, when they heard the rolling store horn, several miles away.

There was no electrical power in those days; therefore, there was very little refrigeration. A few people could afford kerosene-burning units, but most relied upon the iceman, who came each week on a regular basis. He placed the appropriate-sized block in the box on the back porch, where the melt dripped through a funnel, out a hole in the floor, and onto the ground beneath.

Another door-to-door service was the fish peddler. Many people fished the rivers for catfish and would dress them and bring them to your door in big iceboxes built on the backs of their trucks. This was not only a way for the fisherman to make a living, but it provided fresh fish for those who wouldn't be able to make it to the fish market in town.

Others went door-to-door, bringing commodities such as coffee, clothing, lightning rods, and various medicines. Many of these products stick in my mind, but the one that is the most vividly recalled was a salve in a big, round tin can. It was carbolic salve and could be used on animals and growing boys alike. If one of us cut or scratched ourselves, Mama would break out the "cure-all" salve, smear some over the wound, and we would be on our way to healing. If the dog got skinned up, the same salve was applied. If the mules or milk cows needed attention, they got the salve or liniment, which was sold by the same door-to-door peddler.

Another exciting activity for six- to eight-year-olds was meeting the mailman. The post office was seven miles away, and rural routes extended out into the area. We were on Rural Route #1, and you could almost set your clock by Mr. Elbert Hayles, who was our mail carrier all the years of my youth. He came at eleven a.m., and always stopped at our mailbox, because we subscribed to the *Mobile Register*. If nothing else came, the paper came, which was amazing since it was printed just before midnight, sixty-five miles away. Mr. Hayles was a friendly man and would always take a minute or two from his busy schedule to speak a kind word to all the kids who were so anxious to run to the mailbox to get the mail.

Between the ages of six and ten, boys were not quite old enough to handle large animals or the mules that were used to plow the crops, but we were assigned chores we could handle. We would draw water for the livestock, by hand, from the water well, which was a hole, eighteen to twenty-four inches wide, drilled into the ground, and lined with wood planks. A bucket connected by a rope to a windlass, a round wooden spindle with a crank, had to be let down to the water level. A flap in the bottom of the three-foot long, eight-inch wide bucket would let water in; when it was pulled up, the flap would close, holding the water inside. Sometimes, it seemed we drew hundreds of buckets of water, usually in the afternoon, everyday.

There were no pumps or running water, and therefore, no plumbing. Drinking water was kept in a bucket on a shelf on the back porch, where a long-handled dipper was available for drinking. A wash pan was there as well, for washing our hands. When working in the fields, we drank from springs in the branch heads adjoining the fields, using a tin can usually found hanging on a convenient limb. If one was not available, you drank from your cap, or got down on your knees and used cupped hands to bring the water to your mouth.

The toilet facility was a two-hole outhouse, sitting some distance from the backside of the house. Rolls of tissue were unheard of in those days, but there was always newspaper or an outdated *Sears Roebuck Catalog* for your convenience. In the summertime, our bathtub was a number three washtub, filled with water early in the day, and left out in the sun to heat. It was always placed in the back yard, and since we were all boys in our family, no one cared about stripping off his clothes in the yard to get a bath.

Washing clothes was a chore, since it was done by hand. An iron wash pot was a familiar sight at all the farmhouses. It was used to boil the clothes, and a big wooden paddle was used to beat the dirt out. After the clothes were rinsed and rung out, they were pinned on a line to dry. Our clothes generally consisted of kaki shirts and pants, or maybe blue overalls. Mama preferred washing the kakis.

Long before disposable diapers, you could always tell when there was a new baby in the house because there would be dozens of fluttering diapers on the clothesline.

One of the highlights of my youth was walking across the creek on a foot log. To get to the cotton patch on the farther side of the farm, we had to cross the creek, a small stream of clear water produced by springs. You either had to wade, which meant getting your pants legs wet, or walk the log. It was fun trying to walk the log. It was a real balancing act; sometimes we would make a misstep or slip, and we'd get wet all over, instead of just our pant legs. It was still fun going to the back cotton patch.

Chapter 5

Mules, Milk Cows, and Drunken Hogs

When I was about ten years old, the cotton patch took on a much more significant meaning than when I was simply trying to keep up with daddy as he checked his crops. I was old enough to learn how to handle the mules, hold the plow, and do all the other things connected with farming. All farm boys were expected to work. There was plowing, planting, fertilizing, hoeing, chopping, cultivating, and gathering the crop.

We learned quickly; it was expected of us. We all had to do our part. It was not easy to plow a straight furrow, or keep the mule from trodding down the cotton or corn. It was not easy to learn how to hook the mule up to the plow or get him to back up, go forward, or turn to the right or left. The reins controlled the bit in the mule's mouth and how clearly you commanded "gee" or "haw" determined how straight your lines were. "Gee" meant to go right, and "haw" meant to go left. Mules could be very stubborn and hard to deal with, hence the old proverb, "stubborn as a mule." We rode them home for lunch, which was fun. The mule, when it heard the dinner bell ring, even though we were a great distance away in the field, knew it was time to go. We unhooked the mule from the plow, jumped aboard, and headed toward the house. It was always easier to get them going home than to return to the field. Hoeing and chopping cotton were the things I disliked most. A hoe handle just never did fit my hands, but I had to do it, unless I could get Mama to have something at the house she needed me to do.

At a certain point during the plants' growth period, they needed a little boost to spur their growth and production. Nitrate of soda, a white granular substance, had to be distributed by hand, a little portion to each plant. If you didn't take care to do this correctly, a few days after the next rain, your sins would find you out.

During the cultivating season, we would stop plowing at mid-morning for a rest—the plowers and the mules needed it. If we were on the side of the farm near Marshall's store, we could, for ten cents, get a big Royal Crown Cola and a box of crackers, and sit on the plow stock while we ate and drank our goodies.

Milking is one chore I never cared for much. Sitting or kneeling by a cow's side, wiping her bag and teats, and coaxing milk out of them was not something to which I looked forward. On cold mornings, it was worse. Some cows were bad about kicking, sometimes kicking the milk pail out of my hand. Nearly every cow swung her tail, hitting me in the face, which was not much fun, especially when the tail was full of cockleburs.

During the summer months, when the cultivation period had ended and the crops were laid by, we still had chores, like cleaning fencerows and repairing fences and barns. There was never a vacation on the farm. There was always something to do, and as we grew up, we learned to do it all.

Chopping or splitting stove wood was a regular chore. We usually used pine and it burned rapidly in the stove. A wood stove had eyes for the iron pots to sit in so they would heat faster. There was an oven and a water reservoir for heated water. It took a lot of wood to keep it going, and you can guess who was responsible for keeping plenty of wood for the stove. I can hear Mama saying, "You boys get some wood in here; it's getting kinda low."

We always had hogs, and it was a daily job to feed and water them, unless they were grazing in a pasture where there was a stream. We had chickens, too, which were a very dependable food source. First, we had plenty of fresh eggs, with some to sell from time to time. Of course, fried chicken, rice, gravy, and the trimmings was regular fare on Sundays. We didn't have a refrigerator, so we couldn't keep fresh-dressed fryers. Mama would just step down to the chicken yard and pick one out for lunch. She would ring the chicken's neck and pluck the feathers, and in a few minutes, the chicken would be sizzling in hot grease, on its way to our dinner table.

Then, there was the garden. Mama always had a nice garden, with a great variety of vegetables. We had one old mule that was slow and about used up; he was used for gardening. We all had to be very careful when we plowed or worked the garden. If we didn't do it just right, Mama would get us. We learned early how to make holes in a bed and plant sweet potato draws (plants). First, you would make the hole a number of inches apart, then place water in the fresh hole, then drop the draws in, just right; another worker would come along behind with a stick and pat the earth down around the plant. In late summer, we'd dig the potatoes up and place them in mounds, layered with pine straw, covered with planks and dirt, and left in storage against winter freezes. Behind every farmhouse, you could find tepee-like mounds containing that southern favorite, sweet potatoes.

During the great depression in the rural south, the garden was an instrument of survival. Money to buy groceries, or anything else, was very scarce, so every family depended on the garden for fresh fruits and vegetables. Every mother canned fruits and vegetables for the winter. The father dried peas, apples, peaches, and other items for the family, to be used during the off seasons. Corn provided grits, a southern standby that was always on the breakfast table. Cornmeal was a necessity for making bread to go along with the vegetables.

We raised hogs to slaughter for meat and lard, which is fat, cooked down from fried pork, and used for cooking and making soap. There were also pecans to pick up in the fall. This was one of the most back-breaking jobs on the farm. No one really liked to pick up pecans, except Mama. I remember her, in her early nineties, picking up pecans under her favorite tree in the front yard.

One of the most hilarious things that happened during my childhood took place at the cane mill, or syrup mill. We grew our own sugar cane, and in the fall, it would be stripped of its chaff and run through a mule-drawn mill, where all the juice was squeezed out. The juice was piped or funneled to the evaporator pan on one end, next to the fire and chimney, where it was heated. When the process was complete, pure cane syrup would come out the other end, and be stored in one-gallon tin cans. We'd sell some, but we always kept enough back to last us through the year. As part of the process of cooking the cane juice, several people were kept busy skimming off residue and tossing it over into nearby barrels. Over a period of weeks, the residue, which contained some of the cane juice, would ferment, and actually turn into low-grade alcohol.

On this particular morning, we heard the hogs squealing, and when we looked toward the syrup mill, we could see them running backwards, round and round, and doing all kinds of strange things that hogs don't usually do. We couldn't imagine what had happened; then we saw that the hogs had gotten into the barrels of fermented juice and gotten themselves drunk. It was a sight to behold—a herd of drunken hogs running to and fro, making every strange sound you could ever imagine.

Growing up on the farm was a wonderful experience. God bless country folks, especially those from the cotton patch.

Chapter 6

War Changes Things

Teen years have always been difficult. Young people begin to have ideas of their own, yet they are still under their parent's control. My folks were pretty strict with us, and most of the time, knew exactly where we were and what we were doing.

As I grew older, I thought I should be allowed to go places and do things, but Daddy said, "No, you don't need to go; you don't need to be over there."

"But Daddy—" I would say. Daddy's reply, "The answer is no."

There was a time, when I was thirteen or fourteen that I thought my daddy was the meanest man I knew. I was so wrong. As I grew older, I realized how wise he was. I really didn't need to be at some of the places I wanted so badly to go.

For instance, nearly every Saturday night, at somebody's house down below where we lived, there would be a dance. Several guitar, banjo, and fiddle players in the area would gather to make music. Folk pushed the furniture back, and the front room became a dance floor. People came from far and near—some to meet girls, some to have fun, some to get drunk, and some to raise sand and fight. It was no wonder my daddy would say, "You don't have any business there."

There weren't very many places to go, except in the summer, when everybody went to the swimming hole. My folks told me to stay away from the water, so I never learned to swim, which left me out. I would just stand on the bank in my timid way, just wishing I could enjoy what the others were doing. Of course, there were high school ball games that I attended; and as I grew older, I even played a little. Here again, my timidity hindered my ability to play. I didn't like everyone looking at me. I learned to drive by watching my older brothers. The teens were frustrating years for me.

In May of 1941, my oldest brother was killed by a load of saw logs as they rolled off his truck, breaking him up and knocking him into the log pond alongside the sawmill. I remember that day as if it were yesterday. I had never before seen my mother and father totally broken. Their grief was terrible, as they prepared for the funeral and buried their oldest son, twenty-five-year-old Joe Frank.

As was the custom in the country, Joe Frank's body was laid out in the front room of our home. People came by the hundreds to express their condolences, and it left a lasting impression on me. The sadness and sorrow of seeing my parents suffer was embedded in my mind, reinforced by the multitudes that came to his funeral service—cars and trucks were lined up for miles in the procession that followed him to his resting place, in the town of Monroeville, the county seat. His remains lie now beside my father and mother, beneath the shadows of the markers of our grandfather, great-grandfather, and many other relatives, who have long been gone from this earth.

In that same year, on December 7, we gathered around the radio, a big cabinet containing a number of huge batteries, the same radio that many of our neighbors would often gather around to hear the Grand Ole Opry, or the heavyweight boxer, Joe Lewis, knock people out. This night, we heard President Franklin D. Roosevelt announce that the Japanese had attacked our naval fleet in Hawaii. I can still hear him say, "This day shall live in infamy," and "the only thing we have to fear is fear itself." America was at war! What terrible news.

My two older brothers were the right age for military service. In a short time, they were gone. Jeff, who made Major, was in Europe, with General Dwight D. Eisenhower, and David, an MP, was in Puerto Rico. A red, white, and blue flag, and two stars, were placed in the front window, indicating that two from this family were serving their country. Thank God, they both returned, without injury.

The day World War II ended is etched in my mind. I will always hear the bell ringing, as the local Methodist minister drove through the countryside, with a big bell on a trailer behind his car, with a rope hitched to the bell. He rang and rang and rang. Thank God for the victory.

That war changed our lives. Every family had someone involved in the war or the war effort. Many young men went off to battle. Many others went to work in shipyards in Mobile. Busses carried load after load of men ineligible for military service, and women, who took advantage of the opportunities to work in war-related plants such as shipyards and aircraft factories. Thousands of civilians worked at the air bases in Mobile and Pensacola.

People who had suffered during the Great Depression, who couldn't afford the necessities of life, now had gainful employment. Everybody was busy, even children, buying savings stamps and war bonds. The war was on everyone's minds. Although the ration program limited what and how much one could buy, things were looking up, and Roosevelt's theme song, "Happy Days Are Here Again," rang ever so true.

Meanwhile, we rushed to the mailbox everyday, to see if there was word from our brothers or cousins, John Lee and Glenn Lambert, or our Uncle Curtis Lambert, serving with General Douglas McArthur in the Philippines.

Out in the cotton patch, work had to go on. Those who remained, sons of the farm owners and sharecroppers all put forth unparalleled efforts to produce food and fiber to keep our country going.

Mama didn't drive, the older brothers were gone, and Daddy didn't attend church, so we were left without drivers to take us there, which was the only place we could go, except school and work. We didn't have a movie theater nearby, but I remember a field trip our class made to see *The Wizard of Oz*. It was being shown at a theater in Atmore, some twenty miles away. The movie was tremendous. Not only was it entertaining, but also it was educational to country kids, who had never seen anything like it. After the movie, another boy and I went upstairs to the boys' room, while the teacher put all the other kids on the bus. Thinking that everyone was out of the building, the attendant locked the door. When Billy and I left the boys' room and came down to the lobby, we discovered we were locked in. We were terrified that we would be left behind. What a frightening experience. Thankfully, the teacher took a headcount, and found herself two short. Immediately, she came back to look for us. If we had not been so obviously scared, the teacher would have really given us "what for." Instead, we received a mild reprimand.

On late summer evenings, one of our favorite past-times was watching and catching lightning bugs. The smell of cotton opening, combined with hot summer nights, and the stillness of the homestead after a long, hard day was an ideal setting in which to witness farm boys and girls run and play, seeing who could put the most fireflies in a jar.

Another phenomenon that I have never been able to explain is one that I, and many others, have observed on numerous occasions in the summer evenings. Around cotton-picking time, we would see bright lights along the branch heads of the cotton fields. It would become spectacularly bright with the eerie, tiny, flame-like images glistening in the night. Whole areas, a quarter-mile wide, would light up. The country folk called it "foxfire," and I've since learned it is caused by gaseous vapors rising from the ground in those low-lying areas. One thing I do know is that as I remember these awesome sights I realize the impression that was left with me.

By this time, I was thirteen or fourteen years old, and wanting to do anything but plow, pick cotton, gather corn, milk cows, or anything else to do with a farm; all I wanted was to get away. I was a frustrated teenager, and I wanted to be a long way from the cotton patch.

Chapter 7

Sunday Afternoon Ritual

Nearly every Sunday afternoon, we would go to Granddaddy Lambert's house. It was a big, two-story house, built in 1879, on land acquired from a Native American family. It had come into the Dees' possession via a land grant signed by President James Buchanan in 1858.

There was a long lane down to the house that could be seen for a mile across the cotton fields. Over the field and across the road was the church and cemetery, on land given to the community by my grandfather. He was a deacon, an active member of the Poplar Springs Baptist Church for more than fifty years, and was buried along side my grandmother. You can see the cemetery from the porch of the house where they lived and raised ten children.

I remember two things most about Grandpa and the church. One is that he always walked across the field, climbed the fence, and walked down the aisle just as the service began. Sometimes his trouser legs would be wet because of the dew on the plants in the fields he had just crossed. The other thing I remember is that he always took his seat by a window, just to the left of the preacher. There he'd spit his favorite Blood Hound chewing tobacco out the window as the preacher held forth on the word of God. Occasionally, there would be a loud "Amen," which indicated Grandpa agreed with what the preacher was saying.

Those afternoon trips to Grandpa's house, after our Sunday dinner, were like a ritual. On the Sundays we were at home, in the summer, we made ice cream. We took the ice from the old icebox on the back porch, chipped it up, and placed it and a layer of rock salt around a bucket of custard mama had prepared. The rock salt kept the ice from melting. Then the real work began. We'd put the ice cream maker on the edge of the porch, and we boys would take turns standing on the ground and turning the crank, which caused the custard to freeze. After about thirty minutes, we all were able to enjoy Sunday afternoon ice cream.

When we arrived at Grandpa's, we always found him sitting on the front porch. Grandma would usually be in the kitchen, which was out behind the main house, attached by a walkway, to help protect the main body of the house in the event of a kitchen fire.

Grandpa would greet us with a pleasant, but unemotional welcome. Maybe he would make a little conversation, but in those days, kids my age only spoke when spoken to. We sat and listened to my daddy and grandpa talk about the crops or some current issue. It seemed farming and the conditions of the crops were always the main topic. Sometimes they'd discuss politics, although we didn't know what was going on. Mama went to the kitchen, where her mother was, and they talked for hours. We boys would go outside and explore the places we had already been, time and time again.

A lot of Sunday afternoons, other men would come and grandpa would excuse himself to go out by the barn or equipment shed or blacksmith shop. There, they would spend what seemed like hours to me, just sitting on a log, talking. Many times when we would leave, they would still be sitting there. It was many years later, after his death, that I realized what was going on. Why would grandpa leave his family, go out there, and spend so much time with those men, total strangers to us? Well, grandpa was teaching new Masons their Masonic degree lessons. Even in his nineties, he was evidently proficient and very alert in a field where lessons have to be committed to memory and handed down from one member to another.

Grandpa would ride a mule or horse to Masonic lodges for many years, after becoming a member at the age of twenty-one. Later, he helped found the Blacksher Lodge at Uriah, Alabama; it still meets on the Saturday night before the full moon, and is the only lodge in Alabama that does so. The tradition started because early members rode horses and mules or drove buggies to get to the meetings. The moonlit nights provided light to travel the trails and crude, lonely roads, and helped them see wild animals, that might attack them or spook the horses, or anyone who might want to waylay them.

Grandpa became the oldest man to be made a Royal Arc Mason and was honored by his lodge on his one hundredth birthday, in March of 1958.

One of the things most intriguing at Grandpa's house was the big barn with the hayloft. Although warned to stay away, we always found our way, up the ladder, into the hayloft. Of course, afterwards, there always came a stiff scolding.

Another thing we could not stay away from was the storm cellar—a pit dug in the ground and covered with a door. Family members would find safety there during severe weather, such as tornados. Grandma kept her canned vegetables there, and during the winter, she stored her plants in the storm cellar so they wouldn't freeze.

The old, two-story house had a limestone chimney, which was an enticement for boys with pocketknives to carve their names. My initials are still there, more than sixty years after I carved them.

Since our own house was just one floor, the upstairs was an intriguing place. We would slip up the stairs and plunder old books, trunks, and boxes, not realizing, perhaps, the tears and joys that had been derived from some of the artifacts we rummaged through.

The grandparents on the other side of the family, by now had been split up, and were shifted from one sibling to another. There were no nursing homes or assisted living facilities at that time, so children were expected to, and usually did care for their elderly parents.

My daddy's parents did not own a home, but they were well cared-for. Daddy Raymond would be at our house while my grandmother would be at another of their children's homes. Then we'd swap. This gave us an opportunity to get to know them in a different way than our Lambert grandparents.

The first time I tasted Jell-O was at my Aunt Hat's house, in Monroeville. She lived in town and had electricity and a refrigerator to make ice cream and goodies, like Jell-O. I'd never seen anything like this; it tasted good and was cold. I had a hard time keeping it on the spoon, but I tried to enjoy it.

If I'm going to mention my aunts and uncles, I should also point out that my daddy had one of the finest attributes any man could have: he loved his brothers and sisters. He would always stop by for a minute, even if that were all the time he could spare, to see them when he went into their area. He would drop by their store or place of business, or run by the house, just to see how they were doing. Not only did he care for his siblings, his aunts, and his uncles, but he also went out of his way to spend a few minutes with many older folks, just to see if he could do anything for them.

I am grateful for a heritage I can trace all the way to England. I'm glad my great-grandfather came to south Monroe County, clearing the piney woods and preparing cotton patches, so my daddy could become acquainted with Carrye Lambert, my mother and the mother of five other boys.

Chapter 8

Planting, Plowing, and Running From Tornados

The cotton fields of South Monroe County, and the farm on which I grew up, afforded me many experiences that helped mold my life into one of service to my country and my fellow citizens.

As I grew into my teens, more and more in the way of work and farm chores were expected of me. All of my older brothers had been brought up the same way— "There is work to do, and you must do your part." My part apparently included breaking the ground and getting it ready for planting, and then there was fertilizer that had to be put down. Since this was long before my daddy had tractors, all the plowing, preparation, and cultivating was done by mule-drawn equipment.

Fertilizer came in heavy cloth bags and later in hundred-pound paper bags. These bags had to be carried across freshly plowed furrows, quite a task for young, teen-age boys. We carried the bags from the wagon, across the field, and placed them in strategic spots, so the fertilizer distributor was never very far from a refill. An operator guided the distributor by walking behind it, holding onto the handles, while controlling the mule pulling it with the reins. Beneath the hopper was a device that measured the amount of fertilizer released. Depending upon the crop and grade of fertilizer, a certain amount was allocated for each acre. A small plow opened the earth, and the distributor made a clacking sound as the mule pulled it along, which was a signal that fertilizer was being dispensed into the opened furrow. After the fertilizer came the planting.

The distributor opened the furrow and filled it with just the right amount of fertilizer, and then the planter came along, also pulled by a mule, and dropped seed every six, eight or ten inches, as determined by the user. The seed went into the furrows from a container at the top of the planter; specially made wheels covered them over. One had to pay close attention, making certain that the planter was working properly, because if it malfunctioned and the operator didn't catch it, Daddy would know the truth when the seeds sprouted, and the plants came forth. You just didn't want to face my daddy if that happened.

Daddy was a very strict man and wanted everything done just right. One of his sayings was, "If you are going to do something, do it right." He also firmly believed in treating everyone justly, and this meant paying a good day's wage for a good day's work. Of course, in the 1940s, fifty cents per day was the going rate for farm labor. I've seen him write many checks for two dollars and fifty cents, for a five-day workweek. He never kept his workers waiting on their wages, always paying on time, which was something not everyone did.

Another thing we were taught was, "If you are working for someone, give him a good day's work; if you don't like your job, go get you another one; but as long as you are employed by someone, be loyal to that employer."

After the planting came the plowing or cultivating. Cultivating not only covered the small grass and weed sprouts, keeping the foreign matter to a minimum, it let the roots of the plants breathe as new soil was turned up next to them. Every crop required several plowings, until it was time for the plants to begin producing fruit.

Two things required the use of a hoe, a tool I never liked. First, the stand of the plants along the row had to be thinned so they would have adequate room to grow, and ultimately, produce. This is referred to as "chopping." Secondly, a hoe was required to remove clumps of grass and weeds from around the plants. Usually you could make pretty good time covering the fields, but I never enjoyed using the hoe.

On one occasion, in May of 1943, we were hoeing in a field across a branch from the house. A dark cloud was forming in the southwest. We were hoping it would rain, because then it would be too wet to continue hoeing the cotton. The dark cloud moved closer and developed a funnel, which meant it had become a tornado. A younger brother and I, along with a number of farm hands, ran for cover. We threw our hoes down and began to run for the house with all our might. My brother and I made it home, as did the others, just in time. The winds were furious; the skies, dark; it looked like night. The rains came, and then hail—sheets and sheets of hail, as large as marbles. The wind blew so hard that Mama, Maston, and I couldn't get the front door on the north side of the house closed. We pushed and pushed, to no avail. We thought we were doing the right thing, but later realized that if we had closed the door our house would likely have been destroyed. The wind howled, and the hail piled up against the fences along the roadways and filled the rows of every field.

We saw trees, building materials, and all kinds of debris flying by. We were horrified. We knew then that we were in the midst of a monstrous tornado. As boards and tin from the roofs of the barns and houses down the lane flew by, we realized we were in a terrible situation.

When it was over, our house still stood, but the barns were gone. The smokehouse, the chicken house, and all of the outbuildings had been blown away. Later, tin roofing from our barn was found ten miles away.

One of our workers' homes disintegrated around him. Nothing was left. He had a chunk of mortar from his chimney in his overalls' pocket, but he didn't have a scratch on him.

One of our mules, Old Red, now too old to work, had been in a pasture, grazing. After the tornado, we found him in another field, the fence undisturbed. That tornado had blown him right over the fence.

The pecan and other fruit trees had been flattened. The worst was that the cotton crop looked like match stems down the rows; some areas had been totally destroyed. The corn, row after row, acre after acre, was shredded. The entire crop was lost, and it was too late in the year to replant. Were it not for crop insurance, my daddy would have been put out of business. Thankfully, no one was injured.

Farming is utterly dependant upon the weather. It can be too wet, or it can be too dry. Extreme weather conditions will affect the yield of the crop, and of course, a vicious storm will wipe it out in a matter of minutes. This was one reason I never cared to make farming a career; later, you will see how my entire life changed.

There had been several doctors and dentists in the generations before mine; my folks wanted me to be a doctor. I think I could have made a good one. However, it was not meant to be. Although my parents were disappointed at this, and other turns of events, I have had a rewarding life, a long way from the cotton patch.

Chapter 9

A Vision Fulfilled

As the teen years crept by, and I became more experienced with the mule and the plow, I let my mind wander, making speeches that I didn't think, with my timidity, I could ever make. As I plowed, just the mule and me and my favorite dog, Shep, I would dream of places and experiences I never thought could ever come my way. Down one row and back up the other, in fields so big that fence posts at the end of the row looked like toothpicks, Shep would walk beside me. If I stopped, he stopped. When I said, "Get up" to the mule, Shep got up. He was with me every step of the way.

Some days I could see my older brother, Joe Frank, although he had been killed in a logging accident, walking down the road, just as visible as the mule before my eyes.

I visualized brothers Jeff and David, in some far-off place, serving our country, and longed for the day they would come home, dressed in their military uniforms. I was proud of them, and everyday, as I passed their photographs on the wall of our living room, my heart swelled with great pride within me.

About this time in my life, I had a vision that was uppermost in my mind for many years. I still remember it clearly. Some might say I was daydreaming; some might discount it as a flight of fancy, but I call it a vision. I think it had to have been a vision, because in time, it came to pass, just as I had seen it while plowing on that spring day.

Remember, I was a bashful country boy, afraid to say hello to anyone I didn't know. You have to understand where I came from to grasp the magnitude of my teenage vision. In it, I saw myself on a huge platform in an arena, addressing thousands of people. I didn't know what my subject matter was, but I waxed eloquently before a throng of people, totally out of character for a backwards boy from a cotton patch.

Some thirty years passed; I married, was in business for myself, and a Christian. Somehow, I'd wound up in politics. Not only was I active in civic and political affairs, but God had changed my life, completely. It's hard to comprehend the change that had taken place. I'd been blessed with a good mind, and had made good grades throughout high school, but I was plagued with an awful timid streak that kept me from expressing myself as I would have liked.

All that changed after my conversion; I became active in the church. Discipleship Training, known then as the Training Union, in Baptist circles, helped me more than I can express. We had a dozen or so young adults in our class, and most of us became very good friends. Our children were about the same age, went to school together and played Little League ball at the community park. We visited in each other's homes every Sunday night after church. We had great comradeship and enjoyed Christian fellowship with one another. The ham and biscuit snacks with the Tews, the Prestons, the Colliers and others helped us new believers grow in a wonderful way.

In the Training Union class, we would have parts (a verse or two) from a printed lesson on a particular subject. The objective was to try to recite the part without reading it. I'll never forget the first time I gave a small part. I was petrified. I had dreaded that moment all week. The time came, the leader called on me, and I stood up. The few pieces of change I had in my pocket sounded to me like the mint at Fort Knox had just dumped out millions. My knees shook, cold sweat broke out on my forehead, the palms of my hands were wet, and I was about to wet my pants. Somehow, I got through it.

After that, I had many opportunities to share. As time went on, I was able to do better before groups. Many doors of opportunity opened for me to share my faith and experiences. My work in the Baptist Brotherhood and interdenominational men's ministries opened up all kinds of opportunities for me to be before small and large crowds. The time came when I stood before thousands of people, in stadiums, arenas, churches, and convention halls. Eventually, I was elected president of the Alabama Baptist Brotherhood, and then I became only the second layman to ever be elected to the presidency of the Alabama Baptist Convention, which has more than a million members. That gave me even more opportunities to speak, all across America.

Becoming mayor of Mobile opened more doors. Being the mayor of a major city, and an active Baptist lay speaker, made me popular and sought-after. I spoke in a church, somewhere, every weekend. Many times, I flew out on Saturday afternoon, returned on Sunday night and was back at city hall, bright and early, Monday morning. Very few people even knew I was gone.

Everywhere I went, I looked for the place I'd seen in that vision as a teenager. I would walk into an arena, and ask myself, "Is this the place?" and it wouldn't be.

Then one day, I arrived in Dayton, Ohio to address an area-wide men's meeting preceding a citywide revival, where Dr. W.A. Criswell, outstanding pastor of First Baptist Church of Dallas, Texas for many years, was to preach the following week.

When I walked onto the platform and looked out over the hundreds of men from that general area, and when I saw the layout of the arena, I knew that it was the place. I'd seen the same place, more than thirty years before, in that vision.

That was it! God had fulfilled his promise; he had done a mighty work in the life of one timid country boy from the cotton patch, by putting me in places I never imagined I would be allowed to go.

A dream? A vision? You call it what you will, but I know it was God's doing because I was there, in the cotton patch, when it happened to me; and I was there in Dayton, Ohio, the day it came to pass.

Chapter 10

Cotton-Picking Time

As I grew older, my daddy assigned more responsibilities to me. I now took the corn to the mill for grinding. The gristmill was located about a half mile from the house, and was a popular place, especially on Saturdays. It was located next to Marshall's store. The operator, or miller, took a "toll" for his services. The whole-grain yellow corn, already shelled by a hand-driven corn sheller, would be placed in a sack, for carrying to the mill.

The gristmill operator would open the sack, estimate how much corn it contained and then scoop out the amount he charged for his services and toss it in a barrel close by. He would then start up his old Model T or Model A Ford engine, throw it in gear, and the belt would begin to turn the wheels that ground the corn. He dumped the corn in the hopper above the grindstones, and corn meal would start trickling out the lower side of the mill. The same sack used to bring the corn to the mill would be used to carry the meal back home. This operation always fascinated me. As I put the sack across my shoulder, I could feel the meal, made warm by the grinding. Corn meal was a necessity on the farm; vegetables and biscuits just don't go together and there were always plenty of fresh vegetables during the summer, and canned ones during the winter. Furthermore, we didn't raise wheat, so the flour had to be purchased. Flour came packaged in barrels or twenty-five-pound bags, sometimes made of printed cotton that women used to making clothes.

Every farmhouse had a sewing machine, and the woman made many items of clothing. In the early thirties, during the Great Depression, many kids wore fertilizer sack pants and flour sack shirts and dresses.

Quilt making was a popular activity in the evenings at home, and I remember Mama and other women gathering together to make quilts from small scraps of cloth that made beautiful patterns when cut just right and sewn together. They kept many a farm family warm on cold winter nights. Our houses were not insulated and had cracks that let in the cold wind. Sometimes, so many quilts would cover us we could hardly turn over.

Another great responsibility for an early teen was taking cotton to the gin. Cotton gins were scattered throughout the country to accommodate the mule-drawn cotton wagons. It was essential that the farmer get to the cotton gin, as quickly as possible. Wagon sides were raised, allowing enough cotton to be packed in to make a bale. A bale of cotton was five hundred pounds of compressed lint, after the removal of the seed.

Most of the time, there would be a line of cotton wagons waiting to get under the shoot, located beneath a shed adjacent to the building that housed the ginning equipment. Suction pipes, operated by the person who brought the load, carried the cotton, handpicked, then loaded on the wagon, into the gins. The seed was extracted and weighed, and the lint sent on to a compress, where it was bound with a special, course baling material and compressed into bales, wrapped with metal strips. Each bale was numbered and stamped with initials; for instance, Daddy's stamp was "JCM." A sample was then taken for grading. Cotton buyers would come and purchase the bales of cotton, and ship them to cotton mills, for processing into cloth.

One thing I remember well about the cotton gin was the number of hats and caps that were lost to the gin by way of the suction pipe. If one's hat or cap fell off during unloading, the pipe sucked it up immediately and shredded it. There was no retrieving it; therefore, everyone tried to make sure to fit his headpiece tightly to his head.

An awful lot of work took place before the cotton got to the gin. In late spring or early summer, the plants became too large to cultivate with mules and plows, so any large clumps of grass in the rows between the plants had to be removed by hand, with hoes.

The plants then began to bloom, from the bottom up, with beautiful red, lavender, and light colored blooms. Everywhere there was a bloom, a boll appeared, and if it escaped the weevils, eventually, in late summer, would open up, filled with cotton and ready to pick.

As the plants grew, more bolls would appear, until there were blooms to the very top of the plants. In late summer, the fields would be covered in white. From one end of the field to the other, it would be as white as snow, and every farmer prayed for dry weather. Storms and heavy rain would either hurt the grade of the cotton or blow it out onto the ground.

When the crops were ready for gathering, "cotton-picking time," as we called it, Daddy would go to towns twenty or thirty miles away and bring dozens of people in, each day, to help with picking the cotton. Of course, all the Mims boys at home at the time, as well as the regular workers, were right there, going up and down the rows, pulling long sacks with straps over our shoulders, picking cotton. When the sack was full, we packed it in a basket. Everyone had his own baskets.

We never had trouble getting hands to pick cotton; my daddy had a reputation of being fair, and never gave anyone a false weight. He always paid at the end of the day, in cash. Daddy always had an honest scale. In other words, he always paid a picker for every pound he picked. There were, I understand, some farmers who would put lead in the pea, the weight that balanced the scale, making the scale give a false reading, thus cheating the pickers who worked all day in the blazing sun. When a farmer of this caliber was found out, it was very difficult for him to ever get folk to work in his fields again.

Weigh-in, late in the afternoon, just before dark, was a jubilant time. Competition for the day was over. Everyone was anxious to see who had picked the most and would get the most money for the day. The singing that had been going on as the pickers worked up and down the rows came to a halt. A hush fell upon the field as Daddy weighed each basket and tallied up the numbers, announcing the totals so all could hear. A cheer went up for the picker who had picked the most cotton for that day. Usually, the same few came out on top every afternoon. The going rate was something like a penny a pound, and some folk could pick more than three hundred pounds a day. After weighing the cotton, it was dumped into the wagons and packed down.

When we'd finished loading the wagons, either a hired man or one of us boys would take the load to the cotton gin owned by my great uncle. He and another man formed the Hudson-Mims Gin Company and owned several cotton gins throughout the area. (They also owned ice plants that ran trucks out through the country to supply ice to those who could afford it.)

The workers that lived nearby made their way to their homes, and those brought in from nearby towns boarded the trucks for the return trip. Quiet fell over the cotton fields. Smoke rolled out of the chimneys of the tenant houses where the wood stoves were being fired up, and the aroma of fatback meat frying and biscuits baking spread over the entire area. The men were home from a hard day's work, and it was time to feed them. Lightning bugs by the millions lit up fields that had been white as snow with cotton earlier that day. Summer and cotton-picking time in the country are experiences I'll never forget.

Chapter 11

Personalities of My Youth

I cannot write about my years as a boy without dealing with some of the personalities of my youth.

Blind Stafford comes to mind. He couldn't see, yet he walked hundreds of miles up and down the roads of our area. When Mama saw him coming down the road, she would say to my brother, Maston, and me, "You boys go out there and speak to Blind Stafford—if you don't, he'll hear you playing, and if you don't speak to him, it will hurt his feelings."

We would run out by the road and holler, "Hello, Blind Stafford." He'd respond, "Now the first one that spoke was Lambert, right? And the second one was Maston, right?"

We would say, "Yes," and his parting words would be, "You boys be good."

Walking Mary also traveled many miles up and down the road as I was growing up. Some people called her "Crazy Mary." If we referred to her that way, Mama chastised us and threatened to whip us if we did it again. Walking Mary, unlike Blind Stafford, did not talk to anyone. She just talked to herself. You could hear her coming, mumbling and jabbering to no one in particular. She never bothered anybody, but "Crazy Mary" was certainly appropriate.

Bessie Swift and her husband Walter are forever stamped in my mind. Walter could plow more ground than any other man could who ever set foot on that farm, and Bessie could chop and pick more cotton than anyone, man or woman. She was the one who tried to feed me sweet potatoes the day I was born and looked after me when I was young. She was also the one who helped Mama around the house, and for many years, did the washing for all of us. Bessie lived down a lane behind our house, and late in the evenings, after I had already eaten, I would slip down to her house to get some of her biscuits. The smell of biscuits baking seemed to draw me down the lane. Bessie's picture is framed among many of my relatives, and she will forever have a place in my heart.

Anderson Freeman—we called him Freeman—was a convict, released on parole to Daddy's custody. He had spent a considerable amount of time in the state penitentiary for murder, but he had been paroled to work on our farm. He lived in a small house down the lane, but ate every meal at our house. He loved Mama's cooking, just as we all did. On one occasion, Mama set a jar of homemade chow-chow on the table. She could make the very best tomato, pepper, onion, and sugar concoction. It was delicious served over fresh peas and beans, but it was supposed to be applied sparingly. On that particular day, Freeman ate the whole jar. I can still hear Mama scolding him. All he could say was, "Mrs. Mims, that's the best stuff I ever ate, I just couldn't help it." From then on, Mama gave him just enough for the vegetables he ate at that meal.

Freeman was a good worker. He never complained about his duties and carried them out as though he owned the farm. Then one day, after many years, Daddy said, "Freeman, you are free. You have served your time; you may go wherever you want."

Freeman told Daddy, "Mr. Jeff, where would I go? This is home to me." He stayed on many more years before joining some of his distant relatives in a northern city.

Steve Beasley was a huge, black man who worked as hard as any other man did. He was the father of my childhood buddy, Junior Boy. We had all gathered on the front porch of our home one summer afternoon to get out of the rain. The skies were full of fierce thunder and lighting. Daddy said to Steve, who was reared back with his bare foot propped up on the corner post, "You had better take your foot off that post. If lightning strikes around here, it'll run down that post and hurt you."

Steve didn't pay Daddy any attention. A few minutes passed, and "wham!" Lightning struck, knocking Steve backward and scorching his big toe. No doubt, from then on, he didn't keep his feet on the porch posts during lightning storms.

Aunt Lena Ellis was daddy's aunt, who lived a mile away in the old Mims house that my great-granddaddy built when the family first settled in the area. She was a large but pretty woman, well educated and refined in every way. She was active in the Women's Missionary Union and played the piano at Poplar Springs Baptist Church. Aunt Lena had a 1937 black, four-door Chevrolet. When she started the engine, she always gave it plenty of gas, racing the motor. It could be heard for great distances, and she always jammed the car into gear, grinding the gears in such a way that they sounded like they were going to fly apart. I can see her now, ramming that floor-mounted stick shift into first gear, the furthest thing from refined you could imagine.

She always had a beautiful yard, with all kinds of fresh seasonal flowers. Her garden was one of the best around. One of her favorite vegetables was English peas. She knew how to cook the best ones you have ever tasted. Occasionally, she would bring us a mess already prepared. I suppose this is why I like English peas so much today.

Miss Dosha Thomas, a dear black lady, lived up a lane and across the road from our place. Her house was as clean as any house could be. She scrubbed the floors with mops made from corn shucks, and the golden, twelve-inch wide pine boards shone like new money. Dosha was noted for her cakes, and she always had some for us when we went to her house. When she cooked cakes, a pleasant vanilla aroma pervaded the entire area.

Mr. Bernard McGill was a very old man at the time, but a very strong one. The community, for many years, was known as McGill, and I assume the McGills settled there just before or at about the same time the Mims came to the piney woods. Mr. McGill amazed everyone, especially small boys, with his strength. It was demonstrated mostly at cotton-ginning time, when he would back up to a bale of cotton, which weighed between five and six hundred pounds, slam cotton hooks into it, and lift it onto his back.

A Mr. Hayles drove the school bus when I was young. We rode seven miles over a bumpy dusty red gravel road. Every time a vehicle passed, which was often, a cloud of dust came in through the open windows. The thing I remember most about Mr. Hayles, other than his creeping along, was that he was forever tapping the accelerator, which hung down like a big spoon from the firewall of that old Ford. The constant tapping, jerking, and lunging of the bus, and the ever-present bumpy road, made the morning and evening trips hard to forget.

One family I have always remembered is the McDonald family. Mr. George had a number of children, worked hard, and never had much money, as was the case with many farm workers during the thirties. He did not own an automobile.

Every Sunday, he would load his family up on the two-mule wagon and they'd make their way to church. After lunch, they would all gather on the porch or under the chinaberry tree, picking guitars and singing hymns of faith. Shouts of "Amen" and "Hallelujah" could be heard across the cotton fields as this happy family praised God. Their example, over the years, has reminded me that you don't have to be rich in goods to be rich in spirit. The McDonalds were truly a rich family.

Miss Della Beasley, mother of my boyhood friend, Junior Boy, was a trim and proper African-American lady. She sewed well, and her dresses were always starched and pressed. Regardless of the hot, southern, summer weather, Miss Della was always neat, cool, and collected. She was a proud lady and cared well for her family.

In the thirties, we were all poor, compared to standards of later years, but we didn't realize it. We enjoyed life, worked hard, and were thankful to God for what we had. We were just proud country folk.

Chapter 12

The Pretty Blonde
and the Big, Black Buick

My middle teens were difficult, yet happy, years. I was developing from boy to man, and as you will see, there was not much in between for me. I've been told that I've always been kind of an extremist, although it might not make much sense that a quiet and timid boy, teenager, and adult could be an extremist.

I wanted to spread my wings, go to school activities, parties, and other places where teens hung out, but my daddy always said no. I thought he was unreasonable. I became rebellious and hardheaded. I already said it, but it's worth saying again—I thought my daddy was the meanest person in the world, but as I grew older, I saw that he'd had my interests at heart, the entire time.

I learned to drive early. It was during World War II, and my brother's wife, Harriet, was coming to stay with us while he was overseas. Buses ran regularly through Uriah, seven miles away. There were the regular buses and special buses, transporting men and women to Mobile, to work in the shipyards.

The drug store, owned by the Youngbloods, served as the bus station and was a busy place, with people arriving and departing all the time. Harriet was scheduled to arrive this day, but Daddy was busy working as Highway Superintendent. Mama had to get someone else to meet the bus. She wouldn't drive anymore, since she ran into the gatepost going up to her mother and father's house after she was first married. I convinced the fellow she had arranged to pick-up my sister-in-law that I could drive. I had never driven before, but had paid close attention to Daddy and my older brothers, as they clutched, shifted gears and steered.

It was raining hard that afternoon, like dumping water out of buckets. The red gravel road was slippery. Here I was, an early teen, behind the wheel of my daddy's 1941 Chevrolet. He would have had a stroke had he known what was happening. I made it to the drug store/bus station and was able to park without any trouble; I was so proud of myself. The person who was supposed to drive never knew I had no experience at all.

I had some doubts about backing out into the main highway through town when it was time to leave. Despite that, we picked up Harriet, I backed out, and we made it back home safely, never mind the slipping and sliding. Between then and the time I received my license, I snuck around and drove as much as I could. When I did get my license, by circling the Courthouse Square in Monroeville, I went wild. It is only due to God's grace, and his protecting hand, that I can pen these remarks.

Wide open was my speed. The steeper the hill, the faster I went; the stiffer the curves, the more chances I took. As I grew into adulthood and owned my own cars, I remained a fast driver. When our sons came along and wanted cars, I realized how foolish I had been, and prayed that neither of them would follow in my footsteps.

In my mid-teens, as I plowed the crops and worked the fields, I noticed this big, black Buick, driven by a tall, beautiful blonde-haired woman, passing by on a regular basis. She always made a point of waving at me. This was the only Buick in our part of the country, and it belonged to Mr. Billy Phillips, a sawmill owner and operator who lived seven miles down the road, at Little River. He had seven daughters, and the oldest one ran errands for her father, doing banking, picking up parts, and delivering men back and forth to work.

This particular car had a sound unlike any other that drove up and down the road by our farm. I tried to make my way toward the road as soon as I heard the sound of that Buick. She always waved. Just the thought of her paying any attention to me sent my head in a spin.

I asked around, "Who is this? Where does she live? Why does she drive by here so much?"

"That's Billy Phillips' oldest girl, Reecie; she's running errands for her daddy," was the answer I got most often.

She never stopped, although sometimes she would slow down a good bit. It didn't appear that we would ever meet, face to face, in person.

Finally, a friend of mine and I went to revival services one night, at the Mineola Methodist Church, which was three or four miles from our place. About the time my friend stopped his daddy's truck, this big, black Buick pulled up with more girls than you can imagine crammed into it. It was the Phillips sisters and some of their cousins and friends. I had never seen so many girls, but the prettiest one of all was the one driving. I didn't know it at the time, but she had said, "I'll take that one," meaning me! It was the beginning of a relationship, which led to a marriage, which has lasted more than fifty-eight years.

That summer, we went to every revival meeting in that part of the country, regardless of the denomination. Of course, there were only Baptist, Methodist, and Holiness churches in the area. My folks had no problem with me going to the revivals. They had no way of knowing my main purpose was not worship of God, but seeing Reecie Phillips.

I do remember the services quite well, though. It was the hottest time of the year. Service started around seven p.m., and as dusk fell, you could see millions of lightning bugs. They were everywhere. The kerosene oil lamps were the only light, and with the windows open, the lamps drew all kinds of bugs. The song leader and preacher were forever fighting bugs. Everyone had what we called funeral home fans in order to keep the bugs off them. With the windows open, you could hear the mules shaking their harnesses as they tried to rid themselves of flies. Then you'd hear the wagon tongues bumping the trees where the mules were tied.

Many people stood outside the windows to listen to the preacher's fire and brimstone messages. If they stood outside, the men were able to smoke, and maybe even take a swig of whiskey while they listened to the preacher.

One Sunday morning, a man widely known throughout the area for his drinking walked halfway down the aisle, and turned quickly into the pew, whereupon his pint bottle left his pocket and skidded down the oil stained floor, all the way to the riser for the pulpit platform. He politely retrieved his whiskey bottle, while the preacher never missed a beat.

There was a man whose name was Theo Harris. He was brought up in the southern part of the county and in his youth drank hard, and as he put it, "raised hell." He accepted Christ as his Savior and surrendered to preach, going to college and seminary, and for many years pastored a large Birmingham church.

Every summer he returned to our area and conducted revival services in one of the Baptist churches. People came by the hundreds to hear Reverend Theo Harris. Many had known him in his wild days and knew of his conversion. His life certainly gave testimony to the changes he had made. He was a powerful preacher. When he opened the book and began to preach, it was like God himself thundering out to you. There were always great numbers of people converted and baptized when Theo Harris came.

Summer was when crops had been laid and folks needed revivals and fellowship. Sometimes the meetings would go on for several weeks if the Spirit was moving. That's why they were called protracted meetings. Meetings would begin without any set end. The young people were pleased when the meetings were extended. That allowed more opportunity for them to see each other.

I remember the music as the piano player gave it all she had, and Mr. Agee Harris, brother of Preacher Harris, who led the singing. Arms flew and feet tapped as he ran back and forth across the front of the church, leading great hymns like "There is Power in the Blood," "Old Rugged Cross," "Victory in Jesus," and "Just as I Am." All of us young people would sit in the same area. We would sing as loud as we could, and as a group, we made a pretty good choir. We would pack the pews with our young bodies, as close as we could get.

My time with Reecie, during that summer, consisted mostly of revival services. Occasionally, I would see her at a country store or passing by the fields when I was working. She was the most beautiful thing I had ever seen. My young heart would cut cart flips just thinking about her. This was about the time Lauren Bacall was so popular. Since I didn't have a picture of Reecie, I carried a picture of the movie star around with me. Reecie's hair and facial features resembled Lauren Bacall's. Reecie became my Lauren Bacall. I called her the Lauren Bacall of Little River.

Chapter 13

The Place to
Hang Out

By now, I had obtained my driver's license and could drive legally, when I could get the car. If not, I would hitch rides or walk the seven miles to Little River. Reecie would bring me home.

I spent a lot of time talking to Reecie's dad, Mr. Billy. He was a big man, not rich by today's standards, but well to do in those days. He owned a steam powered sawmill, where lumber was sawed from trees harvested from forests in the area and brought to the mill. Much of the lumber was hauled to the Alabama State Docks, in Mobile, where it was exported to Europe and other overseas countries.

Mr. Billy didn't have a son, so I became a son to him. He taught me many things, some good, and some not so good. I thoroughly enjoyed his tall tales and hearing of his escapades, especially the ones committed while he was "under the influence." He always had whiskey and carried it by the case in the trunk of his car. He died at fifty-eight, no doubt due to excessive drinking during his early years. However, he had quit drinking a few years before his death, and all of the family was pleased to see him converted and baptized in Little River Creek.

Little River Creek was the "hang-out" for young people during the summer. The rock bottom of the creek and the rapid flow of the clear water toward the Alabama River, two miles away, made this a choice swimming hole. This was the most famous place for "courting" in the entire two-county area.

Since I had my driver's license, I came up with every imaginable excuse to have to go to the store, and Mama would let me take the car. Daddy would be gone, fulfilling his duties as a State Highway Superintendent, so Mama was the one to say it was okay. I would take off before the school bus ran, and be at Reecie's house at Little River within five minutes. You figure the speed—drive seven miles in five minutes, get Reecie out of the house, spend a few minutes with her, and make my way back home in time for the school bus. It is a miracle that I didn't kill myself or anyone else, as I flew up and down that dirt road.

There was a lot of dust, so the car needed washing often. We didn't have running water, so I would take the car to a rock ford on the Civilian Conservation Corps trail. This organization was formed during President Franklin Roosevelt's administration, to build roads and parks, give young men jobs, and train them in a disciplined work ethic.

At any rate, I would park the car in the rock ford where water would run beneath the car, say four to five inches deep. We used buckets to dip up water to rinse the soap off. Long before automotive car washes, we had a wonderful place to wash our vehicles. That ford is still in existence today.

I became bolder and spent more time at Little River. I became more enamored with Reecie. I still don't know, fifty-eight years later, why she fell in love with me, a sixteen-year-old, timid farm boy, when there were a number of men her own age, who wanted her to look at them. Reecie is four years my senior.

She wasn't just the prettiest girl in the county, she was Mr. Billy Phillips' oldest daughter, and he was one of the most prosperous and well-known men in two counties. Of course, they all looked at her. We spent a lot a time together, always with my friends and her sisters. We had fun. There weren't many places to go unless it was summertime. We were thirty-five miles from Bay Minette, the county seat of Baldwin County, about the same distance from Monroeville, the county seat of Monroe County, and almost thirty miles from Atmore in Escambia County, so there wasn't much for teenagers to do except ride around, which we did a lot. Occasionally, we would use her daddy's Buick, or one of his log or lumber trucks. We spent many evenings on the banks of Little River, roasting marshmallows and, just as it's called now, "hanging out."

There were, of course, in the early summer, watermelon cuttings, where people would bring melons. We would slice them up and sit around eating, spitting out seeds, and talking. There were no drug problems and very few alcoholics because Monroe County was a "dry county," and the nearest beer was twenty or thirty miles away. There wasn't much happening for young people to get in trouble over.

In the fall, there would be sugar cane chews, where several stalks of ribbon cane would be divided among us. The boys would get out their pocketknives, peel away the skin of the cane, and cut it for the girls. All of us boys carried a pocketknife in those days without any thought of ever harming anyone.

Some of the best times were at Little River State Park, where there was a beautiful lake with a spillway. This was the place to be on weekends. Many a romance began on that lake.

Homecoming days and dinners on the ground were big events where everyone, even folk who didn't attend church regularly, showed up for southern fried chicken, chicken and dumplings, and all kinds of scrumptious country cooking.

Living in the country around Little River Creek was an exciting time.

Chapter 14

Married and a
Merchant Before Eighteen

I hesitate to go into this time of my life, because things happened that I couldn't and do not recommend. In spite of the difficulty, it must be told. First, I do not recommend any sixteen-year-old, especially one who had not finished high school, and who was unable to support a family, to think about marriage. It is painful to think about the heartache that I must have caused my parents. As I look back over my life, it seems unthinkable to do what I did, but it has worked out now for fifty-eight years.

That beautiful girl from Little River, four years my senior, was driving me out of my mind. I just couldn't handle the situation any longer. My parent's strict stance on the subject didn't help, and actually made things even worse.

At sixteen, I certainly couldn't obtain a marriage license, so I devised a plan, and it worked. Reecie was twenty and had been in and out of the courthouse in Bay Minette with her father on many occasions. Since she had often taken care of legal matters for her father, she would be a familiar presence in the courthouse, and would have no difficulty getting the license.

I was right. She was able to get the license from the Probate Judge's office without a hitch. We had the license; now, who would marry us? I was more or less running away, so I was sure none of the area ministers would get involved. I had heard of an elderly preacher by the name of Bailey, and I knew where he lived. I had heard my parents and brothers say, "That's where Preacher Bailey lives," referring to an old-timey house by the side of the road, just south of Frisco City. I knew nothing about the preacher, but figured he wouldn't know me or care what I did, since I lived several miles south of there.

We went on Saturday night, August 17, 1946, to Preacher Bailey's house. He agreed to perform the marriage ceremony, if you want to call it that. It was very brief and the preacher's wife was the only witness. We were married. I hasten to say it was not a "shotgun" wedding, for it was six years later that Dale, our first-born son, came into this world. All I knew was that I loved this good-looking gal from across Little River, and didn't think I could do without her. In addition, I was afraid some guy her age or older would get her. There were several who would have liked to go out with her, but thank God, she never gave them the opportunity.

When my parents found out about my being married, they weren't happy, as one can imagine. I certainly understand how they must have felt. I am sorry for the pain I caused them and tried to let them know so, over the years. I was sorry that what I did hurt them, but wasn't sorry I married Reecie. When Mama learned that Preacher Bailey had married us, she exclaimed, "You could have gotten a Missionary Baptist Preacher to marry you."

At the time, I didn't know anything about the difference in Baptist Churches. I later found out that Preacher Bailey was a "hard shell" Baptist and we were Missionary, or Southern Baptist. Mama seemed more concerned about the "hard shell" preacher marrying us than she was about her sixteen-year-old son running off. That was my mama; as wonderful as she was, she was very stern and reserved, and when she spoke, you knew where she stood.

I moved into the house with Mr. & Mrs. Phillips and their seven girls. I was one of six boys, without a sister, and suddenly found myself in a house with seven girls and no boys. What an experience! All of Reecie's younger sisters took to me instantly, while Mr. Phillips took me under his wing as his son. I'll never forget all the things he taught me. As I said before, some were good and some not so good. He had grown up the hard way, but had amassed quite a bit of property: timberland, trucks, tractors, oxen, a sawmill with dozens of employees, and a turpentine still. I admired him very much.

Mrs. Phillips was as good a mother-in-law as one could have; she treated me like a son. One of the things I remember most was gathering at the table for meals. There was so much food. There were always biscuits, and regardless of what other meat was on the table, there was a plate of fried bacon. Mr. Phillips required there be bacon and white beans. I remember he always bowed his head and prayed before we ate.

Sometimes he was so intoxicated that he'd slur his words, and only God knew exactly what he was saying. The beautiful thing was that it was instilled in him in his youth that he should give thanks before every meal. Then he would get out his little bone-handled pocketknife and clean his fingernails. It was a ritual that lasted until the night he died.

I had not finished school yet, which had to be addressed. I was now living in another county, about a mile from the line. The nearest county high school was thirty-five miles away, in Bay Minette. On the other hand, the school I had attended all my life was fifteen miles away, in Monroe County. We decided that Reecie would take me across Little River every morning to catch the bus to Uriah. I would pass right by where I had caught the bus for so many years. Then in the afternoon, Reecie would pick me up. This worked out fine, for that year.

As time went on, Reecie and I opened a small grocery store across the road from the Phillips' home and sawmill. It was more or less a commissary for sawmill and timber crews. We sold Pure Oil Gas, dispensed by a hand pump. You pumped the glass-cylindered tank full and then let out the number of gallons the customer desired. Most customers bought their gas in one-dollar increments. Gasoline was twenty cents per gallon, so one dollar's worth was five gallons. This made things easy to figure.

Salt meat and bacon came in sides and we'd cut off the amount desired with a big butcher knife, and weigh it on a butcher's scale. Bologna and other meats were sold accordingly.

Cheese came in wooden hoops, which we sliced into wedges and then weighed. A customer would point out just the size slice he desired, and—wham—it was cut.

We sold rice, peas, beans, and coffee by the pound, weighed into small, brown paper bags. Soft drinks were five cents each and cooled in a box with crushed ice. Fishermen, on the way to the nearby landings would stop for snacks and gasoline for their outboard motors. We carried a small stock of fishing lines, lures, and poles for folks who might not have enough already.

The workers from the sawmill across the road were some of our best customers. Mama and Daddy had gotten used to the idea of me being married, and Daddy would bring Mama's grocery list to be filled. It was fun being around the hustle and bustle of the sawmill. There was the continual smell of burning wood, because the mill ran by steam from boilers heated by sawdust. There is a special aroma to pine sawdust burning. Someone kept the boiler fired day and night, and one of the most memorable sounds is the whistle blowing early in the morning, waking people up to get ready for work.

At seven a.m., the mill came alive. Saws could be heard singing for a mile as the carriage drew the logs in. Planks of varying widths and sizes came out of the other end of the mill to be stacked and made ready for hauling away.

Watching the men working and putting forth their best, seeing the logs converted to lumber, smelling the fresh pine planks, and seeing Mr. Phillips sitting on his porch, watching and listening to every sound, was an experience. He could sense the very moment that something wasn't right at the mill. He knew when all was well. He could out-figure most anyone around. With only a fourth-grade education, he could add faster than anyone I had ever seen. He was a great man and made me very proud that I married into his family. He treated me as though I were his own son.

We lived in a side room and were always handy for anyone who knocked on the store door when we were closed. Reecie kept books and measured lumber for her dad. She also ran errands for him and took her mother places with the other girls. Mobile was a popular place for us to shop, since it was where most of the wholesalers were located.

Mr. Phillips had established business relations with a number of companies over the years. One of which was the Taylor-Lowenstein Company that sold groceries and supplies, and had a big turpentine plant, where Mr. Phillips sold his "crude dip," as it was called. He had closed his turpentine still by then, and transported what his trees produced to Mobile. "Dip" is the liquid that comes from freshly cut streaks on yellow pine trees. The dip trickles down the face of the cut tree into a metal tin fastened to the tree. Every so often, the person handling the "crop" would have to collect the dip in buckets carried from tree to tree. Full buckets were emptied into barrels placed throughout the area. When all the dip had been gathered, and the barrels were full, the barrels would be loaded on a truck and finally wind up at the Taylor-Lowenstein plant, in Mobile.

We had a number of salesmen from various wholesale companies who called on us. They would come by every week, take orders, and send the merchandise either by their own company trucks or by the Phillips Truck Line. My father-in-law formed the Phillips Truck Line; his brother, Jack Phillips, later took it over as owner and operator. We established friendships with some of the salesmen, and those friendships actually led to our relocation to Mobile, after we closed the store.

During the last year of high school, I arranged with the principal to get my credits from a correspondence school. I kept up my studies, sent in my tests, and graduated with my class in 1948, from the J.U. Blacksher High School.

The many hours spent with Mr. Billy, enamored with his stories, I'll never forget. My learning to drink alcohol, no doubt, would be the worst thing that happened during that time. I will speak more on that later.

Those were interesting, exciting times. Being in business, finishing high school, enjoying those first years of being married, and getting used to seven girls was an adjustment, and it pressed me into adulthood very rapidly. Not many people can lay claim to being married before finishing high school, or to owning a grocery store before the age of eighteen.

Chapter 15

Big City Life

The lumber business was good during World War II and for several years thereafter; however, by 1949, sales had dwindled, the mill was running less and we didn't see much future at the store. One of the salesmen calling on us encouraged me to apply for a job in Mobile with his company. Based on my relationship with him, I was hired as shipping clerk with a wholesale feed and flour company. Reecie and I closed the store and moved, with a few belongings, to Mobile.

Our first apartment was a one-room efficiency, upstairs, in a beautiful home in an older section of town. The area later became one of the several historic districts in this 300-year-old city.

We were just one block from the bus line on Government Street, one of the major east-west streets. Buses ran regularly, but it was not easy catching buses or making transfers, especially on rainy days.

Reecie got a job with a local stevedoring company and worked in the tallest building in Mobile. Since Mobile was a major seaport town, stevedoring, or loading and unloading ships, was a good business, and the company had been around a long time.

We both had good jobs and were very fortunate to get started in what we thought was fine fashion. Reecie always made more money than I did, which could have affected some men; I realized, however, that her business college training and experience helped her to be able to get a better salary than I did.

Until we bought a car, our weekends consisted of walking up and down Government Street, with its massive oak trees, and going to the movie theater, which was something new for me. We spent a great deal of time downtown, which was at that time, a bustling business hub of the upper gulf coast.

We frequently visited Bienville Square, feeding squirrels and pigeons and watching people go by. It was at Bienville Square that I had my first encounter with what we today call a gay or homosexual. A very well dressed man approached me as I made my way to the men's room, located beneath the grand stand. Being the shy country boy that I was, and just getting acquainted with city life, I was totally shocked. I had never heard much about such things, and I was horrified. The first thing out of my trembling lips was, "I will knock your block off, if you don't leave me alone."

I well remember him saying, "Don't be upset," and then I told him I was going to get the policeman, who was on the corner. He turned away and left me alone.

Reecie and I enjoyed seeing the ships come and go out of the port and the seamen from around the world taking in the downtown sights. A beautiful sight was the unloading of the banana boats. Hundreds of workers handled the huge bunches that came on conveyors from out of the hull of the ship and loaded them onto trucks and railroad cars for distribution throughout the country.

Bales of cotton lined the waterfront waiting to be compressed into even smaller bales for export. Corn, wheat, rye, wheat bran, and wheat shorts, unloaded from barges out of the mid-west, now occupied vast areas under the sheds along the waterfront waiting for local feed distributors to haul it away.

Coffee-roasting plants spewed the wonderful aroma of fresh-roasted coffee that permeated the entire business district. Flashing neon signs advertised the bars, cafes, pawnshops, and other businesses on every street in and around the waterfront. Roasted peanuts from the peanut shop attracted many people, and the squirrels were the main beneficiaries. Shoeshine boys, people begging or selling products, and street photographers could be seen on every block and corner. One or two streetcar lines still existed, but they were soon phased out and replaced by diesel-powered buses. These were exciting times for us. We learned much about life in the city and interacting with other people.

It wasn't long before we bought our first car. I was so proud of it. It was a 1940 Buick Special Coupe. It looked good and ran good. The rear seat needed some upholstering work, but I was proud of that black beauty. We were then able to drive back home on weekends, and I didn't have to change buses downtown, anymore, to get to work.

We moved from our efficiency apartment to a larger upstairs apartment down the street. Both houses are, to this day, beautiful period homes in the midtown area, in the old Dauphin Way Historic District.

We went to the movies a lot, but on weekends, we would mostly take off to North Baldwin and south Monroe Counties to visit with our families. We would go up on Saturday mornings and return on Sunday afternoons. It was about a sixty-fives mile drive up there.

One thing that is hard to forget are the miles of automobiles, lined up on Sunday afternoons, trying to cross the causeway, which was a two-lane highway to go through the Bankhead Tunnel under Mobile River. Thousands of cars, loaded with families, returning from the beaches of Gulf Shores, along with the masses traveling coast to coast along the Old Spanish Trail, U.S. 90 and 31, made for horrendous traffic jams on Sunday afternoons. We tried to get back ahead of the worst traffic tie-ups.

One Sunday afternoon, I was flying, at a high rate of speed, down crooked Highway 59, between Little River and Bay Minette. We made it to our apartment safely, but I decided to go to the grocery store. I drove about a half a block when one of the tie rods came loose, and I had no control whatsoever over the steering. Thank God, I was able to come to a stop quickly, without harm to the car, nearby properties, or other cars. If this had happened a little earlier, as I came flying around one of the curves on Highway 59, it's doubtful we would have lived to tell this story. We didn't know much about God at that time, but he was without a doubt looking out for us, and his protective hands were upon us.

We both enjoyed our work, the opportunity to make new friends, and the freedom visit with loved ones who already lived here. I am sure that Reecie's aunt and uncle, Marion and Margie Gates, got tired of seeing us coming. We also spent a lot of time with my brother Jeff and his wife, Harriett. Looking back, we really imposed on both couples.

My job at Cosby Hodges Milling Company consisted of keeping the warehouse crews busy loading trucks, unloading rail cars, filling customer orders, and making sure the trucks were properly maintained. We had a nice fleet of tractor-trailers and bobtail delivery trucks. They were snow white, with advertising on the sides. The company was very strict about keeping the equipment spotless, and this I tried to do. As time went on, one of the boss's sons took over leadership of the company. The headquarters of the mill was in Birmingham, with branches in several major cities. The new "top dog" was very young and thought he knew everything. From time to time, he visited the branches, and he would always find fault, at least, that's how it seemed to me. I made it a point to keep the equipment as clean and presentable as possible. On this one occasion, he reached for the dipstick on an old, but good-looking, REO Speedwagon, pulled it from the oil pan, and splashed black oil all over the sparkling clean white fender. It upset me very much, and being young myself, I had some smart remarks for him. Immediately, I realized I shouldn't have said anything, but it was too late. The big boss never liked me after that, and to make a long story short, I'm sure the incident ultimately led to my termination.

The manager had a hard time breaking the news to me, and assured me that the decision to terminate me had come from headquarters, not from him. It was a blow, being terminated, but it opened the door for me to be back in business for myself.

Chapter 16

In and Out of Business
Before Twenty-Five

W e went that weekend to see our folks. Sitting on the porch, where I had sat with my father-in-law for so many hours, listening to tales that stretched the imagination and fascinating success stories, he said, "Why don't we go into the feed and flour business?" I was very much interested, but I was without any money to launch such a business. I explained that to him, and his response was that he would finance the operation. We had a plan, but no merchandise to sell. He told me to go back to Mobile, put my thinking cap on, and find the products.

On the next Saturday night Reecie and I were at the Gates' house, playing cards. In the background, a radio was tuned in to station WSM, Nashville, Tennessee; one of the sponsors of the Grand Ole Opry was Martha White Flour. I heard Minnie Pearl say "Goodness gracious, it's good! Martha White Flour." Something clicked in my mind. That's it! If we could get the Martha White account for South Alabama, we could go into business distributing their flour and feed in the area. At that time, they had not ventured very far from the Nashville area and their home base, Lebanon, Tennessee.

I made the call, and they were interested. We got together and agreed that we would sell Martha White flour and Fortune Feeds in the same area where I was already acquainted with most of the storeowners.

In those days, there were many mom and pop grocery stores out through the country and smaller towns. A&P was popular in the larger cities, as were a few locally owned chains, such as Delchamps and Greers.

I was excited about the possibilities. I went back to Mr. Phillips, and after going over the plan with him, he too became excited. He agreed to finance the operation, and the Phillips-Mims Feed and Flour Company came into existence. Reecie would keep the books, I would run the warehouse and sell, and we would hire other salesmen to cover routes.

Now, all we needed was a warehouse. We found one located in the Old Cotton Mill building on Craft Highway, in Prichard, which was a thriving city of about forty thousand, located just north of Mobile. We were located on a rail siding so the unloading of merchandise was very convenient. We purchased trucks and placed orders for merchandise; the railcars arrived with feed and flour, which we stored in the warehouse, and we were underway. Flour was sold in fifty-, twenty-five-, ten-, and five-pound bags. Twenty-five pound bags were the most popular size. Two-hundred pound barrels had to be special ordered. However, when merchants ordered flour, they ordered it in barrels. Eight twenty-five pound sacks equaled one barrel.

I was able to sell the first bag of Martha White flour sold in South Alabama to friends who operated a store in Saraland, the first store on the Highway 43 route. Things went well, and we gained a good presence in the stores of the area, but after some time, one of the salesmen working the counties north of Mobile betrayed us. Unbeknown to us, he made a deal to go with a large wholesale grocery company, with the understanding that he would get the manufacturer to take the account from us, and give it to the larger company. He resigned and went to the other company. Our inventory was running low and we couldn't reach the vice-president of Martha White to find out why our rail cars had not been shipped. Finally, I was able to get a call through by not identifying myself. When he heard my voice, he almost croaked. After he stumbled around for a while, he admitted they had given the account to the other company. It was a great disappointment to us. He hadn't had the courtesy to advise us of their intentions, and it left us in a dither. We had routes; we had faithful customers, and we had their trust, but we were rapidly running out of product to sell.

At the time, a large flour company in Chattanooga had a blending and packing plant in Mobile, at the Alabama State Docks. By now, we were living in an apartment not far from the office and warehouse. The man that lived below us, with his wife, worked at the flour plant at the docks. I made arrangements to travel to Chattanooga, where a deal was made for a private label, Kansas Diamond flour, to be packed for us. In addition, our own brand of animal feed, Tip Top Feeds, was packed for us. Our business went on, but our volume dropped, because the new brand of flour didn't take the place of Martha White, which was still being sold. Some merchants, loyal to us, refused to stock it anymore after they found out what had happened. Nevertheless, the new brand's volume never equaled what we had been doing.

Our first son, Dale, was born January 8, 1952. Reecie went to the office every day until then, and as soon as she was out of the hospital, she would bring him in to work with her, putting him in a playpen right next to her desk.

Mr. Billy, my father-in-law, spent a lot of time at the office. He worked a route every Monday, coming through Stockton, Bay Minette, then on to Mobile. He took a great liking to his grandson, and before he was walking, Dale was drinking coffee out of his granddaddy's saucer. Thank God, he wasn't giving him some of the other stuff that he drank!

Our feed business held up pretty good with the Tip Top line. It was a good product, and competitive. Loggers, farmers, and dairymen were not as particular about feed brands as women were about their flour brand. It was before the day of frozen biscuits and mix, and women prided themselves on their biscuit making. Once they were accustomed to a brand of flour that turned out fine biscuits, it was hard to get them to try another brand.

We were fortunate enough to pick up another brand of flour, under the label of Betsy Ross. It was good, hard, wheat flour. Once a housewife tried it, she would continue to use it. To get them acquainted with it, we gave away gold-rimmed dishes, green goblets, and other prizes. It went quite well.

The salesman for the International Milling Company, Charlie, became our good friend. He was very personable and a terrific salesman. He had one fault; he drank a little too much at night. One day, he and I had been out late the night before, and we felt pretty rough the next morning. We were in a store in Chatom, Alabama. Sometime around eight-thirty a.m., Charlie said he was hungry. "These pecan pies look good," he said. "I'm going to try one."

They were about the size of a saucer, served on paper plates. He began to eat, and after he had finished about half of it, he said, "This is good, but the crust is a little tough."

I took one look, and said, "Charlie, it's no wonder it's tough; you're eating the paper plate it's sitting on!" We all had a big laugh.

One amazing thing was how we allowed our little baby boy to go home with Charlie one weekend! He lived one hundred and twenty-five miles away. Looking back, we should have never done such a thing, but Charlie had taken such a liking to Dale and Dale to him that we let them go. It all worked out. Charlie's wife was happy, and the folks at their church fell in love with Dale.

Dale always liked cars. When he was two years old, he'd stand on the front seat, shielded by my right shoulder and arm, and tell you the make of nearly every car we met.

We enjoyed a pretty good business for several years, but we really never made any money. In order to trim expenses and be more centrally located to the customers we served, we moved the business, and ourselves, to Clark County.

Some of my bad habits grew worse, and as business decreased and it became harder to make ends meet, we had no choice but to file for bankruptcy. The dreams of success, and the hope of having a profitable business faded, and the Phillips-Mims Feed and Flour Company ceased to exist.

Chapter 17

Starting Over

We moved back to Mobile, with hopes of starting over. We located an apartment across the street from my brother, and after a short time, agreed to buy a house in South Brookley, near Dog River. Our first house payments were less than a third of what our electrical bill is today.

Reecie went to work at Constantine's, one of the finest restaurants in town, as bookkeeper, and I was able, at the recommendation of a local wholesale grocer, to go to work as a manufacturer's representative for the H.C. Cole Milling Company of Chester, Illinois. I knew the area, and knew how to sell flour, so we made a good fit. The company furnished me with a new car and an expense account, as well as a fair salary. It was a good job, at the time. In the late fifties, you fared well on five dollars a day for meals, and ten dollars per day for a room. One could get breakfast for around sixty-five cents, lunch for a dollar twenty-five, and the balance could get you a good T-bone steak for dinner. We were well on our way to getting back on our feet.

We bought Reecie a new 1955 Plymouth with a V/8 engine. She drove it for several years, and then we sold it to a friend, who drove it for many more years than Reecie had driven it. He sold it to another man; that old Plymouth was around twenty years after we let it go.

Our first long trip in that car was to Cincinnati, to see Margaret, one of Reecie's sisters, and her family. Dale was about three years old and infatuated, as were most little boys, with Davy Crockett. He had his coonskin cap and as we approached every mountain or hill, or went around a curve, he was looking for Davy Crockett, King of the Wild Frontier.

When we crossed the Ohio River, we ran into all the ramps in downtown Cincinnati. I asked Reecie which way to go, and her reply was, "Take your pick."

Well, as you can imagine, I took the wrong ramp. People were honking and hollering something fierce. This was back when Alabama didn't have such a good name, because of racial issues. I will never forget some of the remarks made when people saw our "Alabama, Heart of Dixie" license plates—"Go home, you hillbilly. You [blankety-blank] honkey, get back across that Ohio River, where you belong"— were some of the kinder remarks.

I enjoyed my new job, calling on wholesale grocers and working with their salesmen as they called on their customers, mostly mom and pop stores throughout the area. My territory was South Alabama, South Mississippi, and North West Florida. I kept up with the inventory in the distributor's warehouses, wrote orders for carloads of shipments from the mill in Illinois, and helped the local wholesale distributors develop new customers for our White Ring and Omega flour. On Friday afternoons and Saturdays, the major shopping days, I would conduct demonstrations in retail stores.

Wearing an apron with "White Ring Flour" embroidered on it, and a paper cap with "White Ring" or "Omega Flour" printed in bold letters, I would bake biscuits and cup cakes, and pass them out to any customer who would accept them. I would set up a couple of portable electric ovens and a table to do the mixing right there, as the women carried on over my baking abilities.

The stores would be filled with the wonderful aroma of baked goods, and most of the women shoppers were amazed that a man was there, baking goodies. I made regular biscuits, as well as cheese, tomato, and sausage varieties. Cup cakes in chocolate and vanilla were big hits. I always had a stack of flour nearby, so I could easily place a bag in the ladies' shopping carts. These store sales and demonstrations sold lots of flour, and many merchants wanted me to come to their stores.

Although I made retail calls alone, I spent most of my time working with salesmen who were employed by the wholesalers in my territory. This job gave me the opportunity to meet many fine owners and operators of wholesale grocery companies, as well as their sales and warehouse personnel. I built lasting relationships that you will hear more about as we go on, but the one thing I remember most is the trust and confidence these folks had in me. I was never not able to return to a place I'd been before. I endeavored to be honest with everyone. Most wholesalers trusted me to keep up with their inventory of my products and write my own orders as I saw fit. I never took advantage of them by sending products that wouldn't sell in that particular territory or overloading them with merchandise. When I worked the retail stores, many of the merchants let me write my own orders, saying, "Send me what you think I need." I wouldn't trade those relationships, built on mutual trust, for anything. Many of these friends and customers have passed on, but the beautiful memories will remain forever.

Some of the wholesale owners and managers would call on me to fill in for their salesmen when they were sick or on vacation. They trusted me with their price books and order pads and weren't worried about me collecting money from their customers. Long after I was out of the grocery business, to this day, some of these relationships still exist.

Holiday Inn was just getting off the ground. Before then, most motels had been "mom and pop" operated. There was very little hanky-panky going on in most of those, since the owners lived on the premises and had a watchful eye on all activity. Larger, multi-storied hotels were located in the business districts of the cities. Holiday Inn took off, and its numbers grew like wildfire. For many years, as long as the original partners, fine Baptist men from Memphis, were in charge, there was no alcohol sold at their properties. From time to time, I visited Memphis, and often stayed at the very first Holiday Inn, on Lamar Avenue.

Twice a year, I went to sales meetings conducted by Cole Milling Company. I would leave Mobile aboard the GM&O "Rebel" Passenger Train at three-thirty p.m., and arrive in Sparta, Illinois at about daybreak, the next morning. Someone from the mill at Chester, Illinois on the Mississippi River about thirty miles away, would pick me up.

It was a genuine pleasure working for a century-old company like Cole Milling Company. The same family had owned the company since its beginning. Mr. Austin Cole, Sr., in his nineties at the time, was a very intelligent and forward-looking gentleman. He was dapper in his dress, had a sharp mind, and drove himself to the mill, everyday— or to St. Louis, some miles away. His son, Austin, inherited the company, and it was later sold to another milling company.

The sales meetings were a time to learn about the company's progress and to hear of each salesman's successes. The meetings provided inspiration to sell more, an introduction to new packaging, and rewards for good work, such as bonuses, promotions, and prizes.

One year, I was top salesman, and I was given an expensive Omega watch and a trophy. Salesmen, especially traveling salesmen, had quite a reputation. Unfortunately, it was deserved, because many of them liked to party at night. Most of us had the dumb idea that the only way to sell was to wine and dine our customers. I was no exception. Later, I will show just how wrong I was. Nevertheless, I regret to say that I did my share of partying, at the time.

Drinking at night became more and more a common thing. The grocery salesmen and the fox and coon hunters liked to drink, and I thought it was the thing to do. It came to a point that I looked forward to the time I made my last call, so I could stop at the nearest bar for a drink. I never considered myself an alcoholic, but I must admit, regrettably, because my granddaughters will see these words, I really liked the stuff.

Some of the guys I worked with were just as bad. After the last call, we would stop by our favorite spots and drink for a while before going home. One man, Joe Pope, and I became extremely close friends and spent many hours after work drinking and telling yarns—enjoying just being boys.

Then one day, he informed me that he would never take another drink as long as he lived. I was dumb-founded. I couldn't believe what I was hearing. He meant what he said, and I will explain it all in the following chapter.

After several years of employment by the Cole Milling Company, I approached the company with the proposition of representing them as a broker, which would allow me to take on other product lines. They agreed; it would save them money, and give me an opportunity to build a business of my own. The Mims Brokerage Company was born. I acquired other lines, like Rose's Dog Food, Hatchett's Pure Cane Syrup, Crown Food Products (mayonnaise, jellies, peanut butter, and so on), L&M Tea, and others. These additional lines allowed me to call on other wholesalers, giving me a greater opportunity to build relationships.

The Rose Dog Food line opened an entirely new area for me. It was a new experience, indeed. I called on fox, coon, bird, and deer hunters, and even spent some nights sitting by campfires way out in the woods, listening to hounds running fox or coon, and listening to hunters tell tales about Ole Blue or Doc and Spot, or whatever the name of their dog might have been.

Attending beagle and bird dog field trials allowed me to make some lasting and enjoyable friendships. Calling on feed dealers, and smelling the aroma of ground hay and blackstrap molasses, and fresh cattle and poultry feeds brought back memories of earlier days in the feed business.

Chapter 18

The Greatest Experience

My wife, Reecie, and I were married when I was sixteen; with the help of Reecie's parents, I had my own grocery store before I was eighteen. At twenty-one, I was running a large wholesale business, distributing flour and feed to various grocers in Mobile and southern Alabama.

Although I enjoyed my work and my contacts with our salesmen and customers, I never quite felt I had reached the place I belonged. A feeling hard to describe, a restless sense of frustration and insecurity, haunted me day and night. I had almost everything a man could desire, but somehow, something was missing—something to give meaning to my life.

Like many young people, I dabbled in things I should have left alone and took a certain pride in drinking beer or whiskey with friends. It wasn't long before I was spending more and more time drinking, and giving less and less time to my work. One of the tragedies of modern life is that so many men are as I was then—going through the motions of their work, physically on the job, but doing only a fraction of what they are capable of, groggy from too many drinks the night before.

On one of my sales trips with the H.C. Cole Milling Company, I met a young man who changed my whole life. His name was Joe Pope. Joe was a salesman from Robertsdale, Alabama, who enjoyed drinking and carousing just as much as I did. Many were the nights we spent going from one roadhouse to another, both convinced that we were having the greatest time possible.

I began to notice a startling change in Joe. He was happier than I had ever known him to be, and when we stopped at the restaurant where we often got sandwiches and beer for lunch, I was shocked when Joe said, "I'm never going to take another drink as long as I live."

"Are you kidding?" I asked him.

"Lambert," Joe said, with great excitement in his voice, "I'm a Christian, now! Last week, my friend Billy Faulk invited me to a revival meeting at First Baptist Church. I didn't feel much like going, but Lambert, for the first time in my life, I understand what the Bible is all about, and I took Christ as my Savior. All the things I've done that I'd like to forget, all my sins—they're gone, Lambert, buried in the depths of the deepest sea. I wish I could tell you how happy and peaceful I am now. Sunday, I took my family to church, and it was a great feeing, sitting there with them, listening to the word of God, and singing hymns. Why don't you let God have his way in your life?"

I mumbled an excuse. I was really worried. I was afraid Joe had lost his mind. What he'd said about being a Christian didn't make much of an impression on me, at the time. I had been baptized years before. Most of my friends and customers were Christian, and frankly, I didn't put much stock in the way some of them lived. Nor was I very happy about the change in Joe's habits. He didn't tell me dirty jokes anymore, and although he still spent many evenings with me, it was usually over coffee and cokes. "Holy Joe" told me he had found what he had been searching for, and he tried to help me find it too. There seemed to be a veil over my eyes, though; his testimony meant very little to me.

One Sunday, in the fall of 1956, I got a telephone call from Joe's boss, Bob Linden, with shocking news. Joe had been driving along U.S. 90 when another car crashed into his, head-on. The other driver was a naval aviation cadet from Corry Field, in Pensacola, Florida. The two cars telescoped into each other and swung completely around, reversing directions as they skidded off the road. The cadet was pinned inside his car, which was jammed together like an accordion. Joe was thrown through the windshield. Both men were killed.

I went to Joe's funeral in Robertsdale. As I stood by his casket, it came home to me that there had to be something better than the way I had been living for so many years. Joe had found that way. I didn't realize it, but God was beginning to break the bonds around my sinful heart. Satan was still in the saddle, however. Before I returned home from Joe's funeral, I was under the influence of alcohol. For a number of years, I didn't have any interest in the things of God, and although my heart had been touched, I was still far from my Savior.

Although Reecie and I had lived in Mobile for ten years, and in this community for more than five, I had never been to church, except to an occasional funeral; no one had invited us. The only people in our neighborhood I knew were tavern operators, but when God begins working, he times everything perfectly! On Thursday night, after Joe's funeral, three ladies from the Riverside Baptist Church, where my family and I are still proud members, knocked on our door. They were humble, friendly, kind, and Christ-like. They invited Reecie and me to church, and we promised to go. That next Sunday morning, we were at Riverside Church.

A few weeks later, I moved my church membership to Riverside Baptist. I still wasn't a Christian, but I started going to the men's class at Riverside Sunday School, and here God began to convict me of my sins. I didn't want to give up any of the habits I loved, so for three months, I fought God.

Now it was as though a tornado swept through my soul. I held hard to the things of the world, fearful that they would be swept away. At the same time, I felt the burden of my sins growing heavier and heavier.

Four months after Joe's death, on March 2, 1957, it happened. I attended a sales demonstration in Robertsdale, and tanked up afterward. On the way home, sick at heart from my sins, and sick to my stomach from too much whiskey, I pulled off the road and opened the door to get some fresh air. I fell out of the car—onto my knees.

With the gravel pressing into my kneecaps, I realized for the first time in my life exactly where I was headed. My life was going downhill, and some day, I would be lying in a casket, just like Joe. What then? Joe had found peace with God. What could I take into eternity but sin and shame?

If tradition or ancestry could save anyone, I would have been saved many times. My grandfather had been a deacon in the Baptist church for more than seventy years. The church I went to as a boy had been built on land donated by Granddaddy, with money he and others had given. It was there that I had been baptized in the creek. If church membership alone could save, I had no worries, but I knew I needed something more.

Kneeling there, by the side of the road, I prayed, "Lord, I'm tired of running. I'm tired of sin and the life I've been living. I'm tired of all these heartaches and all this misery. Lord, I come to you, as humbly as I know how, in the name of the Lord Jesus Christ. God, have mercy on my wretched soul."

God heard that prayer. He changed my life completely; it's hard to believe I'm the same man. The fact is I'm not. "If any man be in Christ, he is a new creature; old things are passed away; and become new" (2 Corinthians 5:17). Anything I accomplish is because God reached down into the depths of sin, lifted me up, and set my feet on a rock. He has put a new song in my heart and joy in my soul, and thanks to him, I'm a new man.

Reecie knew something had changed in me, almost as soon as she saw me. My son Dale knew I was a different daddy when I stopped drinking and started praying and reading the Bible with him and Reecie. Now, I wanted to go to church every time there was a service.

Reecie bought me a Bible, and I literally wore the covers off it. I read and searched and dug and prayed; I asked the Lord to reveal his word to me, and God blessed me in a wonderful way. I was like a desert traveler, nearly dead from starvation and thirst, who comes to a green oasis. When I got in my car, instead of turning the radio on, I talked to my Lord. On trips, I would spend hours meditating and praising my Savior. I became actively involved in every part of the church work except the women's missionary society.

A number of people helped me understand the scriptures and grow in my Christian experience, but I give special thanks to my then Sunday school teacher, John Aikens, and two very fine Christian traveling salesmen, Bob Platt and Louis Ferguson.

That time on my knees by the side of the road was by far the greatest experience of my life, but it didn't just happen. Some time later, I discovered one of the amazing links in the chain that finally brought me to God.

While visiting with some sick friends at a hospital, a light-complexioned black man in the corridor strangely attracted my attention. He was wearing a robe and reading a newspaper, and I realized that he must be a patient. As our eyes met, there was a mutual feeling of recognition. My mind started racing as I walked toward him, trying to remember who this man was, and why I knew him. Suddenly, he tossed his newspaper aside, jumped to his feet, and called my name.

At that point, I recognized him. Fletcher English was a merchant from a small town near Mobile. He had been a customer of mine, many years before. His store was the last one I visited on Monday nights, the last call I made after I passed the local liquor store. While I was writing up Fletcher's order and pricing other orders from the day's sales, I would have several drinks; many times, I left Fletcher's store heavily under the influence of alcohol.

Fletcher and I were glad to see each other. After we had exchanged the usual greetings, he remarked that I looked like a new man.

I told him, "I *am* a new man!" I told him what Christ had done in my life, how he had changed me completely.

Tears streamed down Fletcher's cheeks, "Hallelujah!" he said. "Praise God. Thank you, Jesus."

His face was full of joy, and I rejoiced with him, not knowing exactly what was going on but just happy because he was happy. Then I learned why Fletcher was so full of joy. He told me that for years, he and his wife had been praying for me. Night after night, they would get down on their knees and ask God to save me before it was too late. Fletcher went on to say that they had placed my name before their entire church for prayer so that God might spare my life and work a miracle in my heart.

Fletcher and his wife were concerned about me. Their church was concerned. A whole company of believers had prevailed in prayer for me. Ten years before I knew anything about it, these people had presented my name before the throne of grace. Is there any wonder that I believe in God and in the power of prayer?

Chapter 19

A New Door,
Public Service

The most important thing that ever occurred in my life is recorded in the previous chapter. However, the Christian life is a journey. We grow, day by day, and should continue to do so until God calls us home. Many people, for whatever reason, fail to grow or reach their full potential on this earth, thereby missing many great blessings that could have been theirs. The salvation experience is indescribable, but the journey afterwards is a continuous blessing.

There are bumps along the way; the roses come with thorns, and there are ups and downs, but there is one who helps us along our Christian journey. He promises to "be with us always, even to the end of the world." I can testify that God keeps his promises. He has seen me through many storms and many trials and temptations. Pride, anger, jealousy, envy, ambition, moral temptations, and false accusations are but a few of the pot holes along life's highway that only God can help us cross to go on to victory in our journey.

At the age of thirty-five, after eight years of trying my best to serve Christ in the local church's denominational and interdenominational activities, God opened a door for me to spend twenty years in public office.

I had never taken part in any kind of political activity until I began campaigning for the job as commissioner and mayor of my city. Never before had I been connected with a political party, never even carried a political sticker on my automobile. When elections came along, I knew so little about most of the candidates that I'm afraid I seldom voted intelligently. Although I sometimes felt a little guilty because I was doing nothing to further good government, politics just didn't grab me.

Not, that is, until an unusual chain of events began to unfold in a Mobile supermarket. I was checking stock, in connection with my food brokerage business, when a salesman friend, Val Wilheim, came down the aisle with an unusual expression on his face.

"Lambert," he said, "you ought to run for commissioner." The idea struck me as so preposterous I thought Val was joking.

"Yes," I laughed, "and Lassie can run for president."

"No," Val said. "I mean it. You know how corrupt things are at city hall. Unless there's a change soon, Mobile is going to end up the way of other seaport towns, specializing in narcotics and venereal disease. We need men like you in public office. Think about it."

I did think about it, briefly and pleasantly—who doesn't enjoy daydreaming now and then?—but not seriously.

A few days later, I telephoned a friend in the Baptist Brotherhood, and he suggested I get into the upcoming race for commissioner. Again, I brushed the thought aside, but about a week later, when a third friend said, casually, that he thought I ought to run for commissioner, I began to suspect a plot. In fact, the three men were from different parts of the city, in different occupations, and none of them knew the others had urged me to get into civic affairs.

I discussed it with my wife, Reecie, and I wondered if, perhaps, God was trying to speak to me, through what otherwise must be the strangest of coincidences. It was certainly true that something had to be done about the deteriorating city government. I do not intend to point the finger at the administration then in power, but if you will look at any city, where the "ins" has drifted along for too long without a challenge, you'll get an idea of the situation. Mobile needed, better protection against crime, fires, and flooding, and more attention to parks, playgrounds, and youth programs. Instead of the new taxes being proposed, the city needed less wasteful spending and the introduction of competitive-bid buying. There was no question that Mobile needed a change, but the world of politics was new to me, and, to confess the honest truth, more than a little frightening.

I looked at every side of the situation. I had lived in Mobile for nearly twenty years, my wife and I had many friends, my boys were growing up, and my business, the Mims Brokerage Company, had prospered. The people of Mobile had been good to us, and we took pride in the city.

More than a century before the pilgrims entered Plymouth harbor, a Spanish expedition sailed into Mobile Bay and named it *Bahia del*

Spiritu Santo, or Bay of the Holy Spirit. Fort Louis de la Mobile was established in 1702, before there was a United States of America, making Mobile one of the oldest cities in the nation. Admiral Farragut was sailing into Mobile Bay during the Civil War when he gave the famous order, "Damn the torpedoes! Full speed ahead!"

During both World Wars, our city contributed millions of dollars worth of ships and vital products to this nation's security. It has been ruled by the French, British, and Spanish, and has flown the flags of the Republic of Alabama, the Confederate States of America, and the United States of America. Today, Mobile is one of America's leading seaports. The six flags that represent its history point to its destiny as a truly international city of the future.

I had gone to school with a boy named Tom Weatherford. He was a descendant of the Creek Indian Chief, Red Eagle, or William Weatherford, who led an attack against Fort Mims, sixty miles north of Mobile, in 1813. The history of Fort Mims, founded in Alabama by Mims who migrated from Virginia and the Carolinas, and its infamous massacre, were very real to Tom and me. My ancestor, David Mims, and more than five hundred men, women, and children had been slaughtered in that unexpected attack. Red Eagle later surrendered to Andrew Jackson, apologized for the massacre, and was pardoned; he lived in peace and tranquility until he died a natural death. I took pride in the fact that the Mims family had been contributing to the building of my state and country for more than one hundred and fifty years.

I used to dream of the future, back in the days of plowing cotton under the hot summer sun on my father's farm I dreamed of being somebody and having influence on the world. When I moved to Mobile and started my own business, I'd never imagined I might someday become mayor; I just loved the city's thriving energy and fine people. Mobile, with its commerce and industry, Mardi Gras and its thirty-five mile azalea trail, the Senior Bowl game and Junior Miss Pageant, and its gracious memories and hopes for the future must not fall prey to the crime and corruption which have invaded so many cities. Could God want me to have a part in saving this great city from evil?

Reecie was not enthusiastic about the idea of having her husband mixed up in a political campaign. However, we both felt that we owed it to God to make it a matter of prayer.

"Lord," I prayed, "you know I'm active in your work. I witness for you in every way I can, and I want to do your will. If I enter this race for commissioner of Mobile and make a bad showing, it will reflect on you and your church. If I run, I have to win. Lord, make it clear to me what I should do. If you want me to run, I want to know it!"

I was chairman of the deacons of my church, president of the Baptist Brotherhood of Mobile, president of the local Camp of Gideon's, and active in the Christian Businessmen's Committee. Everyone who knew me knew I was a Christian, and the people who had known me before I became one knew something had happened to change my way of life. I dared not bring discredit on the Savior who had changed my life. I couldn't run for public office and win an honorable mention. God's honor would be at stake; Christ's church would be on the line. If I ran, I had to win. To make a bad showing would be a bad testimony. I had to know what to do.

I could picture people who weren't Christians sneering, "That guy's supposed to be a Christian leader, but the Christians didn't vote for him. What kind of leader is that? And what kind of Christians does he think he's leading?"

A lot was at stake. I kept talking to the Lord, in a "man-to-man" sort of way. My wife prayed with me, and I took my problem to some special friends, the men in a prayer group that met every Saturday night.

"Men," I told them, "I'm going to ask you to do something that will probably sound pretty strange. I want you to pray earnestly about a decision I have to make, probably the most important decision I've ever made. I can't tell you what it's about, but I want you to pray."

Those men prayed as I'd asked them to, my pastor prayed, and I talked to the Lord, day in and day out.

Gradually, the answer began to come. God impressed me with his need for Christians to become involved in public affairs. He laid it on my heart that His people must come off the sidelines of life and become participants. I saw that an important area of Christian stewardship is making the world a better place, and I could certainly do this by serving in public office.

I began to realize I was being offered an opportunity to show where I stood, to express my Christian witness in a new way. Deep within me, I felt that God was leading me to seek my place as commissioner. I entered myself in the nomination.

Winning would take some doing; I didn't belong to a party and didn't have a political base, but over a short period, we were able to put together a winning team.

Chapter 20

Organizing to Win

Politics was a completely new world for me; I can't say that I always knew what I was doing, but I had a pretty good idea of what I would have to do to wage a successful campaign, as well as what it might cost.

Television, billboard advertising, and everything that makes a candidate known—it all costs money. At the time, it was a lot of money for a political novice to raise, but it is infinitesimal compared to the amounts spent in campaigns today. Many candidates are hopelessly obligated before they begin—sold out, body and soul, to the people who paid the bills. I didn't intend to be obligated to anyone, and I'm pleased to say that I came through the campaign a free man. I made it clear, throughout, that I would make no deals, of any kind. When I made a decision, I wanted to base it solely on what was right and best for all concerned. The fact that most of our contributions were small ones pleased me more than if a few large ones had financed the campaign.

I made a plan. I visualized every step I would have to take to win the election, and I blocked out, on a calendar, what I would have to do each week until Election Day. In my heart, I was as sure as Reecie was that I could and would win, but I dared not take any chances. I worked hard, as though I would lose, unless I put everything I had into the campaign. I can't think of anything we should have done that we didn't do, or anything we did that we shouldn't have. We just worked as hard as we knew how.

"We" included not only Reecie, but also everyone in the organization we built. Jeff, my brother, became my campaign manager. He was a Catholic who worked just as hard in his church as I did in mine. While I was president of the Baptist Brotherhood, Jeff was president of the local Holy Name Society. Through his influence, many Catholics and Jews united behind me with Protestants who knew me and what I stood for. My best friend, Dennis Moore, was my co-chairman. We rented a campaign headquarters, where dozens of volunteers worked all day and half the nights. Jeff and Dennis practically slept there. It was often two in the morning before we went home.

Our workers were volunteers. This was a change from political operations where ward heelers paid people to work. Our workers had a dedication and enthusiasm that no money could buy. It was a fine thing for our city to have so many people involved in this crusade for better government.

We formed a finance committee of one hundred men. Each member agreed to contact ten men for funds and support. We also set-up advertising, telephone, and ward committees, as well as committees for various other aspects of the campaign.

Volunteers came from everywhere. Housewives, who had never before been concerned with politics, got on the phone, stuffed envelopes, cranked mimeograph machines, passed out campaign literature, and worked for our victory. Businessmen, laborers, church members, young people, and other citizens stepped up to the plate. One man who worked extremely hard was Bobby Tillman, who had lost one leg in an accident. He operated a taxi company, and he worked like a Trojan. A Greek gentleman, Manuel Clikas, who also worked very hard, was about the only person in our whole organization that had had any experience in campaigning. He was perfect on the telephone; he and other workers called everyone they knew or could think of. Hundreds of people who expected only one thing in return, good government, donated countless hours of time.

We arranged for six weeks of meetings at one of Mobile's finest motor hotels and restaurants. Each week, about forty people, from all walks of life—doctors, lawyers, dentists, businessmen, truck drivers, factory workers, farmers, members of churches and civic clubs—were invited to come and hear our platform. I explained why I was running for office, what I was concerned about, and what I proposed to do to create a reasonable and clean government in our city. The response was terrific. Most of those present enthusiastically pledged their support, and week after week, as other interest groups came, the results multiplied, and our organization grew.

All over Mobile, women opened their homes for afternoon teas. They made cakes and cookies, served tea and coffee, and invited their friends in to meet me. I usually spent thirty minutes at these teas, chatting informally and presenting my plan for government, and then I'd drive on to the next place.

When people think of political rallies, they usually think of a lot of noise, drinking, and ballyhoo. Our organizational rallies were altogether different. We generally had a piano and a song director present, and we would open the rally with some singing, beginning with "America" or our National Anthem. Then we went right into business, bringing everyone up to date on recent happenings and filling them in on what we wanted them to do, before we had our next meeting. After that, we had time for fellowship and refreshments. The drinks were coffee or soda, and we ate dessert brought by the ladies. Everyone enjoyed the whole thing. People who had never met before formed lasting friendships at our gatherings. The whole campaign had a very healthy impact on the Mobile community.

I, a political unknown, was becoming organized. An independent candidate, never heard of in political circles, was laying the groundwork for what was to become, according to observers familiar with local politics, one of the finest campaign organizations this area had seen.

We purchased television time, radio time, newspaper space, billboard advertising, and campaign literature. We didn't have an agency. I was my own advertising manager. We laid out every one of our ads and circulars, ourselves. In all our ads, we used the same simple appeals and general motif. Day-glow lettering in orange and black-blanketed billboards and auto bumpers; the public could hardly ignore admonitions like these: "RETURN REASON TO CITY HALL." "VOTE MIMS." "ELECT A BUSINESS MAN TO PLACE THREE, MOBILE CITY COMMISSION."

Some mornings, I got up at three or four o'clock to meet the early shifts of workers in Mobile's factories. Four railroads, four major airlines, and one hundred steamship lines served our city. We had a three million bushel grain elevator, a gypsum company, two paper mills, and a number of chemical plants. Mobile workers built and repaired ships, refined oil, fabricated metal, and produced iron, steel, aluminum, cement, roofing, wood pulp, paper products, clothing, and bakery products. I wanted as many of these men and women as possible to know of my interest in better government. I shook hands with them, passed out my circulars, and asked them for their votes.

Funds came in, a little here and a little there. A Catholic priest (now deceased) contributed twenty-five dollars. We accepted every contribution offered, no matter how small it might be. Once a person has given you a dollar, you have his support.

Autos carried campaign signs. To keep our opposition guessing about where I was and what I might be doing, I often switched cars with friends. One day I traveled in a Pontiac, the next a Chevrolet and the next a Ford or Chrysler. I made certain someone was always with me.

We prayed and we worked. As the days and weeks passed, and we followed the steps on our campaign calendar, a tremendous feeling of good will and enthusiasm developed. People who had never before had any real interest in politics worked day and night with a common purpose. We all had a good time as we looked forward to Election Day.

Thousands of citizens became interested. As the election drew near, we blanketed the city with brochures. Each weekend, we visited every shopping center and saw that we placed a piece of literature under the windshield wiper of every parked car. We distributed bumper stickers and bought hundreds of inches of newspaper space. I made countless personal appearances and radio announcements, and dozens of television appeals.

There were six candidates in the race, including the incumbent and the son of a former mayor. When the votes were counted, the former mayor's son and I were in a run off; I came in second. Our real battle had just begun.

We continued with the plan that had brought me so far, more determined than ever. We made every effort to enlist the supporters of the candidate who had been eliminated in the first run. Our campaign had come a long way, especially for a political novice who hadn't been supposed to win.

I won the final push on television. I wasn't able to pre-record my television appearances as my opponents had, but this gave me an unusual advantage. Years of sales and church work gave me the ability, not only to speak with assurance into a live television camera, but also an interesting additional opportunity. I was able to tie the day's events into what I said each evening, and according to my co-workers, I came across better than my opponents, whose previously recorded statements looked canned—because they were.

Many people freeze when they look into a television camera. I thought of all the people across Mobile, two hundred and twenty thousand of them at the time, looking and listening. They were people who needed a change for the better in their political leaders, and I threw my heart into letting them see that here was one candidate who really intended to work for their best interests. I believe television work is the same as all communication—to reach people, understand them and talk from the heart. You must mean what you say. People can tell if you're sincere or a phony. If you want to convince them, you had better believe what you're telling them.

When Election Day arrived, we knew we had done our best. That morning, Reecie, our two sons, and I met at breakfast, with a sense that everything was now in the hands of the Lord. We turned the whole matter over to him. I prayed he would go behind the curtains with the voters and direct their hands to pull the right levers. I asked for victory if it was his will and if it would glorify him. If not, I prayed for the grace to accept defeat like a Christian.

That night an expectant group gathered at our campaign headquarters. Our workers began phoning in the results as soon as the polls closed, at six p.m. There was an air of tremendous excitement all through the evening. The telephones at our headquarters were in constant use as workers totaled the votes. A television set was brought in, and people milled around with portable radios.

When the votes swept in from the downtown Mobile area, a good many of those present became pretty glum; the majority were voting along party lines. Another group, the silk stockings that consisted of the wealthier and older aristocratic families of Mobile, gave most of its votes to the opponent whose father had once been mayor.

The suburban wards were the last to report, and the tide turned. My strength came from the suburbs, as Kennedy's had in 1960 and Nixon's in 1968. The younger voters, parents raising families and people who had moved to Mobile from other cities, gave me their votes. We had a clear majority. We had come from behind, from second place, to win. What an accomplishment. What a victory! All that handshaking in the suburban areas of Mobile had paid off.

The television cameras zoomed toward me as reporters and media interviewers all tried to ask questions at once.

"Now that you have emerged victorious from this hard fought campaign," asked a television announcer, "what word do you have for the people of Mobile?"

Turning toward the cameras, I thanked people for their confidence in me. I thanked those who had worked so hard to make the campaign a success. I thought of my mother and father, who had been anxiously awaiting the results as they sat by their television set on the farm where I had grown up.

"Mama and Daddy," I said, "I want you to pray for me as I undertake this new task at city hall. I'm a long way from the cotton patch tonight."

Photo Section

Mayor Mims at his City Hall desk.

APWA General Counselor Lambert Mims, 2nd from right, leading Emergency Management workshop in Kingston, Jamaica.

Mayor Mims, while President of American Public Works Association, arriving in Bahamas for a meeting. Mrs. Mims at bottom step.

Mayor Mims with Alabama Governor, George Wallace.

Mayor Mims with President and Mrs. Carter at the White House.

Mayor Mims and Alabama highway Director Marian Wilkins greeting U.S. Senator Jennings Randolph D.W.V., and Chairman of the Senate Public works Committee.

Ambassador Mims in his role of promoting Alabama's waterways.

Mayor Mims presenting Ann Landers with a copy of his book
"For Christ and Country."

Mayor Mims presenting Brenda Lee, country singer, with Key to City.

Mayor Mims with Kenny Rogers, Key to City presentation,
back stage at Civic Center.

Mayor Mims with Mel Tillis, country music star.

Waterways Ambassador Mims at the Port of Mobile.

Mayor Mims with Max Cleland, former VA Administrator and U.S.
Senator from Georgia-at 4th of July Celebration.

Chapter 21

The Bible, a Boll of Cotton, and Remember Lot

That line spoken to my parents was mentioned many times following our first election victory. Little did I realize just how far from the cotton patch I was. On my first day in office, the Mobile Baptist Association presented me with a red leather-bound Bible. It became one of three items on my desk everyday of my twenty years of service, to remind me that I must stand upon God's word, read it daily, and practice what it says, always.

Another item was a boll of cotton, from my daddy's cotton crop that year. It was incased in a shadow box with a glass top, so all could see the fine, pure white locks from the fields where I was brought up. The boll of cotton was to remind me of where I came from—the cotton patch—and my upbringing.

The third was a sign on my pen set that said, simply, "Remember Lot." When Lot and Abraham parted ways, Lot chose Sodom and Gomorrah. It was there he became mayor; the scriptures say that he "sat in the gate of the city." Lot lost his influence and, ultimately everything but his life. Even his wife was turned to a pillar of salt. This was to remind me that I could lose my influence if I did not stay close to God.

The first four years, I spent learning about government and putting forth all the energy I had discovering the needs of my city and doing my best to develop plans to meet those needs. When the three of us who had been elected to the Mobile City Commission sat down to divide the duties, which fell under three major headings—Public Works, Finance & Recreation, and Public Safety—I chose Public Works. I felt that it was there I could make the most impact. Of course, my father's involvement in road construction and maintenance no doubt played a big part in my feeling I could render good service to the citizens of our city.

At that time, there were 216,000 people living in the city. There were more than 1400 miles of streets. Sanitation services, street lighting, storm and sewer services—these were just a few of the activities that fell within the Public Works commissioner's duties. In addition, each commissioner served one third, or sixteen months, of the four-year term as mayor and presiding officer of the Board of Commissioners.

I set out to learn all I could about public works and determined to be the best Public Works commissioner Mobile had ever had. I truly felt that I could do anything I set my mind to do.

At the age of thirty-five, I was the youngest person elected to the City Commission, and became the youngest to serve as mayor. I had gotten my life together. I had surrendered to the Lord. He had saved me and transformed my life. I had studied his word intensely and begun to learn, to some small degree, what it meant to seek and follow God's will.

I truly thought, and believe to this day, that I was in God's will, that what was taking place was according to God's plan for my life. I had found my niche, and my confidence was extremely high. Feeling that God was with me, I felt that I could handle most anything. As it turned out, I would need God's help and wisdom to deal with the many tough decisions and temptations I was to face.

I went home most nights, after a long day, with a tremendous headache. I crammed so much into my brain it was unreal. The burdens of thousands weighed heavily on my shoulders. There were endless meetings with different groups, and then there were the administrative duties, the personnel problems, the zoning matters, and individual citizens wanting to see me about matters that were, to them, the most important in the world.

In addition, there were public appearances and speaking engagements. Every convention expected me to be there to welcome them to the city. There were dignitaries from foreign countries. We had numerous international visitors, because Mobile was, and still is, a seaport town with ships from around the world calling at our port.

The city's infrastructure had needs that had to be addressed. The city limits had been expanded and new streets, drains, lighting, and sanitation sewers had to be provided. The Public Works had been the least addressed department in the years prior to my taking office. No one seemed to care about the condition of the equipment or the level of service rendered to the public.

One of the first things I did was upgrade the public works services. Heretofore, public works personnel, for the most part, were not in the civil service system and were hired and fired at will. The pay was extremely low, so about all we had were men who couldn't get jobs anywhere else or were alcoholics and not able to do a good day's work. This was especially true in the sanitation department.

The trucks were old and dilapidated; they looked terrible and smelled even worse. When the sanitation truck stopped to pick up garbage, a swarm of flies followed it. The garbage was taken to a hundred-year-old dump on the north side of town, where it was burned. An awful stench fell over downtown every night, and the smoke was so bad it burned resident's eyes.

The storm drains didn't function; the least amount of rainfall flooded the streets. My position was—What good is a fine police or fire department, if they can't go where the need is because streets are so bad or flooded they are impassable? The bottom line was that the "rag tag" public works operation had to be upgraded. It would take personnel, equipment, and leadership. I set out to provide all three.

I joined the American Public Works Association and attended every workshop and seminar I could attend. There, I began to learn how to do my job as public works commissioner. I visited other cities and networked with those that had successful programs. I attended equipment shows and conventions to learn all I could about public works. I surrounded myself with people who knew the field, and over time, began to provide the leadership needed to upgrade Mobile's public works department.

One thing I knew for sure was that, in order to provide good service to more than two hundred thousand people; we had to have good employees. They had to have good benefits and decent salaries. Many of the employees had been hired on the spot, and terminated just as quickly. Many did not receive the insurance, days off, and general benefits as regular civil service employees. There wasn't much incentive for them to do a good job. In my mind, all municipal employees were important.

The police and fire departments received the most publicity because of the nature of their job. A big fire created a big media event. A bank robbery or drug bust made the evening news with blue lights flashing all over the television screens. Before I was elected and placed in charge of public works, all the other city activities in fire, police, and recreation got priority in the budget, in recognition, and in public attention. Public works received the most complaints and the least good press. In fact, the press was anxious to criticize my department when potholes weren't filled, the garbage wasn't picked up on time, or the drains were stopped up.

Right off, I decided to take a stand for those who were expected to perform public works functions. When budget hearings came around, I insisted that adequate funds be made available to give salary increases for public works employees. Many times, other city employees received raises, and public works personnel were left behind. I stood my ground, and won in the fight for equal treatment. If one group got raises, all got raises.

In addition, I insisted that all employees be brought under the personnel system with protection, rather than being subject to dismissal, at anytime, without cause. Immediately, moral jumped. People that were more qualified began applying for positions, and the personnel situation greatly improved.

As soon as salary and job security matters were addressed, employees were encouraged to advance in training. The American Public Works Association conducted numerous seminars and workshops, on subjects from safety to sanitation, street maintenance, and storm water management. Many were sent to these seminars, at the city's expense, and in time made a tremendous difference in the performance of all the divisions of public works.

Leadership and personnel were important elements of the program to improve services. However, good equipment was equally important. I persuaded the other two commissioners to go along with me in establishing a budget, which set us on the road to acquiring much needed equipment.

My association with the National Public Works Organization and attendance at international equipment shows helped me learn about the latest equipment. I sought advice from other, more experienced, public works professionals. New fleets of garbage and trash collection trucks were purchased. The old, motley gray color was replaced by sunshine gold and all equipment was marked with City of Mobile decals. An equipment-washing shed with steam washers was installed, with instructions that the trucks be steam cleaned every day. There would be no more stinking, ragged trucks running up and down the streets of Mobile. The entire department took on a new look, and a positive attitude prevailed throughout the city. We began to get great press, just as the fire and police departments did. In fact, they became jealous because of the publicity we received.

A new policy was adopted and signs were posted in every work area outlining our aim: 1. a courteous reply, 2. a quick response, 3. a thorough follow-through. This remained our goal for the twenty years I was privileged to serve, and earned us a reputation as "the nation's finest" public works department.

The great work accomplished by the several hundred men and women in public works was responsible for me being elected to the Board of the American Public Works Association, and ultimately to the presidency of that fine, professional organization. Yes, it was a long way from the cotton patch.

Chapter 22

Challenges and Stress
of Public Service

Those first four years were both challenging and stressful. First, there was the problem of improving city services and providing a sound infrastructure in vast, recently incorporated, areas south and west of the city. Then there was the strain of the economic impact of the closing of Brookley Air Force Base, a materials supply base for the worldwide system of U.S. air bases. Third, these were the days of turbulent civil rights activity. To say that this first term was stressful is an understatement.

Thousands of citizens had been annexed and promised certain services. It was our lot to provide, or at least attempt to provide, everything from garbage collection to street lighting.

To give some idea of the magnitude of this undertaking, try to visualize hundreds of miles of streets, many of which were unimproved dirt roads, hundreds of miles of open ditches and poor storm drainage, no underground sanitation sewers (all homes were on septic tanks), no streetlights, no sidewalks, and no parks. In addition, police and fire services had to be provided, as well as the building of new fire stations.

The financing of these improvements would come, in part, from the municipal property and sales taxes the newly annexed areas began paying. However, these monies wouldn't begin to pay for the services and improvements promised and expected. The city was forced to pursue bond issues, whereby it would borrow funds, to be paid back over an extended period. Sanitary sewers were constructed with revenue bonds, whereby property owners were assessed for improvements and allowed to pay for them over time. Those revenues retired the bonds.

Expert financial and legal advice was sought on these matters; I made many trips to New York City for bond closings, two- or three-day affairs. One day was spent signing the bonds. I'm sure things have changed, but at that time, every bond had to be signed. One company handled this phase with equipment that would duplicate a person's signature on dozen's of bond certificates. It was a tiresome and complicated procedure.

The next morning, a young banker in tennis shoes would show up with a brief case and deliver a multi-million dollar check to us, which we immediately deposited into an interest bearing account; until the funds were expended on projects, the city earned interest on those borrowed funds.

It was on a bond-closing trip that I first had a delicious meal at the *Windows on the World* restaurant at the top of the World Trade Center. What a spectacular sight! Looking down on the Empire State Building, and seeing all the lights miles away, was one of the most awesome sights I have ever witnessed. It was a privilege to take Reecie on several of these trips. The bond folks would entertain us at the finest places— Sardis, Club 21—and we always took in a Broadway play while there. Most memorable was the trip Danny was able to experience with us. I am sure that he will never forget the experience.

The funding of the new projects was certainly a challenge, but so were the planning, development, and construction of the massive public improvement program. It took the city's planning and engineering departments, as well as the architectural engineering department, to plan and coordinate the mammoth undertaking.

Outside consulting engineering firms had to be selected, plans drawn, estimates made, bids advertised and opened, contracts drawn and awarded. It would take years to accomplish it all, but with good employees and excellent consultants, the job was finally done.

As far as collection of garbage was concerned, careful planning was necessary. Residential lots in newer sections of the city were much larger than those homes in the older, historic areas. Older residences had fifty-foot lots, compared to one or two hundred-foot lots. It meant the collection trucks had to travel more miles to collect the same amount of refuse. We came up with a plan to give a truck and crew of three men one route in the older section of the city and one route in the newly annexed section. This meant all crews would have equal responsibilities. There were three pickups per week, when I first took office, which was too much service. Not many people ever put their cans out that often. A carry over from the old days, when the people had a lot of fish heads, shrimp, etc., and the houses were close together—for obvious reasons the three times per week pickup made sense.

It was around this time that the United States was going through an oil embargo, and I saw this as a good time to change pickups to twice a week. We conducted a public relations campaign to make the public aware of the change. We even placed a sticker on every can, to let property owners know which day they could expect a pickup. We put out door hangers, received great help from the media, and the change took place without a hitch. I could say much more about that challenging first term; it was a triumph to accomplish so much over those four years.

I mentioned the economic impact of the closing of Brookley Air Force Base. The announcement to close the vast two thousand-acre complex of warehouses, repair shops, administrative buildings, barracks, educational facilities, streets, runways that would accommodate anything that flew, and docking facilities for ocean going vessels was a sad event. Alabama voted for Barry Goldwater in the 1964 presidential elections, and President Johnson was not happy about it. When base-closing lists were presented, Brookley didn't have a ghost of a chance. Secretary of Defense McNamara became the bad guy who had to proclaim, "Brookley closes!"

I shall never forget that day. Our church, Riverside Baptist, was in the midst of a pledge banquet scheduled for that very night. Many of our members were employed at the base located just north of our community, which was known as South Brookley. We gathered for what was to be a festive occasion at the B.C. Rain High School cafeteria, which is across the Parkway from our church, but because of the news of the closing of Brookley, it was more like a wake than a time of celebration. It was as if a giant water balloon had been dropped on us. As chairperson of the campaign and master of ceremonies of the banquet, I did the best I could to make it through the evening without crying like other folk. Eventually, the base was phased out. Our church and community experienced much change as many of our members accepted transfers to other bases and left our area. Membership in the church dropped drastically, and we have never gained back to the attendance we had before the closing.

By the time I was sworn in as commissioner, in early October 1965, the economic impact was being felt in Mobile and specifically our community. One of the first matters on the agenda when I took office was "What do we do to offset the economic loss?"

Fifteen thousand people or more had worked at Brookley when the closing was announced, and untold thousands were employed in businesses that depended upon the multi-million dollar payroll. Everyone was affected by the loss of income in the area. Everything, from real estate agents and car dealers to restaurants, felt the jolt. Hundreds of small businesses either were closed or severely hampered. Hundreds, even thousands, of homes would change hands in the next several years as the phase-out took place.

What could the city government do? We set out, first, to gain control of the huge piece of real estate and the hundreds of thousands of square feet of buildings. In base closings, the state has first option to buy. In the state of Alabama, only the University of South Alabama had any interest, and that was in acreage near the bay that had been used for housing. It would become educational facilities for the University. The county had second choice, and the commissioners did not choose to tackle such a task. The city of Mobile then had the opportunity to put the pieces together and turn the military reservation into an industrial complex. It was not an easy job. We hit the road, seeking any industry needing the kind of space we had available. We found a large aircraft engine manufacturer to relocate here, employing several hundred people. We were on the way to developing Brookley into the complex we had envisioned. Over the years, although we never replaced the total number of jobs lost, we did create several thousand new jobs, and the base is now a diversified and thriving industrial complex.

The phase-out took at least five years. The strain on the economy affected the community. The loss of friends moving to other places and the closing of businesses was painful. We survived, but the population of the city dropped and has never regained its pre-closing numbers.

There was much stress during that first term when it came to race relations. Although there was never much visible animosity between the blacks and whites, Mobile was, and had been, a very segregated deep south city. The Civil Rights Act of 1964 had been passed, however, and more African-Americans were voting. Change was in the air.

During my first election effort, I had a little support from the black community, mainly because I had spoken in a number of national Baptist Churches, and the ministers knew me. I didn't fare well in the predominately black wards; since my run-off opponent was the son of a former mayor, he received most of the vote in those areas. I couldn't and didn't blame the blacks; they really didn't know me. It certainly did not affect my service and response to them once I was elected. In fact, I set out to help underprivileged areas and began to bring our African-American citizens into the main stream. The city commission set up a bi-racial committee to work on race relations and economic improvements for those who had been, in many instances, excluded.

We were walking a tightrope. On one hand, there was the White Citizens Council that wanted the status quo. On the other, there was the NAACP (National Association for the Advancement of Colored People) and the Non-partisan Voters League, both of which were pushing for change. We tried to reason with both sides, and through the bi-racial groups we were able to keep down a lot of strife that would have otherwise occurred.

We made great strides in getting businesses to open up opportunities for blacks, but in spite of this progress, there was tremendous stress on all office holders at the time. African-Americans had been educated in segregated schools, but many hadn't finished high school. Many felt that they had been held back. Desegregation of the schools was in progress, mostly through busing kids across town. In an effort to balance the population from a racial standpoint, children were taken from their communities to buildings far from their homes. Neighborhood schools always had strong parent-teacher organizations but travel and lack of community pride affected attendance. Change, even for the better, is not always pleasant, yet we went through those years without the turmoil many major cities experienced.

I remember well the day that Dr. Martin Luther King was assassinated. He was in Memphis, in support of a sanitation workers' strike. I had visited the Memphis Public Works operation before as I tried to get an idea of how other cities did things. I hadn't been impressed, one bit, with the way things looked. Their system was antiquated. Crews went through back yards, dumping trashcan contents into huge tubs, which were brought to the street on the shoulders of the workers. Not only was there the danger of injuries to the sanitation workers, but the risk of being accused of tampering with private property. This method had been in effect many years and no one wanted to change.

The workers had many grievances and seemingly, no one would listen. It was an explosion waiting to happen. Dr. King came to assist them in getting the ear of elected officials. Before his visit was over, he was gunned down from the balcony of his motel. The tragic news caused great pain and agony in America. Dr. King's death not only stirred African-Americans, but also grieved all decent folk who wished for better race relations in our country.

A small element in Mobile tried in every way to bring about upset, but levelheaded black leaders and understanding white leaders kept a lid on things. Even though national rabble-rousers came to town, teaching young people how to make firebombs, we were fortunate to get by with little trouble and pain. The stress was tremendous—one side pulling one way and the other pulling the other way, but unlike Washington, Los Angeles, and other major cities, we escaped great tragedy.

Chapter 23

Travel, Trouble, and Trauma

I look back over those twenty years of public service, and I am amazed that I was able to get through them without having a breakdown. I remember one occasion, when I was under so much pressure and wound so tight, my long time friend and political advisor, Dennis Moore, told me, in no uncertain terms, "You are going with me."

"Going where?" I asked.

"It doesn't matter; I'm getting you out of here," he said.

"I can't go; don't you see that line of people out there to see me?" I asked him.

I brought a lot of the strain on myself by being so available. I encouraged people to come to me with their problems, many of which were insignificant, but to them were as big as mountains. I relished it. I was a people person, had established an open door policy, and even had a "Meet the Mayor Day" every week, where people could see me without making an appointment.

The pressure of the duties of the office, the meetings, the conferences, and the pull of the people were almost overwhelming. Dennis won the argument. Mrs. Regan, one of my faithful secretaries, told those waiting that I had to leave. I didn't know where I was going, but I trusted my friend, so for the next several hours he drove me around the adjoining county until I was able to unwind. Faithful friends like Dennis helped me cope with the stress of the office more than they will ever know.

There were times when it seemed that the temptations, trials, demands of the office, and my personal commitment to serving the Lord seemed to get the best of me.

I am reminded of an occasion when I was in the Atlanta Airport, waiting for a plane change en route to a speaking engagement at a church in Tennessee. The pressures of the office during that week had been so stressful I could hardly think straight, and here I was, on my way to try to be a blessing and encouragement to a church and people I had never met. It was a Saturday afternoon, and at the time, Eastern Airlines was the largest air carrier in the East. Eastern had hundreds of flights out of Atlanta, its headquarters. Flights were announced one after the other and they were just about to drive me up the wall. I thought, if they call one more flight, I think I will have to stand up and scream. I finally made my connection to Knoxville. Upon arriving there, a layman from the church picked me up and drove me for an hour or so, and bombarded me with meaningless small talk. He put me up at a small motel where I was the only guest, indicating that he would return later to take me to the church where I was to speak that night and the next morning. Here I was, in a tiny room, about to go up the wall. I couldn't get my mind on my message that, within hours, I was to deliver. I began to cry and pray, and was not doing a very good job of getting through. I was physically and mentally exhausted, and even more spiritually dry. I opened the shade of a tiny window of that little room, and to my amazement, there was a beautiful lake in back.

I made my way around the building and out to the lake. There, I spent the next couple of hours walking around and around the lake, crying out to God for forgiveness of my neglect of my prayer life and Bible study. I repented of every sin that came to my mind, and as I did, God began to lift the terrific load and gave me peace that only he can give. I was once again reminded that he was in control, I belonged to him, and he had promised to be with me always, even until the end of the world.

On another Saturday afternoon, after a hectic week of trying to meet the needs of so many constituents, I found myself in Decatur, Alabama, where I was to speak at a Gideon banquet and a local church the next Sunday morning. I had flown to Huntsville Airport and was met by a local Gideon who transported me to the hotel. I was in no condition to be a blessing to anyone. I knew full well I had to get with God if I was to be an effective speaker in just a few hours. Activity around the motel distracted me from getting quiet with the Lord, so I made my way to the banks of the Tennessee River, where I walked up and down, confessing my sins and asking God's forgiveness. He heard my prayers, forgave me, and set my mind and heart at ease. God supplied the peace I needed and used me in a mighty way that evening.

"If we confess our sins, he is faithful and just to forgive us our sins and cleanse us from all unrighteousness." (1 John 1:9)

It has been said that it is lonely at the top. I can testify to this statement. I remember one night I was expected to welcome three different groups of convention attendees to Mobile. They all wanted me, and of course, I couldn't be at three different places at the same time. My secretary arranged for me to go from one to the other, which is what I did. I went to the first as they were getting started. I took my place at the head table, made my welcome address, and excused myself. Upon arriving at the second convention banquet, they were enjoying a beautiful steak meal with all the trimmings. Again, I made my welcome address and asked to be excused. When I arrived at the third convention banquet, they were just finishing their delicious meal. I made my welcoming address, and still had not a bite to eat. At ten o'clock that night, I was sitting at McDonalds, eating a Big Mac and fries, feeling sorry for myself, having a pity party, and thinking how everyone thought I had it made.

On another occasion, I was invited to speak to a Catholic men's meeting in a northern city. After the usual tough week, I arrived on a Saturday afternoon. The man who invited me, as fine as he was, picked me up and advised me that he was busy and wouldn't be able to spend any time with me. He drove me to the hotel and departed. After checking in and finding my room, I opened the curtain, and all I could see were banks of snow, on what appeared to be industrial buildings. Here I was, having traveled a thousand miles, taking time from my family and personal rest, to be met by a man who was too busy to visit with me, even for a short time, and left alone to look out the window at snow-covered buildings.

Lonely is not the word for how I felt. What was I doing here? My heart was heavy. I had come to be used by the Lord and here I was, the mayor of Mobile, one of the larger cities in America, sitting up here all alone. "Why am I here?" I asked myself. God reminded me that I had not arrived at my opportunity yet. I asked him to forgive me, and his presence blanketed me, as he will always do when one of his own confesses his sins and repents.

That night and the next morning, as I shared my personal testimony and experiences with several hundred Catholic men, God's Holy Spirit took control, and we were all blessed beyond explanation. Yes, it's lonely at the top, but when you have the Lord with you, you are a majority.

The stress of a firefighter strike took its toll on everyone; especially those of us expected to provide protection for our people. Things deteriorated, and some were getting ugly. The attitude of some of the strike leaders and their unwillingness to back off from some of their demands was extremely troubling. The governor sent the National Guard to assist us. The whole city was on edge, and I knew this situation had to be handled, or we would have problems. If we had a big fire, or just several small ones at the same time, it would be difficult to contain them.

Again, on a Saturday afternoon, as was my custom, I was flying out of town to speak at a church or Christian gathering of some kind. As the plane made its approach to the Alexandria, Louisiana Airport, I noticed out the window, a small home engulfed in flames. Children and adults ran to and fro as the flames shot into the air. My heart was so moved that I broke into tears, deeply touched by this family that was undergoing such tragedy.

It seemed that God spoke to me, and said, "You go back to Mobile, and try to bring that strike to a conclusion." I prayed and prayed for my messages for the weekend, but more so for that family I didn't know and the strike, back home.

When I returned Sunday night, I made up my mind to do something to end the matter. I asked several of the leaders of the strike to my home to discuss what we could do. I shared with them and the commissioners what had happened in Louisiana, and how God had spoken to my heart. All agreed that we all had to do some giving, and within a few days, the strike had ended.

God works in mysterious ways. Once again, he turned a stressful situation into a satisfactory conclusion.

As already indicated, being president of the million member Alabama Baptist State Convention, I received many invitations to speak at worship services, men's meetings, and conferences throughout the south. As a Gideon, I had many opportunities to speak at Pastor Appreciation banquets across the country. I was committed to serve the

Lord first and then to serve the citizens of Mobile. I wanted to be the best Public Works commissioner the people had ever had. Many of my close friends didn't understand how I could do both. Sometimes it was not easy, but God's grace is sufficient.

Nature is not always kind to us. Natural disasters like hurricanes, tornados, and floods can be very stressful. I shall never forget September 12, 1979, when hurricane Frederic bore down on the upper gulf coast with winds of nearly 150 miles per hour. When Frederic came around the west end of Cuba and entered the Gulf of Mexico, we began to prepare. You are always hopeful that hurricanes will turn one way or another and miss you. Sometimes they sit in the same spot for days, make a complete circle, and go a different way altogether.

Hurricane Frederick had such force and forward thrust that it was not likely to slow down or wobble. The National Hurricane Center predicted that it would make landfall on the upper Gulf Coast, between New Orleans and the Florida Panhandle. It was headed for Mobile. Emergency management teams from all local governments came together at the emergency operations center to prepare for the worst. We had several days to get ready—if there is such a thing.

We urged citizens to stock up on supplies, board up windows, and secure anything that could be blown around. Folks in low, flood-prone areas, especially near the coast, were evacuated. Vehicles on the evacuation routes were bumper to bumper for hundreds of miles, with people getting away from the coast.

Local government prepared with equipment, supplies and personnel readiness. The closer Frederick approached the coast, the more we doubled efforts to do everything humanly possible to be prepared.

Hurricane Frederick landed just west of Mobile, along the Mississippi–Alabama line, which put the city of Mobile in the worst possible position, the northeast quadrant, where the most damage usually occurs. Federal Emergency Management Administration (FEMA) personnel were on the way and marshaled inland, so they would be on the scene as soon as danger was over.

At daybreak the next morning, we witnessed the greatest devastation most of us had ever seen. It was heart breaking to see a city and county that you love, that you'd worked so hard to improve, demolished. Damage assessments were the first order of the day. Engineers, architects, government leaders, U.S. Army Corps of Engineer personnel, FEMA employees, and public works employees were sent out to assess the damages.

I flew over the city and county in an Alabama National Guard helicopter and could not believe what I saw. Millions of trees were down, virtually every building was damaged, and those near the water's edge had been destroyed. In some cases, only the pilings remained, looking like match stems in the sand. A four-mile long bridge to Dauphin Island had been demolished; concrete sections were toppled into the sound blocking the intercoastal waterway.

I shall never forget how blue the sky was that day, but when you looked to the ground, it was so dreadful. With a disaster like this, the first emotion you encounter is disbelief; this can't happen, this can't be! Then reality sinks in—it has happened; this is real—what shall we do? Then comes shock, and the realization that we have prepared, and it's time to respond. Where do we start? Everything is in shambles, streets are blocked, there's no power, no communications. It's overwhelming! Then comes the positive. We can overcome! We can survive this. We can be victorious. There is a great spirit of unity. Neighbors get to know each other, communities work together, government agencies share resources, and mutual aid becomes a great asset. Federal and state support arrives. Groups of people, the Salvation Army, and church groups from all over the country show up to help.

I remember meeting more than five hundred Baptist men from across the state at the First Baptist Church of Mobile on the first Sunday afternoon after Frederic's landfall. They had chainsaws, fuel, food, rakes, shovels, and anything they might need to assist in clearing the streets. Each team was assigned a certain area, and within the next few days, the streets in the older sections of the city had been opened to at least one lane of traffic. It was heart warming to see so many people involved, from the Red Cross to small civic groups and churches, eager to come to our aid.

Nevertheless, after a few weeks with mountains of debris everywhere and still no power, depression began to set in. Every public building was damaged and many were in shambles. The hurricane had severely damaged city hall, and the seat of government since 1857 had to be moved. This in itself was a major undertaking.

I was to be installed as president of the American Public Works Association at its annual convention, to be held the following week in

Portland, Oregon. This was something I had looked forward to with great anticipation for a long time. A group of our employees and their spouses had plane reservations to this event. They had worked hard to become one of the nation's finest departments, and it was because of their efforts that I was being recognized as leader of this prestigious organization. Needless to say, we could not attend. I taped my address to the organization's members, sitting in my car, outside our ravaged 1857 city hall. Tears running down my cheek, broken in spirit, about as low as I had ever been, I dictated my message, which dealt mostly with the devastation we had witnessed and the great challenge to which we had to respond. I am told that when the message was played to the several thousand members in attendance in Portland, there was not a dry eye in the hall.

It seemed the more we worked to clean up, the more we had to do. It was very discouraging. My determination faded into depression. I began to think I would never survive. There were over two billion dollars in damages, the stress was mounting, and I was worried beyond explanation. The burden was getting the best of me. Stress is a terrible thing. It got so bad, one night my wife exclaimed to me, "Lambert, you do not own Mobile. God has given you the opportunity to lead, but you don't own Mobile. Don't forget that he is in control!"

That was a wake up call for me. Yes, God is in control. I am his and he is mine. I knew it; I just needed a reminder.

Regardless of the stress, God is in control. He is the same—yesterday, today, and forever!

Chapter 24

Experience Is the Best Teacher

Hurricane Frederick was not the first hurricane I had experienced while in office. At the end of my first term, in 1969, the day before the election, Hurricane Camille smashed the Mississippi Gulf Coast. It was a Category IV hurricane and caused hundreds of deaths and great destruction all along the Mississippi coast. Located on the east side of the disturbance, Mobile received a great deal of damage from high winds in the outer bands of the storm. Trees were down, buildings damaged, and power out in many communities throughout the county.

I remember well how we had to bring in portable generators to operate the voting machines. People were cleaning up and trying to get things together from the hurricane, and I was concerned about the voter turnout. Under the circumstances, the turnout would be lower, and for an incumbent this is always something about which to be concerned.

I was well ahead, and unless something terribly unforeseen happened, I would win re-election, easily. Well, something unforeseen had happened, and there was reason to be concerned, but I won without any difficulty. My primary opponent was the man that I was in the run-off with in my first bid for office. I had come from behind and beat him then. His supporters had talked him into running again. He was beaten badly the second time. The next day, he called and said, "You will never have to worry about me running against you again. From now on, I'm on your team."

Cleaning up after Camille had prepared us for our response and recovery from Frederic. As I'd said before, the first four-year term was my training period. It was like on the job training.

The experiences of the first term were a foundation for much progress and production in the years to come. I learned much about governing and government in general, and how to get things done. I learned about leadership and administration from people I had under my supervision, as well as my counterparts across the state and country. If there were anything I did not know or did not understand, I called someone more experienced for advice.

I learned the hard way that I had not "arrived." Early on in my public service, the county commission, located across the street in the courthouse, and the city commission were on opposite sides of an issue. Reporters knew I was always ready to make a statement or give a quote, so one reporter asked me what I thought about the matter. I don't recall what I said, but it was derogatory toward the county commissioners.

The reporter went across the street to get their comments. I'll never forget what this county commissioner, a well-seasoned politician, old enough to be my father said—"Well this young man is not even dry behind the ears yet." His comment was the big news, not the issue. I learned my lesson.

Although I was interviewed hundreds of times, I learned that just because a reporter sticks a microphone under your nose, it doesn't mean you have to speak. If you don't respond to the first question, they will always have another one. Wait for the right question, and then respond, was a good lesson to learn.

I also learned a lot from Governor George Wallace. He was the best I'd ever seen with reporters. He was good at answering a question with a question. What I learned during those first years prepared me for a career of public service.

In 1970, I became the second layman ever to be elected as president of the Alabama Baptist State Convention. It was a great honor to hold this position. I had been a deacon and leader in the local church and active in the Brotherhood or Men's Ministries in the county association of churches, where I was director for a number of years. In addition, I was active in State Men's Ministries and had served as president of the Alabama Baptist Men.

When the convention met in Mobile that year, a well-known minister was also nominated. I hated competing against him, because he was a friend of several years. When the votes were tallied, I had won easily; a majority of the delegates, who were mostly ordained ministers, had voted for me, a layman. I was humbled.

In addition to my duties as commissioner and mayor, I spent nearly every Sunday speaking in churches anywhere from the Tennessee line to the Gulf of Mexico. I received press coverage up and down the state and was in demand as a speaker in churches and at civic gatherings. I would leave my car at the airport on Saturday afternoon or Sunday morning and return Sunday night, and then be at my office at public works before seven on Monday morning.

This traveling was not at the city's expense. The plane fares and other expenses were charged to my personal credit cards. Most of the time, I received enough love offerings to cover the expense. The few times I did not didn't discourage me, because I knew in my heart why I was going, and I trusted God to take care of me. He always did, and still does.

Every morning before seven, you could find me at my office. I loved greeting the workers as they came in, and the ones I missed would see my car in its parking spot as they came by to clock in. It not only showed the workers that I cared, which inspired them to give better service, but also gave me the opportunity to go over important projects with the supervisors. It all made for a quicker response and better service for the taxpayers, whom we were pledged to serve.

In early 1971, I was encouraged to run for the United States Senate. That was certainly an ego boost. I prayed over the matter, and while it was a tremendous undertaking, I felt that it was the right thing to do, that God was leading me to it. Although I did not win, I feel I learned so much that it was still God's will. Throughout the state, thousands of people knew me, or at least of me, which was essential. Others knew my Christian stance and moral convictions—another plus! We were able to put together a good campaign and had enough finances to run a respectable race.

It takes three things to win an election campaign: A good candidate, people, and finances. We had those, but we underestimated the strength of the incumbent. Six years earlier, he hadn't fared well, but did win. Many folk predicted he could be beaten, but he had evidently gained political strength.

I did well raising money, putting together workers, and on the stump. All looked great until a very popular, and pretty, state office holder decided she would run, also. She had run statewide several times and won. She had many loyal supporters who would have gone my way had she not entered the race. She was a nice woman and had had my support in other races. We called each other by first names. In fact, on one occasion, at a Peach Festival in Clanton, Alabama, she had asked me if she could catch a ride from the downtown park out to the Peach Sheds, where other activities were taking place. It put me in a very uncomfortable position, of which I'm sure she's never been fully aware.

It was my policy never to be alone in an automobile with any woman other than my wife. Sometimes I would take several secretaries to lunch, but never just one. I couldn't tell a state office holder no but I wasn't comfortable with the situation. After all, I was in my city car, representing the city of Mobile. I prayed all the way out to the Peach Sheds, several miles away, that nothing would happen and no one would run into us; the last thing I needed was for the headlines to read "Mims in Car Accident with Ms. So & So." I could just see it— "Baptist Convention President injured in car wreck with woman." God heard my prayers. We made it safely, and I was relieved. She never realized how I agonized over this little episode.

When the votes were counted, she had pulled thousands of votes that I would have gotten. She came in second. I was third with a good statewide vote. The incumbent went on to win the primary and the general election, and was re-elected.

There again, I learned much from that experience. One thing I learned was that you don't ever refer to any people as the "little people." In a speech in Montgomery, our state capital, I said that I was the candidate for the little people. I should have said average people, working people, or anything but "little people." The next morning, there appeared in the *Montgomery Advertiser*, a cartoon of me standing at the lectern; in front of me was a great crowd of people, who looked as if they were about twelve inches tall. You guessed it. The caption read, "The candidate for the little people."

One of the best things that came from my traveling over the state was the idea of a major drainage program for the city.

Downtown Mobile is not far above sea level. The newer sections out west are at higher elevations. When it rains, the water rushes down to the older, flatter sections and causes flooding problems. We didn't have any kind of comprehensive drainage plan.

Years before all the growth and annexation to the west, some engineering firm had done a study; it had been on the shelf for decades. Flying into smaller cities at low altitudes allowed me the opportunity to observe what some of them were doing. The thing that impressed me most was the miles of paved concrete ditches. Cities, smaller than Mobile, had far better storm drainage systems than the oldest city in the state. Our ditches were unimproved, costly to maintain, and trapped all kinds of trash and debris that stopped the flow of floodwaters.

I determined that I needed to initiate a "master drainage plan" to handle storm water run off. I went to work on it, sold the other commissioners on it, and started the planning process. The city had three major watersheds, and each was assigned to an engineering firm for study, plans, and estimates. Once estimates were in, bond issues were put together to finance the improvements and construction began.

The second term was a productive time and citizens still enjoy many improvements made then. Much of the city's growth has been because of the infrastructure put in place as I learned from experience.

Chapter 25

Disasters Help
You Grow

My third four-year term, which began in October of 1973, saw the beginning of one of the great strides forward in public improvements to our city.

The multi-million dollar master drainage program was financed by selling bonds to be repaid over time. The three watersheds, or drainage areas, Mobile River, Dog River, and Three-Mile Creek were alive with engineering and construction activity.

There were public hearings on each project. In all cases, right of way had to be obtained, which took more hearings and sometimes condemnation. In such cases, if a price could not be agreed upon, a judge and court would, through "right of imminent domain," set a price for the property, at which time, construction could proceed.

The massive drainage construction, which consisted of widening existing waterways, building new concrete ditches and underground systems, sometimes right down the middle of streets and thoroughfares, caused inconvenience and upset in many neighborhoods. This brought untold hundreds of calls to city hall and enormous workloads on city personnel—especially city engineers and my secretaries.

In spite of the problems, the construction brought great relief in storm water management and had a tremendous economic impact on the area. In addition to contractors and engineering personnel, there were many others involved in the project. Testing firms, equipment dealers, fuel distributors, concrete and asphalt plant employees, and many others benefited economically, which had a tremendous trickle down effect on grocers, restaurants, and other local businesses.

September of 1979 will never be forgotten. That was the month Hurricane Frederic wreaked havoc in our area. The devastation was indescribable; the clean up and recovery took a period of several years. The hurricane had downed tens of thousands of trees, which caused storm water to run off more rapidly, in which in turn caused erosion and flooding .

In May of 1981, a storm system moved from Texas, across Louisiana, Mississippi, and South Alabama. Many areas of the state to our west were flooded. In the middle of the night, the storm system arrived in Mobile and just sat on us for four hours. When it moved on, sixteen inches of rain, or four inches per hour, had fallen on the western part of the city, which is several hundred feet higher in elevation than the older section that is just above sea level.

All of this water came rushing down on the old section near the Mobile River and Mobile Bay, which was at high tide. There was nowhere for the water to go, and we experienced the worst flood of our city's history.

Thousands of homes and businesses flooded, causing tremendous anguish and inconvenience to many of our citizens. Several factors were involved in creating this disaster. The many trees destroyed by hurricane Frederick allowed for more rapid run off. Some of the drainage systems had not been properly maintained because all effort had been put into hurricane clean up. Debris had been washed into drainage systems, causing blockage. The high tide left the floodwaters with nowhere to go. None of this mattered to those whose homes and businesses had been damaged.

It was awful! Refrigerators and other appliances were floated out of mall stores by the rushing waters. One man awoke, with his arm hanging off his bed, touching water that had risen in his home almost up to his mattress.

I took a beating over the flood. No one expected me to be able to hold back hurricanes, but somehow the severe flooding was my fault. I thought I would never survive this one, politically.

The election was in the late summer of the year, and there I was, in the middle of all these flood problems. With the help of FEMA, we set out to acquire some of the flooded homes and to create green belt areas where the homes had stood. In this area meandered some beautiful streams. These streams, because of development, became raging rivers during weather events such as the storm of '81.

In spite of the promises and progress, this effort would take several years. I didn't have several years—I had three or four months until Election Day.

Sure enough, I had a formidable opponent, whose advertising firm came up with a clever ad to remind the citizens of Mobile of the flood, and how I hadn't handled the drainage problem before the crisis occurred. I will never forget those ads. One began with my name, "MIMS," in bold letters on the screen, and then the viewer heard rushing waters and saw tremendous waves come and and wash MIMS away. TV technology would flip MIMS to SWIM and give the viewer reasons why I should not be returned to office.

The outcome didn't look great. It seemed things would go against me, especially with all the money being spent to defeat me.

We all worked hard, trusted the Lord, and did everything we knew to do to win. My supporters really turned out. I will never forget going to my voting place and seeing this man on a walker coming to vote. I didn't know he had been ill. I asked him how he was doing.

"Not too good. I haven't been out in several months, except to go to the doctor, but I had to come out today for you, Brother Mims. We can't afford to see you lose."

Those were the kind of folks that elected me to a fifth term, allowing me to serve twenty years, and to them, I am grateful.

Although there were many sad and difficult days during my years of public service, there were as many happy days and some events that were quite amusing.

One day, the officer on duty on the second floor of city hall discovered a man in the commission chamber, where we conducted the official business of the city, adopting ordinances and passing resolutions, etc. This man was sitting in the middle seat, where the mayor sat as he presided over the meetings, eating sardines and crackers. The officer asked the man what he was doing there. His response was that he was enjoying his lunch. The officer informed him that he couldn't sit there, as it was the mayor's seat. "Well this is Meet the Mayor Day and its open house so I brought my lunch," was his reply. The officer sent the man on his way.

On another occasion, through a one-way mirror, I saw a huge man come into my outer office where my secretary sat. All of a sudden, there were several officers in the outer office, and I could tell we had a problem. Immediately, I went out to see what was going on. The man had handed Mrs. Regan a note that read, "Mr. Mims, five-thousand dollars or die—be cool!"

She had been very cool and pressed a button under her desk to alert the officers that we had a problem. They apprehended the man and were about to take him to jail for booking.

I said, "Hold up a minute, so I can question this man." I could tell that he had some type of mental problem. To make a long story short, I asked him if he knew where Royal Street was. He said, "Yes sir, right out front." The officers didn't want to release him, but I told him to hit that street and never come back. If he did, we would put him so far back in jail, he would never see the light of day. I never had any trouble with that man again.

Another strange thing that happened was when a man was caught trying to chew the antennas off the trunk of my city automobile. There were three of them connected to the radios so I could be in communication at all times. How this poor man thought he could eat those steel wires is beyond me. The officer recognized that the man had a serious problem and sent him on his way.

So many unusual things happened. One of the strangest was when an outstanding, old time type of attorney was before the city commission. He was making his point in the finest southern oratory when he exclaimed, "This is the truth, so help me God!" Just as he said God, with great fervor and annunciation, there was a great thundering sound. It rocked the entire downtown area where stood the historic city hall building. The attorney turned white as a sheet. We were all stunned; about that time word came of an explosion across the river at the shipyard. The attorney was relieved that it was not God speaking, validating his claim.

The fifth term, 1981-85, was a good period. We put forth much effort in seeking industry and pressing for a naval homeport. Many trips to Washington, meetings with our congressional leaders, the Secretary of the Navy, and others were ultimately successful. Mobile's homeport was approved, and construction started on the thirty-eight million dollar facility. Unfortunately, it wound up on the base closure list before it was completed and never opened.

Governor Wallace was re-elected and state and economic development personnel gave a good bit of attention to Mobile and south

Alabama. Brookley Industrial Complex was attracting more industry and things looked well for the economy. Many of the public improvement projects were coming to completion. City government was clicking and accomplishing lots of work.

I must give credit to the good people I worked with for my twenty continuous years of service and the great progress we made. There were loyal supporters who stuck by me and hundreds of volunteers who gave their time and talents to serve on the numerous boards, commissions, and committees of city government, without who we could not have been successful. I had experienced leaders who did tremendous jobs but it was the hundreds of ordinary people who made things happen. I am grateful for all who joined in the effort to make our community a better place to live.

By U.S. court order, a change of government election was proposed, and the people voted to change the form of government from a three-member at large, commission form of government, to a seven-member districted council and mayor form of government. This was done to allow more minority involvement in government. I certainly had no problem with seeing more minorities involved, but my sincere conviction was that the form of government we'd had for over three-quarters of a century was the most effective and efficient form of government a city could have. The people received more bang for their buck with it; however, the people spoke, and since 1985, the mayor-council form of government has existed.

Toward the end of the term, I decided that, after twenty years, at the age of fifty-five, I would step down and not seek re-election. I felt tremendous peace about this decision and have never regretted making it. I was grateful for twenty years of service and the wonderful opportunities God gave me during that time. I had been in meetings with presidents, governors, ambassadors, and leaders from around the world.

It had been my privilege to greet and present "keys to the city" to hundreds of visitors from all over the globe. It was a joy meeting many famous people, such as Elvis Presley, Kenny Rogers, Mel Tillis, Hank Williams, Jr., Minnie Pearl, Boots Randolph, Brenda Lee, Jerry Clower, Norman Vincent Peale, Robert Schuller, Ann Landers, and various dignitaries from around the world.

On Elvis Presley's last visit to Mobile, not long before he died, I was delighted to have the opportunity to go backstage and present him with an Honorary Citizen's certificate and the keys to the city. He was without a doubt the most difficult person to communicate with I have ever encountered. He was sullen and withdrawn, and I had to pull every word out of him. Colonel Parker, his top advisor and handler, was by his side, and most of the conversation was between the colonel and me. Elvis did give me one of his scarves, however, that I am keeping for my granddaughters.

Another wonderful thing during my years as mayor-commissioner was meeting hundreds of great pastors and spiritual leaders across the country and being allowed to speak in many outstanding churches of the land.

The journey has taken me a long way from the cotton patch, but during good times and hard, I was able to grow mentally and spiritually.

Chapter 26

Life After the Mayorship

After my decision not to run for re-election in 1985, other doors opened. At fifty-five, I was not ready, financially or otherwise, to sit down and do nothing. The experiences of twenty years of public service, and the knowledge I had gained in positions of leadership in other organizations needed to be shared.

We opened an office in a historic 1888 building we purchased at the corner of Church and Dearborn streets in downtown Mobile. Dale, our oldest son, who had taught school and coached high school basketball, was now a real estate broker, and needed space to conduct business.

We formed a company—Mims Sales and Development Co., Inc.; to own, repair, and sell real estate and do any other lawful business it might choose. Danny, our youngest son, professionally known as L. Daniel Mims, Attorney at Law, had just graduated from Cumberland Law School of Samford University, and needed a place to hang his shingle and set up his law practice.

I formed a consulting firm, Lambert Mims and Associates, and began to represent a few clients. The executive director of the American Public Works Association asked me to work under contract with the Association. I agreed, and was named general counselor, which has nothing to do with the legal profession. My duties involved giving advice on public works matters to member cities and counterparts across the country. I was also to work with the education foundation of the association and conduct workshops around the country on various subjects relating to public works. This required a great deal of traveling, which was tiring yet enjoyable, as I met new people in every section of our great country.

I would usually do two workshops a week, in different parts of the country. Then, two or three weeks later, I would do another set somewhere else. I also prepared a workbook and manual on Emergency Management in Public Works and spent a good bit of time attending Federal Emergency Management courses at the Emmitsburg, Maryland training center.

Now if that was not enough traveling, I took on even more, at the request of Governor George Wallace. The governor asked me to be Ambassador for the Alabama waterways. Most people don't realize it, but our state has more miles of navigable waterways than any other state, and most of them lead to Mobile, the seaport that connects our state with the world as far as water transportation is concerned.

The great public works project, the Tennessee-Tombigbee Waterway, involved constructing a channel and a series of locks and dams between the upper reaches of the Tombigbee River and the Tennessee River. The Army Corps of Engineers supervised this project in three states: Alabama, Mississippi, and Tennessee. It was one of the most massive ever undertaken by the corps, and was completed at great expense to our government. It connects the port of Mobile with cities along the Tennessee, Ohio, Mississippi, Illinois, Missouri Rivers and all those other navigable rivers in all those areas. The president of the United States, Richard Nixon, came to Mobile for the dedication, which indicates the significance of the project.

Naturally, Governor Wallace was very proud of these assets and wanted them promoted to the fullest, therefore the Alabama Waterways Agency set up offices in the International Trade Building at the Alabama State Docks. I became the ambassador of the Waterways for Governor Wallace. My duties required that I travel, speaking to civic, waterway, and port groups; as well as meeting the press in the cities east of the Mississippi River and along the Gulf Coast and eastern seaboard.

This was a great opportunity and experience for me. I developed a slide presentation and brochures that I used everywhere. My assistant arranged speaking engagements in New York, Chicago, Pittsburg, Cincinnati, and other places. These visits always involved speaking to at least one group and a press conference to promote Alabama's waterways and the Port of Mobile.

Another aspect of the promotional position was requesting the leaders, the movers and shakers of industrial cities located along waterways, to come to Mobile at the governor's invitation and at the state's expense.

A typical trip would start with the invitation on behalf of Governor Wallace to join several other city leaders to see our dock facilities at Mobile. The state jet would be at their airport at eight a.m., we would bring them to Mobile, have a tour of the docks on the state yacht, enjoy a great seafood meal at the Trade Club, and have them back home by five p.m. No CEO of any corporation or community leader turned this invitation down, allowing me to get to know some of the most influential people in the East and Midwest parts of our great country.

The pilots and I made sure we were there before eight a.m., and we never had to wait on anyone. We departed at eight and within an hour or so, depending on the distance, we were in Mobile. Along the way, I pointed out the various waterways and let them know that most of them led to the Alabama state docks, where we were headed.

I made dozens of these trips, and we received tremendous media coverage on both ends. The media carried the event at the departure and at Mobile. These were memorable times, productive in promoting our state, waterways, and port.

One might ask how I could do more traveling. The Public Works Association and Waterways traveling amounted to a full time job, yet on Sundays, I spoke at various churches, which sometimes required even more air travel. Sometimes I had to look for signs to determine in which airport I was. The Memphis and Atlanta Airports became very familiar since they were connection points for most flights out of Mobile.

The Ambassador for Waterways position ended when a new governor took office, however my position as an ambassador for Alabama, Mobile, and especially Christ continues until this day.

Chapter 27

Falsely Accused in
the Middle of the Campaign

F our exciting years had passed. I was pleased with my life after
public office. I had met many new people across the country and
had thoroughly enjoyed promoting Alabama for the governor and
leading workshops for the American Public Works Association.

It was time for an election. Many people were unhappy with the
new form of government and some of those elected in 1985. My supporters began to urge me to run for mayor. After considerable prayer
and research, I decided to run. Surveys showed that I was still popular
and could win. The adrenaline was pumping, and the political fire
once again burned within me.

A campaign organization was put together, a plan of action laid
out, and an announcement day set. Many of my long-time supporters
were enthused, as was the candidate. I will never forget the great
number of people who showed up for the announcement. There were
more people than at any previous announcement. The hotel staff had
to open ballrooms to either side of the stages. We had scheduled the
announcement so all of the television stations could go live during the
six p.m. news. Electronic media and the newspapers were well represented. Everyone was interested in my taking on one of the wealthiest
and most powerful political figures in this area.

We received great coverage, and our campaign was off to a tremendous start. We had one of the best campaign headquarters
locations we had ever had in. The organization came together beauti-
fully, and everyone was working with great fervor. A few financial
supporters made connections with the incumbent administration running for re-election, and many dollars I would have otherwise gotten
went to the incumbent.

All went well until July 3, 1989, when a U.S. Marshal walked into my campaign headquarters in the Festival Mall and handed me a stack of papers, with a cover letter indicating the document was from the United States Attorney's office of the Southern District of Alabama. It was an indictment by a federal grand jury. I shall never forget reading, "The United States of America vs. Lambert C. Mims," charging me with conspiracy, violation of the Hobbs Act, and racketeering; all of which was supposed to have happened more than four years earlier, before I left office in 1985. If there had been any kind of violation, I should have been charged at least four years before, while I was still in office or shortly thereafter.

During the mid-eighties, there was an investigation into wrongdoing at the county courthouse involving the government's main witness in my case. A county commissioner was indicted, primarily (I learned later) on the testimony of this same man, who evidently turned state's evidence to avoid prosecution.

I was accused of violating the Hobbs Act by causing him to enter into a business arrangement with another man to obtain the city's refuse, for the purpose of operating a waste-to-energy plant. Of course, the partnership of these two men was unknown to me.

Since all of the municipal waste of the area was needed for the production of steam, the investigation turned to the city of Mobile and me, as commissioner in charge of public works. After the fact, I learned the government set its sights on their star witness in the county case, and he began to court me. Several years before, the city had given him an opportunity to put together a steam plant proposal, although I was never sold on the idea, as records show. The individual could not get his project financed, because it just wasn't feasible, which I knew all the time. The city of Mobile had a more economical garbage collection and disposal system than any other city its size. Over time, he pushed the project, or the government pushed him to involve others in its scheme.

During the eighties, the FBI set out to trap as many public officials as it could. In my opinion, this was part of the plan to eliminate political opposition at local levels of government. County commissioners throughout the south were indicted through sting operations involving purchases of pipe, asphalt, and other materials. Many were trapped, convicted, and put out of office.

This individual, the steam plant man, was in and out of my office so much that he became a nuisance. I couldn't turn around without getting a visit or a call from him, offering some new twist on building the steam plant. He even went so far as to get his minister, one for whom I had great respect, to contact me on his behalf. Out of courtesy to the minister, I gave the promoter more of my time. The more I heard, the less I thought of the idea. However, many powerful business interests were putting pressure on the other commissioners. The local newspaper was promoting the idea, since the price of oil had risen and this plant would help local industry obtain much needed steam at a reasonable price. Such a deal would help the area economically, they thought.

I finally agreed to accept proposals, and the ball began to roll. Little did I know—I was being investigated. Later, I learned I was a target.

During that period, the government's star witness admitted that he had participated in as many as one hundred secret tapings, a few of which were played during trial. This all started in early nineteen eighty-four, a year and a half before I stepped down from office, not running again in 1985.

It is unbelievable that only one secret recording of any conversation with me was played to the jury, and that was one made on my very last day in office, in October of 1985. It was with an FBI agent posing as vice-president of a company taking over the steam plant project. The thrust of the conversation was the ability of a certain local company to construct such a plant. My response was that all things being equal, I always preferred local companies, in order for our citizens to benefit. After all, that is a duty of an elected official—to look out for his constituents.

There was nothing on the tape to incriminate me or anyone else. It was a waste of time to play and replay it. However, the prosecutor alleged that I had become wise to them and given a "Chamber of Commerce" speech to the agent. No other recordings of my conversations were played. If they had played others, they would have shown my resistance to the whole steam plant concept. I will always believe tape recordings that would have revealed my true feelings about the steam plant were held back; and someday I hope to get to the truth through the Freedom of Information Act.

Those responsible for this malicious prosecution will never let anything like this come home to roost, but we often see law enforcement withhold evidence, misstate, misrepresent, conspire and do all kinds of things to make cases and get convictions, often sending innocent people to prison.

The justice system should be about more than who wins or loses, or presents the best case for or against; the justice system should be for fairness and justice.

One Supreme Court justice, many years ago, wrote, "It is better for one hundred guilty people to go free than for one innocent person be incarcerated."

It is also interesting to know, as I learned five years later in 1989, that a sealed indictment had been put in a file at the federal courthouse in 1984. If there had been any case against me, it should have been brought to trial then, not when I ran for mayor in 1989.

I am confident that if I had run again in 1985, the indictment would have been opened just before that election period. Instead, it was held until 1989, and in the midst of my campaign, opened; I was charged, thus ending my political career.

It is a matter of record (a signed affidavit), that the incumbent mayor's son-in-law stated, when I announced I was running for mayor, "Jeff (now U.S. Senator) says Mims won't be around by then, anyway."

None of this should have made a difference because the record is abundantly clear that no Hobbs Act violation was ever committed. There was no *quid pro quo*. The truth is that no crime was committed, and as you will see later, there was no evidence presented during the trial showing a crime was committed. I will always believe it was a political prosecution designed to keep me from being elected as mayor again.

There were powerful people, rich and influential in state and local politics, afraid that I would win the election and unseat the state chair of one of the major political parties. Of course, none of these folks would ever let such a thing touch them, and would deny to the highest heavens that they had anything to do with a plan to ruin me.

The mayor, whom I had served with during my first term as city commissioner, was the chair of his state party and close friends with other leaders throughout the state. His position gave him power of approval over all Alabama presidential appointments—federal judge-ships, U.S. attorneys, U.S. marshals, etc. If the state chair did not approve an individual, then the president wouldn't let that name go to Congress for a vote. The long and short of it was that the U.S. Attorney and the U.S. Marshal owed their prominent positions to the incumbent mayor.

Most of the federal judges were the mayor's political buddies, and in many cases part of the old Mobile establishment.

During trial, it was brought up that the first mention of my indict-ment was not in a U.S. attorney's office. It was in a meeting in a private attorney's office with a man close to the mayor and who, in my opin-ion, stood much to gain financially if his friend was re-elected.

I was arraigned before a U.S. magistrate, where I pleaded not guilty, was fingerprinted and released on my own recognizance until a trial date could be set. We asked for a speedy trial, hoping for a date before the election, but knew in our hearts it wouldn't happen. One interesting thing about the fingerprinting was that the Marshal charged with this responsibility said, with tears in his eyes, "Mr. Mims, in all my nearly twenty years on this job, this is the hardest thing I have ever done. I believe you are an innocent man." His voice trembled and broke. He said, "You are, without a doubt, a modern day apostle Paul." That's when I cried.

The toughest job I ever had was completing that race knowing very few people were re-elected to public office while under indict-ment. It was hard making speeches, meeting the public, shaking hands, and making television and radio commercials. It was hard to hold my head up. In fact, only two things kept me going. One, I knew I had not knowingly committed a crime, and two, the Grace of God as he had promised was sufficient.

Some support dropped off my campaign effort, and money was harder to raise, but hundreds of my friends and supporters stuck with me. One wrinkle appeared in the plan of those who devised this scheme to keep me out of politics. The indictment, which was sealed for four years, was opened, and I was served on July 3. The qualifying date had not passed, and a man running for one of the council seats decided to jump into what had been a two-man race for mayor.

I came in third place, and the run-off was now between the incum-bent and the other person. When that election was held, the newcomer won and the incumbent was defeated. Evidently, the people who had voted for me went with the new man. The scheme to save the incumbent backfired, and he lost the election in spite of their actions.

The first person I called when the indictment was served was my mama. My father had passed away several years earlier. "Mama," I said, "there is going to be some sad news on the television today and I wanted to alert you." I went on to share with her what was happening and she said, "It's going to be alright, I still believe in you." Thank God, for Mamas who believe in their children.

Chapter 28

The Jury Sings in
the Longest Trial

It was a long period between July and January, when my trial was to begin. Our youngest son, Danny, who is an attorney, was very helpful. I can never say enough about him, or his brother Dale, who stood with their daddy like giants through the trial—a trial that never should have been—and the days that followed.

We selected one of the best defense lawyers in the area, Thomas Haas, as the lead attorney. We began to map out our strategy and started to raise money for expenses. Tom Haas' fees were reasonable enough, and he spent many hours on my case. Danny also spent many hours, without one cent for his time, when he needed to be working on his law practice and other paying cases.

I tried to pay my lead lawyer each week, on Thursday. One day, I was a thousand dollars short on attorney fees for the week. Reecie and I prayed that the money would come—that morning.

When we arrived at the Federal Building, my brother David and his wife, who had been loyally driving each day from Monroeville to be with us, handed me a tightly folded check. I stuck it in my shirt pocket. Knowing my brother's circumstances, I figured it would be a few hundred dollars. At break time during that morning's proceedings, I slipped the check out, opened it up, and to my amazement, it was for one thousand dollars! The money was just what I needed to meet my obligations for that day. Tears streamed down my cheeks, and I praised God for his goodness.

I was on trial with several other men, some of whom I did not even know, over matters of which I had no knowledge. We tried everything to get the judge to sever my case from the others, but to no avail. If we had, there would have been no case against me.

We sat there for ten and one-half weeks, in the longest running trial ever conducted in the Southern District of Alabama. There, we listened to testimony relating to others about tax fraud, paper mill contracts, water board contracts, and on and on. I am confident this was part of the plan, to throw me in with all the rest, and really smear my name.

I will try to explain this case in layman's terms and reserve the legal aspects for another time.

I am told that the local state district attorney at the time had received treatments for what everyone gathered were drug abuse problems. He also, in my opinion, suffered from paranoia, and for whatever reason, seemed to think I had something to do with a police officer arresting him on one of our busiest streets for driving under the influence. He also had it in for one of the best-known and most respectable local contractors, who had supported someone against him in the previous election. This contractor was a good friend and supporter of mine, as well as many other local, state, and federal office holders. He was a hard worker who built a tremendous company that employed upward of eight hundred people and held large contracts, all of which kept many families employed with good incomes.

He was the kind of man who wore work clothes and boots and would get down in the trenches with his men. Many people loved and appreciated him and respected him as one of the hardest workers around. He was not the office or executive type. His son-in-law and others took care of that end of the business, while he was hands-on in the field and spent much of his time rounding up contracts to keep his people busy.

For some reason, the district attorney got the idea that this contractor was a political kingpin and was calling the shots in a shadow government. Nothing could have been farther from the truth. My contractor friend never put any pressure on me, nor asked me do one thing out of the way, much less anything illegal. He was always looking for business, however, in an effort to keep his employees working.

Through the media and word of mouth, he'd heard of a proposal for the city to make its solid waste (household garbage) available to a company that converted garbage to steam. He was interested in building the plant if possible, and let it be known to all. This particular person was not popular with some people, because he and some associates were able to get a franchise, some years earlier, to own and

operate the dog track. Some thought he was crooked, but as I understand it, he just out-politicked and outworked the other group. The
fact that the contractor was part of this dog track ownership was always a burr under some sides. There were also alleged tax issues with
the contractor, the so-called kingpin.

The district attorney hired a former FBI agent, who wouldn't have
known the truth if it had sat on him, to assist in the investigation. If
there had been any kind of ethics violation on my part, the prosecutors
should have charged me under state law. The district attorney went to
the U.S. Attorney in an effort to make this a federal case.

As already mentioned, the investigation was going on before I left
office in 1985, and an indictment was sealed until I ran for office in
1989. By then, through lies, innuendos, threats, and other unethical
tactics, a number of people were brought under an umbrella charge
known as the RICCO Act, which covers racketeering influences, corruption, and organized crime.

I had no knowledge of racketeering. I always endeavored to be
straight and honest, so much so that I turned down gifts and trips
from individuals and corporations because I didn't want to be unduly
influenced by gifts.

The others accused under the RICCO umbrella were the contractor,
the owner of one of the competing companies, water board supervisors, employees at Scott Paper Company, and others.

The courtroom was filled with attorneys representing all of these
individuals. Some had four or five. Others, as in my case, had two.

We were thrown several curves before the trial actually began.
First, the U.S. Attorney had his sights on higher offices and was the
golden boy of the Republican Party at that time. He became the Attorney General of the State of Alabama, and later was elected to the
United States Senate.

The female attorney he assigned to prosecute the case was the
granddaughter of a U.S. district judge, and had aspirations of someday
becoming a judge herself. Later, she was appointed to a lifetime position as district judge in the Southern District of Alabama.

The first curve thrown us was the denial of severance, which
meant I had to go to trial with everyone else. The second was a denial
of our request for a change of venue. Since this was such a high profile
case, we felt it would be better to move the trial. This petition was de-

nied. The next curve had to do with the jury pool. We were given an extensive list of potential jurors. A jury consultant spent considerable time studying the list and advising us on favorable and unfavorable potential jurors. We felt we could get a fair jury from this pool.

Just before the jury was struck, we were informed that we could not use that pool; and were given a much shorter list, with no time to research them. Then there was the problem of agreement on which jurors we wanted and ones we wanted struck. Since there were so many charges and so many different personalities all being tried at the same time, it was hard to come to a happy medium. I wanted one type of person, and others wanted the opposite. For instance, I preferred church-going, professional, middle-American people; others didn't want churchgoers who could be prejudiced against someone who owned part interest in a dog track where Para mutual betting was legal and permitted.

Here we were, in this huge, wood-paneled courtroom, with eagles, flags, and portraits of judges of days past. Some of the people on trial as well as spectators and witnesses were intimidated. Many people, including jurors, think the defendants must be guilty of something, or they wouldn't be here. "Surely our justice system wouldn't accuse innocent people."

Hear me out! Let me make it very clear. Just because we live in the United States of America, or the city or county of Mobile, doesn't mean the government is always right. Thousands of people, every year, in this great country are falsely accused, tried, and convicted.

The trial lasted ten and one-half weeks. The media had a field day. Television cameras and newspaper photographers caught my family, my lawyers, and me every time we approached the steps of the federal courthouse. They listened, and they reported. No one could ever figure out what I had done wrong. As my lawyer put it, "It was like fighting air."

To this day, he has tears in his eyes every time my case is mentioned. He states, "Lambert Mims is the most innocent man I ever represented, and it seemed we could do nothing to avoid him being done in. It is the greatest injustice I have ever witnessed."

What the government presented was that I used my influence as a public official to force two companies to merge in order to obtain the city's refuse, to make steam, to sell to a local industry.

The two principals, one on trial and the other the government's star witness, testified that I had nothing to do with them meeting, and that I had absolutely nothing to do with them merging their companies.

It was the government's claim that I had violated the Hobbs Act— that I had used my influence for gain. To support my claim of innocence, and the very fact that no evidence was presented that I received anything of value for any decision I ever made, I am including the following for your consideration; see the last paragraph on the next page.

2404 Hobbs Act –
Under Color of Official Right

In addition to the "wrongful use of actual or threatened force, violence, or fear," the Hobbs Act (18 U.S.C.ξ 1951) defines extortion in terms of "the obtaining of property from another, with his consent...under color of official right." In fact, the "under color of official right" aspect of the Hobbs Act derives from the common law meaning extortion. As the Supreme Court explained in a recent opinion regarding the Hobbs Act,

> "[a]t common law, extortion was an offense committed by a public official who took 'by color of his office' money that was not due to him for the performance of his official duties...Extortion by the public official was the rough equivalent of what we would now describe as 'taking a bribe.'" *Evans v. United States*, 504 U.S. 255 (1992).

In order to show a violation of the Hobbs Act under this provision, the Supreme Court recently held that "the government need only show that a public official has obtained a payment to which he was not entitled, knowing that the payment was made in return for official acts." While the definition of extortion under the Hobbs Act requires obtaining property from another with consent induced by force, violence, or fear, the under color of official right provision does not require that the public official take steps to induce the extortionate payment: It can be said that "the coercive element is provided by the public office itself." *Evans v. United States*, 504 U.S. 255 (1992); *see United States v. Margiotta*, 688 F.2d 108, 130 (2d Cir.1982), *cert. denied*, 461 U.S. 913 (1983) ("[t]he public officer's misuse of his office supplies the necessary element of coercion...").

This theory of extortion under color of official right has resulted in the successful prosecution of a wide range of officials, including those serving on the federal, state, and local levels. For example: *United States v. O'Connor*, 910 F2d 1266 (7th Cir.1990), *cert. denied*, 111 S. Ct. 953

(1991) (police officer accepts payment from FBI agents posing as crooked auto parts dealers). *United States v. Stephenson*, 895 F.2d 867 (2d Cir. 1990) (International trade official in Department of Commerce accepts payment to influence ruling). *United States v. Spitler*, 800 F.2d 1267 (4th Cir. 1986) (state highway administrator accepts money from road building contractor). *United States v. Wright*, 797 F.2d 245 (5th Cir.1986), *cert. denied*, 481 U.S. 1013 (1987) (city prosecutors accept money for not prosecuting drunk drivers). *United States v. Greenough*, 782 F.2d 1556 (11th Cir. 1986) (city commissioner accepts money for awarding city concession). *United States v. Murphy*, 768 F.2d 1518 (7th Cir.1985), *cert. denied*, 475 U.S. 1012 (1986) (judges accept payment to fix cases). *United States v. Mazzei*, 521 F.2d 639 (3d Cir.) (en banc), *cert. denied*, 423 U.S. 1014 (1975) (state senator accepts money from landlord seeking government office lease).

In *United States v. Stephenson*, 895 F.2d at 871-73, the defendant, who was a federal official, unsuccessfully contended that the Hobbs Act only applied to state and local officials, and that prosecution of a federal official for extortion would have to be exclusively brought under 18 U.S.C.□: extortion by officers and employees of the United States. The court found that the government could seek a charge under whichever of these two overlapping statutes it thought appropriate. Moreover, "it is not a defense to a charge of extortion under color of official right that the defendant could also have been convicted of bribery." *Evans v. United States*, 504 U.S. 255 (1992).

GENERAL RULE: the usual fact situation for a Hobbs Act charge under color of official right is a public official trading his or her official actions in an area in which he or she has actual authority in exchange for the payment of money.

Some cases, under certain fact situations, however, have extended the statute further. For example:

- Some courts have held that a Hobbs Act violation does not require the public official to have *de jure* power to perform any official act paid for as long as it is reasonable to believe that he or she had the *de facto* power to perform the requested act. *See United States v. Nedza*, 880 F.2d 896, 902 (7th Cir.1989) (victim reasonably believed state senator had the ability to impact a local business). *United States v. Bibby*, 752 F.2d 1116, 1127-28 (6th Cir.1985): *United States v. Sorrow*, 732 F.2d 176, 180 (11th Cir. 1984); *United States v. Rindone*, 631 F.2d 491.

I want everyone to know that there was never a shred of evidence presented that I ever expected, or received, anything in exchange for any official action I ever made.

As we sat in the courtroom waiting for the proceedings to continue, we could hear, from the judge's chambers, the jury singing "Happy Birthday" to the judge. I had a terrible, sinking feeling. My heart dropped within me. Until then, it had seemed that the jury, at least the ones that were awake, was somewhat sympathetic, but now, as the party in the judge's chamber grew so enthusiastic, things began to change.

A jury that has your life in its hands is singing "Happy Birthday" to the judge who is supposed to be conducting a fair and impartial hearing.

How can this be? One must understand that the system is set up to favor the government. The prosecution team sits just beneath the jury, where their every move and facial expression is visible. The defendant's team is on the far side of the room, and cannot see the raised eyebrows and body language expressed by the prosecutor's team of investigators, sitting at a table facing the jurors; however, some onlookers sitting nearby could see these "communications."

The judge was cognizant of the jury; every morning, he gave them a little pep talk, telling them how proud he was that they were doing their civic duty by serving. He made every effort to meet whatever need they had and make them as comfortable as possible. In my opinion, he was overly solicitous—so much so, I believe they fell in love with him.

At lunch break, marshals transported the jurors to nice restaurants, where they dined on scrumptious food at the government's expense. One could become accustomed to this kind of treatment over a ten-week period.

During this time, someone (perhaps a marshal) told the jury that the judge was going to observe his fiftieth birthday. Feeling a genuine rapport with the marshals and the judge, someone came up with the idea of providing a cake and party for the judge. Whether this thought came from a juror, or a suggestion from a marshal, we don't know. However, our attorneys were approached about giving their consent for the jurors to take some time out from the trial to have a birthday celebration in the judge's chamber.

We were put in a box. Although I objected to the idea, my attorneys felt that if we didn't agree to the celebration, the jury would be upset and take it out on us in the verdict. Consequently, the trial was interrupted. As court personnel entered the judge's chambers, we saw black balloons and the jury gathering to wish the judge a happy birthday.

My stomach churned, my heart fluttered, and when the loud refrain of "Happy Birthday" came from those chambers, my spirits fell. I felt as if I were the lamb before the slaughter.

I cannot prove this party had any bearing on the final verdict, in my opinion, however, a fair-minded judge would have declined such an offer as being unethical, without ever involving the attorneys for the defendant.

I believe this could have been just one of a number of things that caused my part of the case not to be dismissed. The bottom line is, however, that the government never presented any evidence that I violated the Hobbs Act.

The government did not present my financial records, because there was nothing there except the salaries and income my wife and I earned legally through hard work. I was tried, convicted, and served time for a crime I never committed. Many people believed that those who tried me were guiltier than I was.

Fortunately, I was acquitted of several counts including racketeering, but was convicted of violating section 18 U.S.C.: ξ 1951 the Hobbs Act, which was a tremendous injustice. Hundreds of people, as well as my attorneys, my family, and I have a hard time accepting that I could be guilty of gain from official acts when there was not one shred of evidence that I was promised anything, or accepted anything of value in exchange for any decision I ever made.

A sentencing date was set, during which time United States probation officers came to my home for a PSI, a pre-sentence investigation, which is supposed to aid the judge in determining the length of the sentence in a case.

The pre-sentence investigation report indicated that guidelines suggested twelve to eighteen months' confinement. When the sentence came down, I faced ten years and a ten thousand dollar fine. A ten-year sentence under the old law would allow parole after serving one-third of the sentence. Three and a third years is a long time to be incarcerated, especially when one is not guilty.

Most people, even those who never voted for me, felt I got a raw deal and that the whole thing was a travesty.

As a boy, I stumped my toe many times while plowing in those cotton patches back home, but this was the hardest, toughest stump I had ever hit.

Chapter 29

Convicted and Sentenced

Sentencing day came, and everyone heard the judge's ruling—ten years, a ten thousand dollar fine, and I was released on my own recognizance. I was convicted of a felony and became #03949-003 in the federal justice system.

I stood on the courthouse steps, with dozens of baffled and disappointed supporters behind me. I was able to stand tall because of the grace of God and the fact that I knew that I was not guilty. As I faced the throng of media representatives, I once again declared my innocence and moved to appeal my conviction to the Supreme Court of the United States.

The first step in the appeals process was to file an appeal of the district court decision to the United States Court of Appeals for the Eleventh Circuit, headquartered in Atlanta. The Eleventh Circuit handles appeals from Alabama, Georgia, and Florida. The judges on this court came from these states, where many had served as district judges. Circuit judges are often friends with district judges. The district judge's decisions are rarely overturned. All of these positions are political appointments and are life terms. Regardless of their stand-alone attitudes, everyone is beholden to a powerful individual or party committee. I do not accuse them of open and deliberate collusion, but it makes sense that these private, personal, and professional friendships can't help but influence decisions, especially in high-profile political cases.

My world had come crashing down. Twenty spotless years of public service to the city of Mobile and all the work for the State of Alabama was now tainted by this unjust conviction.

My consulting business was doomed. The Waterways position and agency had been abolished. I gave up my position with the American Public Works Association, my speaking engagements dried up, and my campaign was derailed. Time stood still. Petitions for appeal took forever. The court system dragged its feet getting the transcripts to the appeals court. The days grew longer and longer, and the load became heavier by the day.

Many people were praying for my family and me, and we could feel the presence of God in our lives. We tried to stay upbeat, as we knew that thousands of people who knew of our Christian faith were observing us. We had to be strong and be a good testimony for the Lord. The thing that helped me greatly was our first grandchild, Lindsay, who was born on March 5, 1990, while I was on the stand testifying in that ten and one-half week trial.

I came from a family of six boys, Reecie and I had had two sons, and now there was a girl. She was precious. Reecie and I kept her while her mother worked and her father, the lawyer, built his law practice.

What a glorious time. Everyday I took her down by the river in our front yard, and we went back and forth in the swing for hours. I sang and prayed—for her, for myself, that what had happened to her Big Daddy would not cause any problems in her life, and most of all, I prayed for those who had put me through this nightmare.

At one time, I had been the most recognizable person in all of southwest Alabama, and although I had some negatives, I was still the most popular public official in the area.

I taught an adult Sunday school class at the Riverside Baptist Church, where we had been members for many years, and liked to spread my Bible and commentaries on the kitchen table as I prepared for my lessons. Every time I tried to study, I thought of the investigators, the prosecutors, the judge, and those responsible for my predicament. I confess I had a hard time with this. I asked God to forgive me and help me overcome the obstacle affecting my study and eating away at my innermost being.

One morning it seemed that God spoke to me, saying, "Do you think these people are thinking of you today? They did this to you, and they have gone on to something else. You must give them up. I'll take care of them."

With that, I forgave them all and felt relief that the bitterness I had would no longer eat away at me. I was delivered from their hold and completely free—which brings me to another place where I felt completely free.

It was a moonlit night. The ripples on Dog River sparkled in the moonlight. I had been fretting over where I was going to come up with the money needed for attorney fees. The costs were mounting. The trial had cost big bucks and the appeals, and especially if we had to go to the U.S. Supreme Court, would cost tens of thousands of dollars.

We had been blessed with a beautiful waterfront home on Dog River. It had appreciated in value considerably since we acquired it. Three hundred plus feet of waterfront property and nearly three acres of land on the wide and high part of the river was worth a good bit.

I had often said I would live and die on Dog River. I really meant it, but I never say that anymore. You see I had to give it up— at least in my heart. The moon was full as I walked out onto my pier. It was quiet; a slight breeze caused the river to ripple and the moonlight to sparkle upon its surface. I looked into that full moon and poured my heart out to God. I said, "God, you gave us this beautiful place. You know I've said that I would live and die on Dog River. I will not make that statement again. I am willing to give it up, if need be, to raise money to defend myself against these false accusations. You know better than anyone that I am not guilty, so Lord, I will be willing to live in public housing if I have to. Tonight, I surrender it all to you. Please help us through this ordeal. I commit it all into your hands."

An indescribable peace came over me. I felt completely free—the same feeling I'd had as a boy chasing lightning bugs in our front yard next to the cotton patch.

We filed the appeal with the Eleventh Circuit, and it seemed it took forever to get an answer. Finally, we were granted a hearing where oral arguments were heard.

A three-judge panel with one judge from Montgomery heard the case in the federal courthouse in Montgomery. The Alabama judge presided, and he had it in for me from the get-go. He had close ties with former state party officials, through whom he received his appointment, and knew of my connections with former governor, George Wallace.

He appeared to be pro-prosecution, and cut my attorneys no slack whatsoever. Sometime later, our petition was denied, and stamped, DO NOT PUBLISH, which meant no one would ever know the judges' thoughts or reasons for denial. We filed for a re-hearing before the entire court, in what is known as an en banc hearing. Again, we did not get relief and were forced to proceed with a cert petition to the U.S. Supreme Court.

Danny contacted well-known Harvard law professor, and nationally recognized attorney, Allen Dershowitz, about handling our case. Because of other pressing cases and commitments at Harvard University, he referred us to his brother Nathan Dershowitz of New York City. We worked out the financial arrangements, and Nathan Dershowitz proceeded to file the petition in the Supreme Court.

In the meantime, the district judge ordered me to report to Maxwell Federal Prison Camp at Maxwell Air Force base, Montgomery, Alabama.

Chapter 30

Incarcerated, Reporting to Prison

January 18, 1994 was the worst day of my life. The previous week, Dale and I had been in Dallas, Texas for a trade show, where we had a booth displaying his Deerlift, an invention that assists hunters in lifting wild game onto an ATV. On Saturday night, the call came ordering me to report to Maxwell Federal Prison Camp on Tuesday, January 18, before 2 p.m. I don't think I slept a wink after the call. We arrived home in the wee hours on Monday morning, which meant I had just one day to turn myself in.

The U.S. Marshal's office furnished a list of items I could take into the facility: underwear, shaving lotions, toothpaste, etc. We hurried around getting everything together, but discovered when we arrived that it all was to no avail. The right hand didn't know what the left was doing. Policy had been changed, as you will see.

It was the longest trip I had ever made. Going to prison for something you didn't do is a very bitter pill to swallow. I remembered what had happened to Jesus and tried to be encouraged by his words—"I will be with you always, even unto the end of the world."

Reecie had misread a word from God that I would not be incarcerated. She kept saying when we got there, they would tell us to go back home. I tried to get her to be realistic. The system doesn't work that way. I had been convicted and ordered to turn myself in, and nothing would change unless the same system, the U.S. Justice Department, ordered me released. She would not hear it. When the time came, and they drove off without me, she had a very hard time.

Reecie and our two sons drove me up to the compound gate. The trunk was popped, and they were getting my things out, when an officer shouted, "Get that junk back in that car. All you bring in here is what's on your back." He was so ugly. I couldn't help but wonder what I was getting into. Thankfully, this was the worst encounter I had with any officer while there.

I began to cry; my sons and wife began to cry. Dale was terribly upset. He had never heard anyone speak to his father in that manner. Later, he said it took all of the restraint he could muster to keep from causing lots of trouble. Thank God for his restraint.

They drove away, all of us crying, as I was escorted to the nearby receiving area for processing. I had to strip down to my birthday suit. "Stick your tongue out; wiggle your ears; spread your cheeks; flip your private parts." It was the most humiliating thing I had ever experienced.

I was fingerprinted, asked all kinds of questions, and had a mug shot taken that appeared on my record with my number, 03949-003.

The officers issued me underwear, blankets, a few toiletry items, some thin tan pants, a white t-shirt, and canvas shoes. I was told I would be issued clothes the next morning. I was then directed to the clinic, where a physician's assistant examined me.

There are no locks on the doors of a minimum-security prison camp. An inmate can walk off the campus, but must suffer the consequences if he does. When caught, he would be confined to a penitentiary, placed behind bars and razor wire fences.

They assigned me to Montgomery Unit, E-wing. Mobile and Birmingham were the other two units. From my second story dorm, I could see the state capital dome in downtown Montgomery, a building where I had many times visited governors and other state officials. My brother Maston had served there in the legislature as a state representative and a state senator. My brother Jeff had served as one of Governor Wallace's key cabinet members.

As I was taken to my dorm, several hundred men ran down the walkway. I did not know what was happening. Some were hollering, "You shouldn't have done it! Look at you, new man on the compound." Some laughed, some mocked; I didn't know what was going on. Later, I learned that their dorm had just been released to the chow hall. The three dorms rotated which would go first, second, and third. The last one would be released after the second group had entered the chow hall. By then, the first group would have finished their meal and exited.

By the time I got upstairs, and was taken to my cube and bunk, most of the men had already gone to dinner. The officer instructed a black inmate to show me where the food service building was located. In a few minutes, we were on the way, although after my traumatic day, I was not hungry.

When we arrived, I immediately observed more racial segregation than I had ever seen. There were two lines leading to the serving counters, one all white and one ninety-nine per cent black. As we made our way to get our trays, several white guys said, "You don't need to be over there," meaning I ought not be in the line with the blacks. I later found out why, but this being my first experience at the chow hall, and since I was following the man who brought me there, I proceeded to the right, to the side of the building filled with blacks.

Now some of the comments from the whites, "You don't need to be over there," were from purely racist, and same feeling was on the other side—the blacks wouldn't sit with the whites. Spanish-speaking men, especially the Puerto Ricans, had a special area where they ate.

It did not take me long to realize that I really didn't belong on that side of the dining hall, and it had nothing to do with race at all. It had to do with the language. It was horrible; it was as if I had been dropped into hell. I have never heard such cursing and vulgarity in my life. In fact, I heard more profanity in the first ten minutes than I had heard in my entire sixty-plus years.

From that first night on, I sat with the mostly white Christian men. A few blacks sat with us. Occasionally, I would sit on the other side, to let the blacks know I wasn't racist and in the hope that I could influence some of them for the Lord. When asked why I didn't sit on that side more often, my response would be, "I can't stand the cursing, swearing, and vulgar language," which everyone seemed to understand.

I had never been in the military service, required to sleep in a barracks. I had never been in the scouts, forced to camp out with other boys. I had never slept in a room with thirty to forty other men. I had never slept in a bunk bed, much less an upper bunk. That first night, I had a hard time climbing the ladder and getting into the top bunk. I was almost in the bed when a sudden a cramp hit me in the leg. I thought for sure I would tumble backwards to the floor, but I finally made it.

The next day, as I continued with the physical examinations, a very compassionate, young, black physician's assistant (PA) gave me a bottom bunk. He said, "You are old enough to be my father, and you deserve a bottom bunk." The next day, I was assigned a bottom bunk.

There were two men to a cube, which was about seven by nine feet, with concrete walls about five feet high. When you stood, you could see the rest of the dorm. When seated, there was some degree of privacy. Each person had a locker for his belongings. There was also a small desk for reading and writing. The metal beds were labeled. After the first few nights, my bed was labeled Montgomery E-11B. When the officers came through at night, counting, if an inmate was not in his bed, they would know immediately who was missing.

At four, every afternoon, at all federal facilities, there is what is known as the four o'clock standing count. When officers screamed count time, everyone hit the floor and stood by his bunk. Every inmate in the entire system is counted physically, recorded, and I am told that notice of the total number is provided to the Federal Bureau of Prisons in Washington, D.C.

After the four o'clock count, an officer brings the mailbag for the unit and everyone crowds around looking for cards or letters from friends and loved ones. I was told that I received more mail than any other man did. Letters and cards came from all over the country and were a genuine blessing to me, but I felt sorry for men who always came to mail call yet never received a piece of mail. They expected to hear from someone, but no one ever wrote. I don't see how men without a support group made it. It is hard enough to be confined, but even worse when no one cares.

After returning from the chow hall on that first evening, a group of Christian men came to my cube. One gave me a pair of shower shoes, another a coffee mug, another some cookies; there were more gifts from others, but most of all they gave me encouragement, that everything would be all right, they would help me adjust and do whatever they could to help me.

One man, a former pastor of a large church, was most helpful, and he and I became fast friends and a great support to each other. His encouragement meant more than he will ever know and on the eve of his being released, he wrote me a note saying, "The best part of being in prison was meeting you." We are close friends until this day.

I didn't sleep much, if any, that first night. I cried, I prayed, I looked back over my life and could not believe I was incarcerated for something I did not do.

I said, "Lord you know that I am not guilty. I don't know what this is all about, but use me while I am here." That first night, I went to the chapel, where the pastor and a group from Snowdon Baptist Church were conducting a service. This same church had ministered at Maxwell every Tuesday night for many years and had been a great influence on many men. Most people have never heard of Snowdon Baptist Church, but millions have heard of Chuck Colson, one of President Richard Nixon's Watergate figures. His life was changed by this church a number of years ago, when he was incarcerated at Maxwell.

That very first night, I was allowed to give my personal testimony, which according to the men was a blessing to them, but it was more of a blessing to me.

Many of the several hundred inmates had heard of my case, and the media had let the whole state know that I was to surrender to Maxwell that afternoon. The Lord opened the door for me to share my faith that very first night, which set me on the road to a wonderful and productive ministry while I was there.

My dearest and best friend, and long time political supporter and advisor told me on the day I was sentenced, as we gathered back at my office, "Well, just look at the opportunities you will have to do prison ministry." At that moment, I had been in no mood to hear this, and to tell you the truth, I resented his comments very much. I thought if the Lord wanted me to be in prison ministry, he could have just told me. At any rate, my friend Dennis Moore's words turned out to be true. Those years of incarceration were like being on a mission trip. No, it was not easy being away from family and friends, and I looked forward to visiting days with great expectation, but in spite of the injustice, God took what people did for evil and turned it into good, just as he did in Joseph's life, as recorded in Genesis 50:20.

Bright and early, I reported to the A&O (admissions and orientation) officers, something all new inmates had to go through. Orientation included getting familiar with the rules, procedures, and layout of the compound. We were required to pick up cigarette butts when classes were not in session, and for a few days, I was assigned to picking up cigarette butts and trash around the compound. This was a humbling experience. There I was, one time mayor of a major city, head of hundreds of people in public works and trash removal activities, picking up cigarette butts and paper. If this couldn't bring a person down, I wondered what would.

There was a young man, an attorney from South Florida, who checked in the day before, as I had done. As we walked over the compound, I began to find out about him and got into the status of his spiritual life. He informed me that his father was a Jew, and his mother was a Catholic, and no one had ever said anything to him about God. He said, "I am nobody." My response was that there were no "nobodies" in God's sight; everybody was somebody in his eyes. It was hard to convince him that anybody cared, much less God. For several hours, we talked as we made our rounds. As time went on, I could tell that the Holy Spirit was working on him, and he was softening his position considerably.

Thank God, before the day ended, beside a rail fence on the backside of the compound, near the banks of the Alabama River, I was privileged to pray with this young man and hear him ask Christ into his heart and life.

My prayer, uttered that first night of incarceration, was being answered. Untold hundreds of opportunities to witness were given to me in the days to follow.

Chapter 31

Working at
the Chapel

E very inmate was required to have a job. Most of the men worked at the Maxwell Air Force Base in offices and shops. Others labored at keeping up the grounds and golf courses. A number were assigned to various departments in the compound—grounds, building maintenance, commissary, mess hall, various warehouses, and janitorial positions, etc.

Some were assigned to Gunter Air Force Base. A few had duties at a veteran's hospital at Tuskegee, some forty miles away. All the men who worked off the compound went to a marshaling area and were transported to and from their job sites by bus.

I prayed God would put me where I was supposed to be, to do the most I could for him and the kingdom.

The associate warden, a Christian gentleman, in reading my pre-sentence report and having knowledge of my Christian activities while I was mayor of Mobile, assigned me to the chapel. I will never forget that night about two weeks after I arrived and had gone through A&O. I saw my name on the call out sheet. The call out sheet was posted in each dorm, and indicated whether you had a medical or dental appointment the next day. It also gave new work assignments. When I read, "03949-003 Lambert Mims, report to the chapel," I began to weep tears of joy and praised God at the top of my voice. Many of the men with whom I had already become acquainted were happy for me. A few thought I was getting preferential treatment, but I knew it was God opening the door for me to be a blessing to many men.

The associate warden had indicated that I would be good at the chapel, but he had some reservations about my being there. God must have spoken to him, because he made the assignment. At the time, there was no chaplain; the previous one had been transferred, and the new one wouldn't arrive for several weeks.

There were menial tasks, like cleaning the chapel and vacuuming, but I had lots of time to talk to the men as they came in seeking spiritual help. I began working with the ministers who came in to conduct services, like those from Snowdon Baptist Church on Tuesday nights. The Catholic priest came in on Saturday afternoons; the Church of Christ folk on Sunday nights, and the Episcopalian priest came one night. In other words, there was ministry going on every night and Sunday mornings.

When the new chaplain came and assumed his duties, I was allowed to do several things that blessed the men and gave me the opportunity to share my faith. He was a Baptist and had attended Southern Seminary in Louisville, Kentucky. He knew many leaders I knew, and we had much in common.

He was a good preacher and loved that part of his work. It might not have been in accordance with the rules, but he allowed me the opportunity to counsel with men, one on one.

On Sunday nights, after the Church of Christ service, we had a large number gather for Bible study, with several of us inmates rotating the teaching. There were many lives restored and scores brought to faith in Christ in the Sunday evening meetings. After the night service, a number of us would gather around the fountain that was more or less the centerpiece of the compound, to share and have prayer under the canopy of God's beautiful moon and stars. Other nights, we gathered in the visitor's yard having Christian fellowship and eating popcorn from the movie in the auditorium.

One of the most popular and beneficial activities the chaplain allowed was my posting a board in the small library of the chapel, near a heavily traveled sidewalk. I called it the "good news" board. It could be seen from the sidewalk. Everyday, I would get up at five o'clock in the morning, go to the TV room and listen to *CNN Headline News,* and make notes. I would then post several items on the board under the heading "Today's News," and right under that was a section called, "The Good News." There, I would post a different scripture verse every day. Many men would pause, look through the window, read today's news and the good news and be on their way.

During the day, men who were on the sick list, awaiting an appointment at the clinic next door or on the evening shift would come into the library where I would explain the scripture passages, receive prayer requests, and offer prayer. Dozens of men had their lives changed because of this ministry.

Another ministry was making a goody bag for new inmates. Interested men would buy packaged cookies at the commissary and bring them as their tithe or offering. I would place the cookies, along with a New Testament and some tracts, into a brown paper bag and distribute them to newcomers. We tried to always have a Christian brother in each dorm wing that looked out for new men. It was important that a new inmate, perhaps incarcerated for the first time, receive a kind word and an expression of love from someone who had already experienced this traumatic event.

From the chapel, I could see the men come into the R&D (receiving and discharge) area. Many were just as I had been, crying as their families left them, and crying over what was transpiring in their lives. I could see the buses (rolling jails) as they unloaded men from other institutions.

After the processing at R&D, they all came along the same sidewalk I traveled my first day there. They came right by the chapel. I did something I don't think had ever been done before by anyone working at the chapel. I made it a point, as much as possible, to make my way to the sidewalk and greet as many new inmates as I could. I would tell them about services, invited them to come over as soon as they were settled in, and offered to pray with them. Many welcomed my offer, and I would stand there on that sidewalk and pray for them, their families, and their needs.

I saw those faces—white, black, and brown—beam as I held their hands and prayed God's blessings upon them while at Maxwell. There were many cases of one on one sharing. I didn't try to keep up with all of the decisions; God keeps those records. He knew my heart, and he caused those who needed a word of encouragement to cross my path.

One case that comes to mind is the man who came to the chapel after hearing that his wife, on the way home from seeing him, had been killed in an automobile accident. The poor man, as could be expected, was in shock, not knowing where to turn. I took him into the chapel and began to console him.

I said, "You know the Lord is the only one that can help you through this terrible thing. Do you know him as your personal Savior?"

He explained he was Catholic, and my response was that we were not talking about religion or denomination. I wanted to know if there was ever a time that he confessed his sin and invited Jesus Christ into his heart to forgive him of his sins. He said, "No!"

"All right," I said. "That is the first order of business. Let's get down on our knees, here by the front pew, and talk to God."

There he cried out to God to save his soul, confessing his sins and calling upon Jesus to come into his heart. Afterwards, I shared scriptures of consolation and prayed that the Holy Spirit would comfort him as he went through his loss.

Another case I am reminded of involves a man from South Carolina who had not been to the chapel before. On this particular day, he rushed into the chapel from the telephone room. It was his twenty-fifth wedding anniversary, and he had just called his wife. A special day turned into a terrible one when she informed him to get lost; she didn't want to see him, ever again. She told him that she had moved in with his best friend and would be seeking a divorce. It broke his heart. When he came through the door, he was sobbing and tears flowed down his cheeks. I took him into the library, where he told me his sad story. I told him as I told so many, "You cannot handle this alone; only God can help you. Do you know the Lord? Was there ever a time you surrendered your life to Christ and asked God to forgive your sins?"

His answer was no. I explained that this was his greatest need; he agreed, and we prayed right there that God would save him. He confessed his sins and asked Jesus Christ into his heart. His countenance changed. He looked like a different man. He was a new man. We talked for a long time. He had a hard time forgiving his wife and his business partner and best friend, but he finally saw that he must do so, because God had forgiven him.

About a month later, he received a letter from his wife, asking for forgiveness and stating how sorry she was for making such a dreadful mistake. She asked him to call collect, and he did—the marriage, and most of all, his soul was saved. Praise God!

Another difficult case was the one where my roommate's (roomie, bunkie, or cellie in prison terminology) little son died on the way home from visiting him. His wife and two-year-old son from the Rio

Grande area of Texas had visited and seemingly had a very pleasant time. They were both beautiful people. The little boy had sat on my knee earlier that day, as both of our families were in the visiting area. On the way home, in the wee hours of the night, the little boy developed a high fever and a stop was made at a Beaumont, Texas hospital. He had scarlet fever, which sent his body temperature skyrocketing. When the word came of what had happened, and the son was near death, my roommate came to me, as distraught as anyone could possibly be.

It was very difficult for me to counsel with my roommate before he left. It was comforting to both of us that he was a Christian and had the Lord, who is the only one who can help us through such a time. It seemed he would never be furloughed to join his family, but finally, all the papers were signed. By the time my friend got to the Beaumont hospital, his son had died.

Upon his return, we learned of the tragic outcome. It was even harder then to deal with the situation. All we could do was to pray for God's consolation. No one can understand such a thing; but true believers know that "all things work together for good to those who are called according to God's purpose" (Rom. 8:28).

There were two cases where the men were not allowed to go on furlough when loved ones passed away. One case was that of a man's mother passing, the other was a man's son. In both cases the warden, other prison officials, and local prosecutors, wouldn't allow it. In both cases, we received permission to use the chapel for memorial services for the inmate's loved ones. I was asked to conduct the services. Several of us read scriptures and led in singing and did everything we could to console our fellow inmates in their loss.

One afternoon a new man on the compound came into the chapel with tears streaming down his cheeks. I hardly understood what he was trying to say. He was sobbing, half in Spanish and half in English. I tried to console him, but he never opened up to me. After a while, the chaplain arrived and took him into his office. When the chaplain finished talking to him, he was escorted to R&D and taken off the compound. His medical examination had revealed he had AIDS, which caused him to be sent on to a hospital, away from other men.

God gave me many opportunities to share his love. I wish all had accepted it, but that was not the case. I had a dream, shortly after arriving on campus, in which three children, ragged, dirty, and cold huddled by a big stone fireplace where the fire had died. In that dream, as I tried to speak to the children, one cursed and spit at me, one showed no emotion whatsoever, and one warmed up and came to me.

My ministry in prison came down this way. Some couldn't stand me or what I stood for; some didn't seem to care about anything; but thank God, some listened and as a result, their lives were changed, and so was mine.

Unfortunately, only a few black men came to Sunday night's Bible study. We would usually have upwards of fifty, mostly white, inmates who would attend. Several of us rotated the teaching. Sometimes it would take several weeks to complete a study or theme or book of the Bible. Then another would take over. Some of the black inmates started calling this a Klan meeting, which was ridiculous. In prison, people say all kinds of things. It was a Bible study, open to all, and over several years, it was a blessing to hundreds of men as they came and went.

To the regret of many, a new female warden came on the scene, and some of the black men convinced her that the Sunday night Bible study was a racist gathering. She issued orders that inmates could no longer lead meetings such as we were having. How unfortunate, but wherever God is working and blessing, the enemy comes against that work.

Although those Sunday night, inmate-led, meetings stopped, no one could stop us from talking about the Lord. Several of us would share on the compound, at the chow hall, at the ballpark, on the track, or by the fountain. True believers obey God rather than man.

Visiting days were days of excitement for those who had friends and loved ones that cared. Inmates anxiously listened for their names to be called out over the public address system. It meant that there was someone visiting them. I was fortunate to have family come to see me every visiting day. There were others, too—deacons from our church and friends who were on my visitor's list who came regularly to see me. Religious leaders received special permission through the chaplain to visit me.

Visiting days were good days; we talked and shared the week's events, prayed and witnessed for the Lord. Reecie came to know a number of the spouses of inmates. They stayed overnight at a local hotel so they could return for a visit on Sunday. Actually, Reecie developed quite a ministry, encouraging women who were not as grounded in the faith as she was. Lasting friendships developed over those years, and God used both of us to help others by pointing them towards Christ and encouraging them to be strong, in spite of the circumstances.

I am grateful for the way God blessed my family and me throughout this ordeal. As it was with Joseph in Gen. 50:20, so it was with me—"What men meant for evil, God meant for good."

Chapter 32

The Rolling Jail

The time arrived for me to appear before a representative of the U.S. Parole Commission to establish a date for my release.

I told one of the officers, a black woman who knew of my background and seemed to like me that I would be going to Atlanta for a parole hearing. She called me into the small office and said, "I'll pray for you." I thanked her, and she prayed one of the most beautiful and meaningful prayers you could imagine, for which I was very grateful.

The hearing was to be held in Atlanta, Georgia at FPC Atlanta. We expected that several inmates would travel to the hearing by van and return the same day, which was not to be the case.

Four of us, a Jewish fellow; a big, black Baptist guy from the Mississippi Delta; a Spanish-speaking Catholic, and this Baptist layman were called to R&D and placed in a small holding area with no outside window, where we waited for what we thought would be a Dodge van. After some time, what sounded like a diesel engine roared up to the front door. I said, "Men, this doesn't sound like a Dodge van to me. It's a rolling jail, a bus with bars, for transporting real desperados."

A few minutes later, we heard what sounded like a wheelbarrow full of chains being dumped out on the tile floor in the adjoining room. I said, "Men, we need to pray."

I heard them say, in one united voice, "Would you pray for us?" I will never forget that day, when the four of us stood in a circle with arms around each other's shoulders, and I asked God to be with us in what was ahead.

I had never been handcuffed before. I had self-surrendered to this institution, so there had never been a need for them. The officers called us out, one by one and asked us to turn our backs, then immediately placed leg irons on us that were joined with a short connecting chain, allowing steps of about twelve inches. Then they turned us around and handcuffed us. I felt completely helpless, as tears flowed down my cheeks, but I remembered the words of Jesus when he said, "I will be with you always, even unto the end of the world." This promise strengthened me, and I completely surrendered to him.

Officers stood by the bus with shotguns, while we were led to the door of what seemed to be a regular, over-the-road bus. Inside, however, we could see the bars all the way around the bus, inside the windows. Just behind the driver's seat was a divider of steel bars. When everyone had boarded, the door was locked, with the driver and one officer in the front compartment. At the rear of the bus was a cage constructed of steel bars, where another officer sat with a shotgun across his lap. He was opposite the latrine where the inmates were to urinate.

The bus was about half-full of guys from a higher security institution north of Montgomery. These were, in many cases, hardened, violent criminals with long prison terms being transferred to other institutions. Their language was horrible and their conversations so gross, I could hardly stand it.

I took a seat by a young man who had been Christian since his boyhood. He had been away from his family for a number of months. I shared with him how God was a God of second chances, and if he would only confess his sins, he would be restored to the fellowship he once knew. In a few minutes, he lit up like a Christmas tree, and I knew that in his heart, there on that rolling jail, he had asked for forgiveness.

The bus left Maxwell and headed down I-65, but instead of taking I-85 to the east and Atlanta, it kept going. I knew then that we were not headed to Atlanta. We went a little farther, and the bus turned toward Florida. That night, weary and tired, we arrived at the federal prison in Tallahassee, Florida.

It was a long trip; handcuffed and shackled, it was nearly impossible to eat the snack we were served. One of the inmates was unchained and became the busman who passed out the food and drinks. I didn't drink anything, because it would increase my need to urinate. I had not had anything since early morning, for fear of having to go too much.

In the afternoon, I became very uncomfortable, to the point of pain. I hobbled to the latrine, but with my hands bound and a shotgun to my back, as much as I needed to urinate, I could not bring one drop forth. I made my way back to my seat and continued to suffer, asking God to help me. Somewhere on a Florida road, I said, "Lord, surely there were times when the crowds pressed upon you, and people wanted you to minister to them, and you could not break away. Surely you must know the strain I'm in. Won't you please help me make it to wherever we are headed?" I want you to know that I made it into the night and did not relieve myself until we settled in at Tallahassee. Even after the bus was unloaded, I could not go. Imagine forty men in a small room, with a toilet in the middle, where everyone was staring at you. It just wouldn't work.

The bus pulled up to the prison. There was razor wire everywhere and armed guards in pickup trucks circling the area. The bus entered a secure yard, and we were put in a holding area. From there we went through the entire admissions process, including being stripped down, finger printed—the works, which took several hours. Finally, into the early night, dead dog tired, the group was divided, with the real high-risk inmates going one way, and the rest of us sent to another wing, or cell unit.

Three of us from Maxwell were sent to cellblock A, and upon arrival we discovered that army cots had been set up wall to wall, with barely enough room to walk between them. We were assigned cots, with the Jewish man on one side and the black Mississippi guy at my feet. They never let me out of their sight. This was all new to us, but evidently, I was the glue that held us together. Of course, they knew my Christian testimony and remembered how we had prayed together before leaving Maxwell.

The first person I saw when placed in cellblock A was the officer in charge, a real dark African-American man with pearly teeth, a broad smile, and the countenance of an angel. He assured me that I would be safe there, and he would make things as easy as he could for us. He informed us that we would leave for Atlanta early the next morning.

The first thing I looked for was the toilet, where I got relief for the first time in more than twelve hours. We were given a bite to eat, and I used the phone to call my family, who were anxiously awaiting my call from Atlanta. When my wife gave permission for the collect call, the first thing she asked was, "Where are you?"

I replied, "I am in a real jail in Tallahassee." That was a shock to her and our sons, who were standing nearby. I explained what had happened; they could tell how washed out I was from what was the worst trip I had ever made.

Several Christian men told me of a Bible study on the mezzanine, and I told my buddies from Maxwell. They said, "Let's go," and we did, and were blessed as we all read from the Bible and shared our faith. My Jewish friend took it in readily; it was nothing new for him to hear me talking about Jesus Christ.

There was little sleep, and the night was short. At two in the morning, we were told to get up and get ready. We went through the same routine as when we came into the facility. Finally, about daybreak, we were handcuffed, shackled, and boarded another of the rolling jails. We were on our way to Atlanta, and it was another long day, a duplicate of the day before.

We arrived at the U.S. Penitentiary in Atlanta, a place where folk like Al Capone and other criminals had served hard time for decades. It was an awesome place. The walls were high and thick, and I'm told that they go forty feet into the ground. They are topped with row after row of razor wire and sharp spikes. There are wires streaming across the open areas so helicopters can't get in. It is next to impossible to escape this maximum-security lockup. There are guard towers on every corner and along the massive walls. The story is that the only person ever to escape did so in a choir robe with a group who had come in for a worship service.

The bus came up to a massive steel door; lights were flashing as we approached. The lights turned green and the door opened. Once the bus was inside, the door closed behind it and we were in a secure chamber. A number of armed guards appeared on the scene. We again hobbled off the bus and slowly made our way through a series of steel doors and bars.

We went through the same humiliating strip search, exposing our private parts, fingerprinting and questioning. By then, I was just about past going. The rough trip from Montgomery to Tallahassee, with very little sleep the night before, and many hours on the bus without using the bathroom had taken its toll on me.

Arriving at four in the afternoon, at shift change, was not good. The officers were ready to go home and upset because this busload of inmates was interfering with their plans. These officers were the rudest, meanest people I have ever seen. They were hollering and shouting, some even cursing. I was already at the point of breaking, when one asked, "What's an old man like you doing in prison?"

I broke down, crying, as I said, "As far as I'm concerned, it's because of political prosecution, the FBI lied, and the judge allowed it to go on."

Then I heard a voice saying, "Ya'll leave my mayor alone." It was like the voice of an angel. The very nice black supervisor came to me, and said he had grown up in Mobile and now was with the Federal Bureau of Prisons. He knew my work and reputation, and indicated he was sorry I had to go through all of this. The other officers did back off a bit after he interceded.

My Jewish friend and I were taken to a cellblock where we would be locked up for the night. It was an awful place. There were hundreds of men cursing, swearing, and screaming to the top of their voices. The echo was terrible. The sounds vibrated off the brick, concrete, and iron. Again, it seemed I had been transported into hell. It was hard getting a call through to my family, and when I finally did, it was difficult to hear because of the noise.

The next morning the guards let us out of our cells and took us to meet a man from the camp next door to the penitentiary. He was a kind, well-mannered black man, who said, "Come on, you are going with me to the camp. There will be no need for cuffs and shackles."

What a relief—someone seemed to care. After the rough treatment we had received, it seemed a miracle. We walked through corridor after corridor until we came to a gate, where we boarded a van and were transported out of the prison to the camp.

After our tiring trip, the awful experience of going through the Atlanta Penitentiary, and going six hundred miles out of the way through Tallahassee to get there, the Atlanta Camp was a welcome sight.

God's grace is sufficient!

Chapter 33

The Atlanta Experience

The Atlanta prison camp lies just outside the eastern wall of the penitentiary, literally in the shadow of the place where some of the country's worst criminals were confined.

The Atlanta camp was different from the Maxwell camp in many ways. It was smaller and much more laid back. The rules were not as strict, and the officers didn't seem to be as interested in making names for themselves. It was my understanding that officers rotated between the penitentiary and the camp; it was a great relief for them since they had just come off duty from behind the walls with high-risk inmates, some of whom were incarcerated for horrendous crimes.

The facility was smaller, with all ground-level buildings, and housed fewer men than Maxwell, occupying less ground space. It was as clean and comfortable as a prison camp could be, yet not as pristine as Maxwell, where the Air Force monitored the buildings and grounds, and every blade of grass had to be just right and in place. The food was much better, with a greater variety, and to my knowledge, there were no complaints whatsoever. The commissary had far more items than Maxwell, with easier access and shorter lines.

There was a nice chapel for religious services, and a number of church groups came in to conduct services. My Jewish friend from Maxwell accompanied me to all the services and listened intently. From the prayer meeting at Maxwell, when we had the bus roll in, he hardly let me out of his sight, except when we were assigned to different tasks.

Admissions and Orientation (A&O), where new inmates became acquainted with the camp, the same at all institutions, was the first order of service.

A new supply of khaki clothes was issued, which was something of a relief from Maxwell's dark green. During A&O, while not in class, policing the grounds was the order of the day.

I've always felt that any job done should be done well, so I did my best picking up paper around the grounds. Although I was to be there for only a short time for the parole hearing, I still wanted to do my best and prayed I would get the right job assigned to me. Many of the men at the camp worked behind the wall at the mattress factory or other production type jobs. I didn't really want the hassle of going back and forth into the penitentiary everyday. My prayers were answered.

The administrator observed the way I worked around the administration building, came out one day, and told me he would assign me to grounds and wanted me to pick-up around the administration building and the front of the penitentiary, every day.

The next day's call out sheet had me going to the grounds department. Upon arrival that morning, I discovered the familiar "turf battle" situation that is prevalent in most large organizations, especially government bureaucracies. The superintendent resented my being there. "I didn't request additional personnel. I run this department; what are you doing here?" he asked.

I replied, "You need to take it up with the administrator. I didn't come here to cause problems; but the administrator told me he wanted me to clean up around the building and up front, especially where the warden parks everyday."

"Oh, alright, take this bag and go to work," he snapped. I am pleased to say that over the few weeks I was there, the grounds superintendent warmed up and turned out to be a pretty nice guy.

I was determined that I would make the most out of my weeks there as I waited for August 19 and my appearance before the parole hearing officer. I kept busy, sharing my faith with everyone who would listen, and discovered that a number of the men there were Christians. We leaned on one another's shoulders and encouraged each other as the scriptures exhort.

As I made my rounds in front of the penitentiary, my heart went out to the families of those inmates who were or had been incarcerated in the maximum-security facility. There is a burial ground outside the wall where men who die there, with no one to claim their bodies, are buried.

Crime surely does not pay. It affects so many lives—the victim, the victim's family, the perpetrator, the perpetrator's family, and many others. As I made my rounds, picking up paper, I spent a lot of time talking to the Lord, not only about my own needs, but also about the needs of the tens of thousands of children whose fathers were behind those walls, and walls like them across the country.

There were people, mostly staff of the penitentiary, coming and going for shift changes, so there was a lot of activity in the parking lots. Of course, everyone could tell I was an inmate, but it was very rewarding for me to have so many congratulate me on the way I was handling my duties, even if it was picking up paper.

I was reminded of the case of the Greek general, whose enemies set out to embarrass him by stripping him of power and reducing his duties to garbage collecting. He said, "If the job will not reflect glory on me, then I will reflect glory on the job."

These congratulatory remarks even from the administrator and the warden pleased me to no end, but there were some who tried to trick me. I shall never forget an incident that took place on my first or second day at the Atlanta camp. I was to clean out one of the pick-up trucks used by camp personnel. I didn't mind doing what I had been told, but when I opened the passenger side door, I saw a ten-dollar bill on the floor mat. I closed the door immediately and returned to the office. There are many do's and don'ts in a prison compound, but none will get an inmate in trouble quicker than having paper money in his possession. When I saw the paper money on the floor of that truck, I was sure it was a test. The money didn't tempt me at all, and I knew not to let my hands touch it. I told the officer what I had seen and explained that I couldn't touch it. If he wanted me to clean the truck, he would have to remove the ten-dollar bill. He responded, "I must have dropped it. I'll go and get it." I could tell that he had tried to set me up, but it hadn't worked.

On another occasion, I was making my rounds by one of the watchtowers and heard a voice. "Hey buddy, look in my car there, and get me a pack if cigarettes. I'll drop this bucket on a rope if you'll put them in there for me."

Again, I felt this was a set-up. An inmate wasn't allowed to touch any vehicle; I was not about to go near the car, much less open the door. I told the officer high above me that I was sorry, but I just couldn't touch his car. He said okay, and I continued on my way.

While I got away with being caught up in possible set-ups, I narrowly escaped "being sent," as it is called, behind the wall. The last place I wanted to be was next door in the U.S. Penitentiary, but the threat was real.

Periodically, inmates are called in for a urine test. It seemed each time I was called, I had just been to the restroom and was unable to urinate. On this occasion, there were about a half dozen of us called. I was the last one to be tested, but I still had no urge to go, especially with the officer breathing over my shoulder. After trying desperately, without any success, I was told to try again in fifteen minutes. If I couldn't urinate then, I would be sent to the prison behind the wall, for refusal. I prayed as hard as I could that the Lord would intervene. Before the fifteen minutes were up, I heard the officer who was handling the tests tell the other one, "I have to go; do what you want to with Mims."

In a few minutes, I was called in and the officer said, "You look like a Christian, and I doubt if you ever had any drugs in your life. Get out of here." My prayer had been answered.

The same thing had happened to me at Maxwell. I heard my name called over the public address system, "Mims report to the captain's office." I had known what it was about, but again, had just gone to the restroom.

I tried and tried, to no avail. The officer said, "I'm compelled to call the captain and have you shipped, but I'll wait a few more minutes." The two-hour time limit was coming to a close. I was frantic! I literally cried out to the Lord for help. I did not want to be shipped for refusing to give a urine sample. Five minutes before the end of my two hours, I tried again. The officer was standing so close to my back that I could feel his breath against my neck. I, in desperation, cried out, "Please give me a little room." He stepped back a few feet into the hallway, and my prayers were answered with five minutes to go.

The date of the parole hearing arrived. Tom Haas, with tears in his eyes, pleaded my cause, as did my son Danny, the attorney. Danny and Tom had driven up from Mobile to be with me. Each applicant was allotted a certain amount of time. The hearing officer was a very nice lady from the Midwest, and as I found out, a good Christian and very understanding. Letters from the district judge and supervisors at Maxwell were presented. Some are included:

United States Government
M e m o r a n d u m
Federal Prison camp
Maxwell Air Force Base
Montgomery, AL 36112

Date:	June 30, 1996
Reply To	
Attn Of:	Carlton Fisher, Jr., Chaplain
Subject:	Good Letter For Lambert Mims, 03949-003
To:	Bryan Pownall, Unit Manager
For:	Central File

I have known Lambert Mims since my arrival in September 1995 at FPC Maxwell, as Mr. Mims was assigned to work for me as a chapel orderly.

Mr. Mims worked for me for approximately three months and then was transferred to another position because of administrative needs. If the decision had been left up to me, Mr. Mims would still be working for me in the chapel.

While Mr. Mims worked for me, he was completely respectful and loyal. He went out of his way, even during "off" hours to find ways to help in the chapel.

He saw his chapel position as more than a job, but a ministry. Recalling his own sense of grief when he became incarcerated, he spends much of his time and still does trying to help newly incarcerated men transition into their new surroundings.

Since Mr. Mims left the chapel position, he has certainly been no stranger to the chapel. He attends nine different chapel programs on a weekly basis and attends any special Christian events that we sponsor. He is ecumenical in his Christian approach, attending both Protestant and Roman Catholic services. He is recognized as a leader in the Christian community and assists me in leading a weekly prayer service.

Mr. Mims has a wife who faithfully comes to see him for every available visit. From past conversations with him, I know that Lambert deeply loves her. He also is not getting any younger.

I do not believe that Lambert Mims is a threat to society in any way. For the sake of his family and the remaining quantity and quality of his own life, I hope that within the law, there might be a way to grant him leniency in his sentence.

UNITED STATES GOVERNMENT
M E M O R A N D U M
Federal Prison Camp, Montgomery, AL 36112

Date:	6/27/96
Reply To	
Attn Of:	C. E. Hudson II, Recreation Supervisor
Subject:	Reference Letter for inmate Lambert Mims (#43949-003)
To:	Unit Team for Lambert Mims (Montgomery E)

It is my understanding that the above inmate is meeting with the Parole Board on August 19, 1996. Because of this I am relating certain relevant facts that could be considered in determining the character and work ethics of this inmate.

He attended all of the wellness courses that I taught in the Recreation Department. These include Weight Loss, Nutrition, Stress Management and Disease Prevention.

He is a personable individual who is constantly trying to counsel with new inmates on their arrival. He tries to help them with the beginning orientation to prison life.

It is my understanding that he worked in the Chapel for the first 20 months of being in prison. He was then transferred to CO-8 Custody and works daily with the new inmates who are on the unassigned duty list.

I have noticed that he is busy daily doing his work of picking up trash on the compound. He appears to be busy all of the time.

I made my appeal as follows:

"Although my incarceration, as the record indicates, is a result of no direct fault of mine, I am terribly sorry that an impeccable record of twenty years of public service has been tainted. I regret the appearance of any wrongdoing, and if any citizen thinks any less of me because of this, I am deeply remorseful.

If I had it all to do over again, I would try my best to know more about what my "friends" were saying out of my presence and would be more careful in meeting with people I didn't trust just because some friend, preacher or otherwise, urged me to do so. As unfortunate as this situation has been, much good has come from the experience.

1. My family and I are much closer and more supportive of each other than at any time in our lives. 2. My real friends mean more to me

than ever before. 3. I've been given a rare opportunity to see men hurting in a way I've not known before. 4. Although I did not choose incarceration, I did choose to serve my fellow man while incarcerated. Helping men through one of the most traumatic experiences of life, the transition into incarceration, has been very rewarding. 5. There has been ample time to assist men as they went through separations, divorces, family illnesses, deaths and other tragedies, while working in the chapel and on the compound at Maxwell FPC. 6. All of these experiences have better prepared me to serve others in the future; and have helped me to maintain my faith and integrity.

I respectfully appeal to you for relief, and would appreciate your serious consideration based on the following:

1. The recommendation of the PSI, Salient factor 10, Severity factor IV, guideline range 12-18 months (see PSI). 2. The Judge stated that his intention was for me to serve only 40 months (see letter). The Prosecutor agreed. 3. A clear record of conduct during my 31 months of incarceration (see progress report). 4. According to others I have managed to accomplish some good in my effort to help other inmates (see letter). 5. My outstanding work record - Chapel and CO8 Custody. 6. My present age of 66. 7. My wife's present age of 70. 8. My positive outlook on life and the future, without bitterness. 9. My past contributions to my fellow man, what I can do in the future, and my sincere desire to do so. 10. This instant case is the first and only blemish on my record. 11. Anyone who knows me knows that I am not a threat to society in any way."

Respectfully Submitted,

The hearing went well. The hearing officer stated that she would recommend I be cut loose after serving one third of my ten-year sentence (40 months). Of course, the Parole Commission in Washington, D.C. had to make the final decision, which meant it would take several weeks to get an answer.

Unfortunately, when the answer came, I was required to serve an additional six months, because a co-defendant had earlier received that determination.

We appealed the parole commissions decision but the original decision stood. I would have to serve forty-six months for a crime I never committed, and for which there was no evidence.

Shortly after the parole hearing, I was returned to Maxwell. My possessions, toilet items, books, Bibles, alarm clock, etc. were packed up and one morning, at two o'clock, Eastern Time, I was awakened and told it was time to go. I, along with several others, was led to the door of the U.S. Penitentiary, where we were taken to a secure area. There we sat on the concrete floor for several hours. Once again, we were required to go through the same strip and search procedures, and cuffed and shackled. Sometime near mid-day, we boarded a bus that took us to Talladega Federal Prison where most of the men were destined. Afterwards, a few of us were transported to Maxwell.

It was a trip that I shall never forget, the most stressful of my life, and one that cost the taxpayers of America untold thousands of dollars. It was a waste of resources, especially since my family had agreed to suffer the expenses if I had been sent on a round trip that should have taken less than one full day.

Chapter 34

Prison Stories

There is so much to tell. My life has been filled with unbelievable events. My prison experience is no exception. Neither time nor space will allow penning all of the events, but some must be shared. Some are long tales, others are brief. Some can be presented as short stories.

SHORT STORIES

FAMILIES INCARCERATED—FBI agents lie; prosecutors develop theories; jurors lean toward the government and judges, appointed for life, throw the book at people—sometimes at whole families.

FAMILY #1:

The father was so angry with the son that he would not speak to him for months. The younger man was blamed for getting the whole family involved in a drug conspiracy. The wife was serving a one-year prison sentence. His sister and mother-in-law had been indicted, but cleared. The father had nothing to do with the case, but he was serving time in the federal prison camp adjoining the FCI (Federal Correctional Institution) next door, where the son was confined. He was bitter. He was angry. He was filled with hatred. He never wanted to see his son again. The son was grieved, saddened, and deeply hurt that his father had been indicted, but the pain of the father's attitude far outweighed it all.

Then one day, the counselor called the son to the unit office. "You have a call."

"Hello," the son reluctantly said into the telephone.

"This is your daddy," was the response on the other end of the line. He was just a few feet away, but it seemed like thousands of miles because of the past hard feelings. "I'm sorry," said the father. "I think it's time we got on with our lives and put this matter behind us," the father tearfully explained.

The son, with tears streaming down his cheeks, said, "You are forgiven. I've wanted to talk to you for so long, you are forgiven!"

FAMILY #2:

The father was a full-fledged redneck. The son was a chip off the same block. You never saw them without their jaws packed full of chewing tobacco; each could win a spitting contest.

They hated authority. They despised the federal government. Hatred and bitterness filled them. Profanity was the normal manner of speech and racism flowed from their tongues.

The wife and mother was a tough little woman, who expressed herself in the strongest of words and actions. She was a scrapper from the word go, but no one ever was a greater support than she. She visited as much as possible, except when running the family grocery store prohibited her from traveling the several hundred miles to the camp where her husband and son were confined.

The father had his circle of friends and the son had his, but wherever they went, they cussed the government, the justice system, and anything else that crossed their minds. They didn't have time for chapel services or anything of a spiritual nature.

They served their time, the next day being like the first, and waiting for the day that they could get back to their grocery store, where they had been found guilty of food stamp fraud.

FAMILY #3:

The two younger of five brothers were left at home, through a plea agreement, to run the family's vast farming, oil, and cattle operation, along with their eighty-five year-old mother, who stood at the airport window to wave goodbye to her three older sons. They were on the way to a federal prison camp six hundred miles away, to begin serving up to five-year sentences on charges of bank fraud.

The older brother was the banker/business leader of the operation, known to thousands in their state and nationally throughout the agricultural business community. The operation, started by their now deceased father fifty years before, spread throughout their state and into faraway ones. It was the American dream come true, the result of hard work by their father and mother, and continued by the brothers, some who served on various boards of banks and other powerful co-operatives.

For many years, the operation borrowed, through the bank founded by the father and controlled by the family, huge sums of money from other financial institutions. It all tumbled down when bank examiners discovered the funds were not spent dime for dime on specific operations, i.e., a lump sum was borrowed to make a crop for a season or the year, and the money was used on all divisions of the operation. From this discovery, although the loans were always re-paid, came the indictments and threatened indictments in each district touched by the vast agricultural operation; and hence the three older brothers' plea agreement to let the other two remain free.

The three older brothers self-surrendered, and the rest of the in-mates immediately dubbed them the "Brothers Three." Except during work hours, where each was assigned to different details, they were inseparable. When you saw one, you saw the other two. They lived in the same dormitory, in the same area of the unit. They came to chow together and shared the same friends. They were well liked, respected, and known for their hard work.

All went to parole hearings together, only to be denied relief, but motions pending before the trial judge were considered; although they had different sentences, the judge ordered all three cut loose after serv-ing sixteen months.

A happy mother and two younger brothers welcomed the "broth-ers three" home, after many tears and many dollars spent, to get on with their lives back on the farm.

FAMILY #4:

There were three brothers in law enforcement. The oldest was the elected sheriff, and the two younger became deputies. They were clean cut, well thought of public servants, known throughout the mountain counties by everyone. The parents were proud of their sons and so were the citizens. The brothers kept the law, other public officials praised them, and the public appreciated them.

Then came a government informant trying to save his own skin with campaign contributions and a deal only the government can make up, and the bottom line is—all three were convicted and sentenced to twenty years each.

The sheriff was assigned to one institution and the two younger brothers were assigned to another, the two always remaining together. They all worked hard at Unicor, which offers the highest paid jobs in the federal prison system.

They were quiet, hard-working, family types who loved God, family and their fellow man and caused no problem for the institutional staff. After serving several years, they went back to court and were able to get their twenty-year sentences reduced to ten.

Their families visited them often, and they still have much support in their home county with many of their fellow citizens, who declare that if they were on the ballot they would be re-elected, in spite of what has happened to them.

FAMILY #5:

There are three brothers and the father-in-law of one, all serving time at the same institution. The brothers were involved in convenience stores and evidently had done quite well. The government's theory was that they sold something illegal, and thus they found themselves incarcerated.

They are very different in every way. They don't look alike. They don't act alike. Their personalities are diverse. One likes to play sports, one keeps up with the stock market, and the other is a regular attendee at Catholic Mass. One is vocal, one is quiet, one is very bitter. This family, in prison jargon, is doing its time and their families make their way to the distant institution regularly, to give their support.

FAMILY #6:

It was a father and son team. The father was a rural county sheriff and the son was the chief deputy. They were popular, well respected, and appreciated by their fellow citizens and carried out their law enforcement responsibilities well. The wife and mother was a sweet woman who works for a public agency and drives two hundred and fifty miles every visiting day to see her husband and son.

All was going well for this middle class, very public, family until federal agents, through paid informants, involved the father and the son in a so-called illegal activity, and both wound up in a warehouse for human beings.

The father and son were quiet, nearly always together and talking with each other. They attended the movie every night, but kept to themselves.

They went back to court, using the same reasons in their motions. The son was released, but the father was not, and although not particularly vocal, he carries a heavy burden within himself about the whole thing, especially not being released. Yet he hopes the judge will, in time, rule in his favor, as well.

He never showed any interest in chapel services, although he did say that when a Methodist speaker came, so would he. However, a Methodist spoke a number of times, and he never attended.

FAMILY #7:

You could not believe they were born of the same woman. They are 180 degrees apart, like east and west. One looks for the day he can return to his calling, preaching the gospel, and the other longs for the day he can hit horse tracks or casinos. One is well educated, a powerful and an articulate speaker, and the other is as rough as a cob, a drinking (not in prison), cursing scrapper who is not afraid of the devil.

They were big operators in the health care field. Their company operated in several states and had thousands of employees. The preacher brother and CEO was a friend of politicians, preachers, and important people everywhere, and he zipped around the country in his Lear jet, the way most folk would drive around their community. Full time pilots waited to fire up the jet to go to Washington and other points at a moment's notice.

Everyone in the small town where their headquarters was located knew when the preacher brother came screaming into the small airport at night.

The entire family was involved in their business venture. When they were indicted for fraud, tried, and convicted without audits, as the government so often does, their sister and other brother were indicted also, but later released.

The mother is a saintly woman, nearly eighty years old, and has been a rock to her sons and the entire family.

One brother was released early, but the other brother, the preacher, is serving a fifty-one month sentence. He lost everything in the way of material goods. He spent nearly two million dollars on legal fees, and the government took the rest.

There is another side of the story, however. He admits he took a wrong turn when he went from pastoring a large church to a position in a state cabinet. His grand mistake was running for governor, after which the feds began to check into his affairs, and ultimately indicted and convicted him of charges that he completely denies.

His own testimony is that he went from paperboy to preacher by age fourteen, from pulpit to politics, from politics to prison, and from prison back to the pulpit. He has gone full circle and can't wait to return to his first calling—preaching.

FAMILY #8:

This whole family is in prison. The mother, her brother, and her three sons are in for drugs. The government, in its customary fashion, exaggerates the numbers, and makes street corner crack peddlers into kingpins with boatloads of dope. The prisons are filled with folks who broke the law, but not nearly to the point the FBI, DEA, and other agencies theorize. Unfortunately, judges go along with these unrealistic, unproved theories.

Such is the case in this family. The mother was sentenced to life in prison, without parole. The uncle was hit with a long-term sentence, and the sons were given ten years. They, through their counselors, are able to make calls from one institution to the other on a regular basis.

One son is very religious, having become so in prison. The other, serving his time at the same institution, is not so committed. The one is at peace, serving his time, and his God by helping others. The other is scheming, slipping, and sliding, trying to "con" his way through at every turn.

The mother, the other son, and the uncle are all doing their best to cope with the fact that their entire family is incarcerated because the government painted them to be a big-time drug ring, and the judge believed the prosecutor, throwing the book at every one of them.

FAMILY #9:

Numerous husband and wife teams are in prison—not in the same prison, but one in one place and the other in another place. The stress is great and few of the marriages last. Nearly ninety percent of marriages fail when one of the partners is incarcerated. The chances of a marriage surviving when both parties are incarcerated are about zero. The marriage mortality rate is another downside to the U.S. having more people incarcerated than any other civilized nation.

With permission, letters can be exchanged, and through counselors, phone calls can be arranged on a quarterly basis. Family members, particularly children, have a hard time visiting both parents, especially since most are institutionalized many miles apart.

DIVORCE, DEATH, DISAPPOINTMENT & DESPAIR

DIVORCE

CASE #1:
They wrote often, sometimes every day, but as the wife served her sentence in one place and the husband in another, they grew further and further apart. It was the second marriage for both. Their respective children from their first marriages would visit occasionally. A mother or brother, from time to time, would come on visiting day. The phone calls between them became fewer and fewer as they were transferred from institution to institution.

The glue that held them together was gone, the money was gone, the prestige, the good times of long ago became a faint shadow, and the marriage was gone. Divorce papers were exchanged and the penal system won another victory.

CASE #2:
It's his twenty-fifth wedding anniversary. It is normally a very happy time; but to this particular inmate it was the saddest day of his life.

He rushed into the chapel office. He burst into tears. He shook and trembled as he stood before the inmate who had counseled with many on all types of problems.

As he gasped for breath and struggled for words, the inmate with an eighteen-month sentence sobbed these words out, "It's all over, on our twenty-fifth anniversary, my wife has told me, 'Get lost, I don't ever want to see you again.'

"What happened?" the clerk asked, as he tried to console this devastated man.

"She took up with my best friend and moved him into our house," the inmate answered, choking and coughing with a broken heart.

This is a common thing among incarcerated persons. So often the other mate, home alone with problems never encountered before, becomes very vulnerable and decides that they can't make it alone. Friends take advantage of the situation and drive wedges between mates already separated by incarceration. Another marriage becomes a casualty of "the system."

CASE #3:

Sometimes inmates, after they are released, move in on other inmate's spouses, met during visiting days at the institution where both served time. A high-profile family went to prison. The father, his second wife, and the son and his wife all were convicted and sentenced in a multi-million dollar case. Somewhere along the line, the son's wife, incarcerated at a then co-ed facility, met a man with whom she fell in love. Released before her husband, she arranged to bring the children to see their father. For a time, she faithfully visited her husband, giving him the opportunity to see her and their lovely children. Then the visits became further and further apart. The wife was enjoying the pleasure of a big home, fine cars, the luxuries of life, and the satisfaction of her own lusts.

Then one day, the news came. She would not be back. Someone else could bring the children. She was seeking a divorce and was going to marry the inmate she had met while incarcerated.

One more victim left bitter and dejected by "the system."

CASE# 4:

They lived in a large house, were members of the country club, active in the city's largest church, and doing great in their business, where they worked together. They had both been married before, producing children by those marriages, but had been married to each other for seventeen years. He thought everything was fine between them.

Although several years of indictments, trials, re-indictments, and re-trials had taken a toll on the marriage, the most damaging thing was pride on the part of the wife and her parents. They couldn't stand the embarrassment of him being convicted and sentenced to a federal prison camp on income tax evasion.

This couple had been close friends of their pastor and his wife, who were known throughout their city, visiting in each other's homes frequently. No one would have expected pride to overcome this wife as it did.

The pastor and others counseled her, to no avail. He begged, he pleaded, he did everything he could to dissuade her, but she insisted on divorcing her husband. His incarceration was too much of an embarrassment for her and her prominent parents.

The divorce papers came; he lost his wife of seventeen years—another victim of "the system."

DEATH

CASE #1:

Death in prison is something no one wants. Although it can come when least expected, and inmates die while incarcerated, really no one ever dies in prison. I am told it's always listed as DOA (dead on arrival) when they arrive at the hospital.

Inmates, whether they are non-violent, minimum-security prisoners, when stricken, are carried away in handcuffs. One inmate in his fifties died in the restroom at about four o'clock in the morning. To the CO's credit, he worked as hard as he could to resuscitate him—to no avail. Anyone could see this man was gone. The ambulance came, the authorities came; everyone acted as though he might have a chance, but he was DOA when he reached the hospital.

CASE #2:

Another was stricken on the track late one hot, summer evening. Overweight and out of shape, he had attempted to jog and was overcome by an apparent heart attack. Witnesses said he was dead. The ambulance took him away, but he was DOA when he reached the hospital. Records show that he did not die at the camp—he died en route to the hospital.

In some higher-level institutions, where violent criminals are confined, inmates lose their lives at the hands of other inmates. Shanks (homemade knives or pick-like weapons) are popular instruments of death. One inmate gets it in for another, for whatever reason—snitching, lying in court or for dozens of other reasons—and at the right moment and place, the victim falls to the floor and bleeds to death.

Over the years, correctional officers have lost their lives at the hands of inmates. Inmates hate some officers, especially in maximum-security prisons, and men die in the line of duty because of an anger-filled, out of control inmate. At the Atlanta U.S. Penitentiary, a marker stands just to the left of the front entrance as a memorial to those who have died in the line of duty. "All gave some, some gave all" is the inscription on the gray marble tablet, a constant reminder to all who pass that he could be the next to face death. Death takes a different turn when the inmate's loved ones fall. It is a frustrating when an inmate gets word that a loved one has passed away. He can do so little to help in such a time of need.

Policies differ at the various institutions, depending on the warden or administrator, when it comes to visits during a time of loss. They consider many factors, such as the severity of the offense, time remaining, conduct, and custody level. The warden can grant emergency furloughs to inmates who have community custody. Special exceptions can be made in cases where the custody level is higher. Escorted furloughs are sometimes permitted where the inmate is not allowed to go alone or be escorted by a family member.

Inmates with long sentences are routinely denied the opportunity to attend their loved one's funeral. Some wardens will permit an inmate who meets certain criteria to have a bedside visit, if the attending physician documents that the patient is terminal. In these cases, the inmate can elect to have a bedside or a graveside visit, but not both.

Death, no matter whom it comes for, is a traumatic time for those incarcerated.

DISAPPOINTMENT

There is always hope a motion will be granted for an early parole, a change in sentencing, a rule 35, a rule 2255, or anything that would allow an inmate to go home sooner.

Many who can afford attorneys spend untold hundreds of thousands, some even millions, of dollars on legal fees, always hoping for a miracle. Others use "jail house lawyers," persons who, over the years, have acquainted themselves with the law by spending hours in the law library, studying cases. Then there are those who were attorneys, well educated, trained, and experienced, who assist in filing pro se motions for relief.

Whatever the case, there is always hope until a negative decision is made. Then comes disappointment and depression. Inmates walk around in a daze. Their hopes are dashed. Then another motion or avenue to take appears, hope springs forth again, and the circle continues.

When all funds are gone, when the family can't afford another attorney fee, when every avenue is exhausted, and every jailhouse lawyer has gone through every motion available, hope ends—legally. Disappointment then turns into despair.

DESPAIR

When all hope is gone, disappointment turns to despair. When there are no avenues or approaches to take, and there is nothing to do but serve the time, the bottom falls out. All hope for getting a sentence reduction is gone, and the weight and reality of it presses down. The inmate becomes despondent, and he begins to feel—what's the use? He doesn't care anymore. He doesn't want to get up. He withdraws from his friends. He is distant to his family; life is not worth living. Thousands in state and federal prisons are trudging through life with no hope. Many can't even remember the details of the offense for which they were charged and convicted. Their shoulders slump, their feet are like concrete blocks. They are in a sea of despair. Many never come out of it.

Others, through a higher power, spring out of it and find reasons to stay on top. They become involved in chapel activities, hobbies, crafts, sports, or anything that makes life worth living, even after hope fails.

CORRECTIONAL OFFICERS:

THE GOOD, the BAD, and the UGLY

"I'm not a guard! I am a correctional officer," responded the officer in the visitor's parking lot in answer to a visitor's question. Not many correctional officers enjoy their work. Who wants to spend day after day and night after night with convicted felons? A few correctional officers, who are on ego trips or enthralled by their authority, might get kicks out of having handcuffs, keys, and a radio on their belts.

Most work in the field of corrections because it is a job. The pay is fair, the benefits are good, and the retirement program is great. Some dream of being a lieutenant, captain, counselor, unit manager, or even warden if they endure long enough.

Some see the Bureau of Prisons job as a continuation of military benefits and GSA opportunities, and some just mark time and are as anxious to get out as the inmates they oversee. Some say to inmates, "Someday you'll be out, but I have to build my twenty years."

Regardless of why correctional officers are on their jobs, they all fall into one of three very definable categories: the good, the bad, and the ugly.

The Ugly

It's not about looks; it's about disposition. Some very beautiful people can be downright ugly, especially when they put on a uniform and have some authority. To a former high-ranking official, fresh on the compound, a female officer screamed, "What public office do you hold this morning? What authority do you have today? We will see how much power you have here."

"Come to me, baby," howled a giant of a lieutenant, from across the courtyard, at an inmate who walked off the sidewalk, onto the grassy area. "I got you now," screamed the hulk, with keys clanging, handcuffs swinging, and a fist pounding into the other hand. "I got to have you," he said, prancing like a commanding general, who had just won a long, hard fought war. "Ten hours of extra duty, and I'll tear up the shot [an incident report in BOP jargon]," the lieutenant yelled. On any given night, he would get a dozen men to pick up trash. He was one of the ugly.

"Get that junk back into the car," said an R&D officer to a man self-surrendering at a federal prison camp. The inmate-to-be had received a list of items from the marshal's service that he could bring in. His family spent many dollars and hours of time shopping for items that one branch of the Justice Department had said could be brought into a camp. Things like underwear, tennis shoes, radio, and shaving and toiletry items, at the scream of one ugly correctional officer became "junk." The person self-surrendering, nervous over events of the recent past and in pain over having to part with his wife and two grown sons, stood horrified at the demeanor of a paid correctional officer. To make matters worse, while the man grasped his three-year-old grand-daughter's photo, the officer shouted, "You can't have that. You have to mail it in; all you need is what's on your back. Get the rest back into the car, and come with me."

"Junk," the ugly officer said. "Get it back into the car."

On another occasion, the same man had been chained hand and feet all day while in transit to another facility. His strength was exhausted. The strain had taken its toll. A lack of opportunity to take care of ordinary bathroom needs had made him dull, and the pressures of the trip, the noise, and the physical restraints had drained him.

He finally arrived at a U.S. Penitentiary Detention Center unit (DCU), well within the walled confines of this awesome penal complex.

"Come on old man," shouted the mean officer in Receiving and Discharge (R&D), "We don't have time. Get your clothes on. Get your shoes on. Let's go 'pop,'" hollered the middle-aged man in gray pants and white shirt, as a sixty-six-year-old inmate wrestled with his clothes as fast as he could. "We don't have all night. What's an old man like you doing in jail?" the officer asked, pressing even further.

With teary eyes and a trembling voice, the weary inmate was able to get out only a few words, "The FBI lies."

"Why are you here," the three-hundred-pound counselor snapped, as the inmate moved through processing at a U.S. Penitentiary. Not understanding what she meant, the inmate asked, "I beg your pardon?"

"What's a man your age doing in jail?" she barked back. As if he was not humiliated enough by his circumstances, he is humiliated further by a screaming bureaucrat who tries to punish when there is no need to do so.

As he calls the roll for the unassigned, the status all new inmates find themselves in as they await A&O (Admissions & Orientation), the officer of many years shouts to a former public official, "Oh, you are that big shot politician I've been reading about. I've heard about you for a long time," he says, in front of a dozen or so men. "How do you feel today?" he asks then, in a derisive manner, and moves on to another inmate.

He is inconsiderate, he will not stand still, he will not let anyone finish a sentence, and he barks half-statements and phrases and acts like a nervous wreck. He is an accident waiting to happen. He is a lieutenant in the Bureau of Prisons. Definitely, this is not a good one, but there are some.

The Good

The ugly—Yes! The bad—Yes! But there are many that are all business, yet considerate and compassionate. They are good.

She is tall, very blonde, a little chubby, walks like a soldier on the way to battle, and barks very loudly. She is tough; she comes across on the PA system like General Patton. She means business and rarely ever smiles. She is in control. She is a lieutenant. She is hard, but she is a good officer. You know where she stands. There are many officers like this—all business—no play, but fair.

The inmate made his way, chains jingling as they bumped the tile floor, toward R&D to be processed into a DCU. It had been a hard day. This inmate had never before been handcuffed. He had never been transported before, much less with twenty-five others on the same bus for three hundred miles. Never had there been so many deprivations. The bus trip and the restraints had knocked the wind out of his sails. He dragged through processing and was finally taken to the lock up where he was to spend the night. As the door opened, the officer in charge greeted the inmate with a smile from ear to ear. "I know you've had a rough time on the trip today. We want to make it easy on you tonight," said the kind officer. "My orderly will show you around and try to make it as comfortable as possible during your layover."

Although many officers are there just to make time, hit the clock, and go home, there are good ones, who are kind, considerate, and compassionate. To them, inmates are not to be treated like animals, but as human beings, with respect and without partiality, regardless of background, offense, race, color, religion, or otherwise.

In all due respect to the correctional officers, some have become hardened and impenetrable because of years of dealing with con artists.

However, not all inmates are bad; many are first time offenders, non-violent, from good backgrounds and respectable families. They may be truly sorry for the offense they committed and cause no problems at all. That kind of inmate balances the correction officer's behavior and leads them to treat inmates like humans instead of animals.

The good, the bad, and the ugly; thank God, there are more of the good than the other.

Jail House Religion

Some inmates are reluctant to go near the chapel or get involved in any religious activity for good reason—ridicule! Inmates that care little for their soul, salvation, or self-respect mock those drawn toward spiritual activity. Those who live, as if there is no tomorrow, no hereafter, and no eternity are the first to poke ridicule at those who do. They accuse those who seek spiritual help of being weak and without strength to serve time like a man. It is "sissy" to depend on God, to pray, worship, and spend time enriching the soul—according to the tough guys.

Jailhouse religion, some say, is for those trying to make points with officials. Chapel attendance looks good on the progress report, say scoffers. Critics are quick to charge that some will do anything, including "get religion," to cut time or make points.

It is easy to stand on the sidelines and criticize those who are sincere. Come join us; it's better to be with us and a few hypocrites, than be outside with all the hypocrites, say those who have a relationship with God. There are plenty of play-actors, but in the same goes in all the churches, synagogues, and mosques of the world. Prison has no corner on hypocrisy. They are everywhere, and those who use this excuse don't have much of an argument.

Of the two million people incarcerated in America, the highest number in any country, there are untold thousands seeking divine help. Many inmates have life-changing experiences during this most traumatic time.

Incarceration, like any adversity, will make one either bitter or better. Most are bitter. Some learn to hate more. Many learn to become real criminals, and go out worse than when they came in. Some, because of bitterness and hatred, are always in trouble and get "shots" for infractions. Some become mean and disruptive and have to be transferred to higher-level institutions. On the other hand, thousands are better, and growing to spiritual maturity.

Because of the hundreds of prison chaplains and the First Amendment provisions, giving all faiths and denominations the right to worship, every inmate has an opportunity to find the spiritual relationship he or she desires or needs.

Groups such as the Prison Fellowship and Campus Crusade for Christ provide volunteers, on a regular basis, to conduct sessions, seminars, workshops, and religious services in prisons throughout America.

Other organizations such as the Bill Glass Ministries and Mike Barber Ministries bring in athletes for crusades and revivals, while many other organizations provide printed materials and videos for religious programs.

Every major denominational group has staff to assist prison chaplains in their work. Millions of hours are donated each year to helping the incarcerated find inner peace, build self-esteem, and restore their families. All ministries give opportunities for inmates to be better, rather than bitter, during their incarceration.

Some fall through the cracks, and some have jailhouse religion that they leave there as they go out the gate, but others find that religion changes their lives, gives them a purpose for living, and an opportunity to find the divine plan for their lives. They walk out of the gate better. Call it jailhouse religion, if you want. It's bitter or better, and it's much better to be better.

Shiny Floors are Deceiving

The floors of the "grand corridor" are sparkling shiny. No hospital floor could be cleaner. You can almost see yourself in the granite and marble, but to either side there is misery.

Men by the thousands are hurting. Their hearts ache and break from loneliness. Some are lifers; some have twenty, thirty, fifty years or more. No one has less than ten years. The shining floors are deceiving, because not far away are warehoused men, who in most cases, have given up. They see no way out. There is no way out from a physical standpoint.

From the entrance to the circular driveway, you can tell it is a place of incarceration. The massive, hundred-year-old structure, six stories high, with many barred windows, tells one that this is a super jail.

As one approaches the granite steps on the lower level, one can see that even the steps to the first landing are spotlessly clean—wiped and power washed everyday.

From the landing, and up the second level of stairs, the massive columns stand like guardians on each side of the entrance. Higher up, above the entrance, is razor wire lining the eaves of the enormous hulk of a building. Even higher, the copper cupola stands tall to cast its eerie shadow over the front doorway, stairs, and sidewalk of one the toughest prisons in the country.

As one leaves the lower landing, and walks up the second level of steps, one can see words, three feet tall, chiseled in granite above the front door—UNITED STATES PENITENTIARY. On the glass doors, sparkling clean, is etched—United States Department of Justice, Bureau of Prisons, U.S. Penitentiary.

The lobby gleams with cleanliness. To the left is the warden's office, and to the right are other offices. Straight ahead is a series of doors, actually bars, which open at the will of the officers in the control room. Through these barred doors, you can see a long corridor and gleaming, shiny floors.

The first door opens. Inmates are escorted between two sets of doors, and the next will not open until the first is closed. As you go through a series of security checkpoints, you make your way down the grand corridor that connects the three main buildings of the prison. Through this corridor, thousands of men have trudged along in the prison shuffle, a walk acquired after years of prison life. These men have been convicted of every crime known to humanity—murder, rape, bombings, bank robbery, train robbery, mail fraud, and on and on. You name it—they have been there.

The gleaming walls and shiny floors are deceiving, because to the right and left are corridors leading to hundreds of small cells where men are locked up like caged animals. Some are dangerous. Some are not. Some are angry. Some are sad. Some are dejected. Some have no one to love them. Their entire support group may have forsaken them or died. There are no letters, no contact—only loneliness and despair.

The sparkling walls and shiny floors are deceiving because many men have lost their lives just off these corridors, stabbed by other inmates with improvised picks or knives—shanks, they are called.

Officers have died at the hands of men filled with hatred and anger. The monument to the left of the front door says it all—All gave some; some gave all—referring to the deaths of correctional officers while on duty. Certainly, some criminals will do anything to anyone who crosses them, and deserve to be watched and shunned. There are multitudes, however, who have never harmed anyone and wouldn't do so under any circumstances. Nevertheless, the COs (correctional officers) must be alert.

Some COs are kind, mild-mannered persons; some are arrogant, hateful, and provoking to those in their charge. So over the shining floors of the "grand corridor" walk all kinds of people, both employees and incarcerated.

The shiny floors are deceiving.

In Transit—Herded Like Animals

All are treated the same, whether convicted for driving on a military reservation with an expired license or mass murderer. When in transit, all are herded like animals from one institution to another.

Whether it is to a camp (FPC), correctional institution, (FCI), a United States Penitentiary (USP), or a super-maximum institution (SMI), there is no difference with the transportation division of the Bureau of Prisons.

Some go through detention center units (DCUs), also known as holdovers, and others through Federal Transfer Centers (FTC), but regardless of where they travel, they are treated like animals.

Some inmates are transported by car, some by vans, some by over-the-road buses, and some by airplanes, but it is always the same—animals to the market.

Most common are the chains, handcuffs, and leg irons—and a grueling experience that takes the energy out of the best. The emotional stress, physical drain and noise of angry inmates are indescribable. The impatience, arrogance, and abuse of power by correctional officers add to the stress, and take many almost to the breaking point. Add to it the strain of not being able to relieve oneself because of crowds of gawking inmates and restraints, and one has a most miserable trip. Some spend weeks and months being transferred from place to place, and on any given day, there are hundreds counted as "in transit." In prison terminology, this is called diesel therapy. A person can lose thirty, fifty, or as much as sixty pounds during these trips, especially if it includes stops over a period of three or more months in several time zones and numerous institutions. Many times, city and county jails, where the food is pitiful and sanitation conditions are poor are used by the BOP as holdovers.

A typical transfer includes a call to R&D to pack out. Inmates are not told the day they will leave because of security reasons. If the prison announced a specific time and place, the danger is that it would alert someone or some group, making a hijacking a real threat. When it is time to leave, the inmate is called to R&D and he or she never is allowed back on the compound.

The case manager organizes the inmate's central file, which includes all pertinent information about him, and goes with him wherever he goes. Guards strip the inmate to his birthday suit and go over him with an electronic device to check for any metal. Then comes the examination—wiggle your ears, open your mouth, flip your private parts, spread your cheeks, lift your feet and show me the bottoms. Get dressed. Then the routine you put your white t-shirt and under shorts back on, followed by a thin pair of tan pants—no pockets, no belt—just elastic in the waist. A cheap pair of blue canvas shoes with no support is provided.

The bus arrives—the diesel engine roars, and the bus lieutenant, driver, and rear gunman throw an armload of chains and handcuffs to the floor. It sounds like a dump truck load. The inmates flinch; you are taut, and your lips are tight.

Put your hands out—the chain goes around the waist, with one end slipped through a link. The handcuffs are fixed to the chain. First one wrist, and click; then the other wrist, and click. The cuffs and the chain around the waist secure your hands. Turn around, chains rattle. The leg irons are clicked on the first ankle and then the other. A twelve to sixteen-inch chain limits the length of the steps.

Maximum-security prisoners with long terms and violent records are black-boxed, which means a rectangular box is fastened between the wrists, which limits movement of the hands to next to none.

Inmates are marched out to the bus. COs stand by with shotguns, as their prisoners stumble up the steps and through the door between the driver and lieutenant and the inmates. The windows are barred. A cage, accessible only from the outside, is to the rear, where another CO sits with a gun across his lap.

Everyone staggers and stumbles to a seat and flops down for a long, uncomfortable ride. The files and records are carefully loaded, and the bus is off.

A small box containing a sandwich and an apple is all you have to get by on until the next stop. It's hard to eat, bound with chains and cuffs. The cuffs dig into your arms. The orderly brings a cup of water, but it's too difficult to drink and moreover, too much trouble to urinate. You hold it, and the trip becomes more discomforting. The leg irons will not let you stretch out your legs.

The noise is deafening. The profanity is unbearable. The vulgarity is sickening. Hatred spews from men's tongues. Some even curse the officers. "What can they do to me?" is the attitude. "I'm already locked up. I'm in chains. What else can they do to me?"

The bus roars down the highway. It looks like any other over-the-road bus, but it is a rolling jail with prisoners in transit. When it reaches its destination, the process is repeated. Hurry up, get in here, go in this cell, come on, we don't have all day, do this, do that, go here and go there.

Like herded animals—inmates are in transit.

Locked Up Too Long

The big over-the-road bus, gleaming white, with orange stripes down its sides, rolls inconspicuously along the interstate highway; but for the bars down each side and at the front, and the rear concealed by dark windows, it looks like any other commercial transport bus. This bus is different. It has a government tag, a driver and lieutenant up front, protected by bulletproof vests, an officer in a cage on the left rear side, with a shotgun across his lap; this bus transports federal prisoners.

Some inmates are maximum-security, which means they serve their time behind a wall or fence, and others are minimum-out. They are campers, confined to a minimum-security camp with no fences or bars. All are handcuffed and shackled during transport. Only the high-risk ones wear the "black boxes" — a devise that fits over the cuffs between the wrists, making it impossible to move your hands.

There are nearly thirty men aboard, from all security levels. Some are headed to a maximum-security prison, others to parole hearings, some back to court; most are on disciplinary transfer, having been involved in a riot or burning of a library or hobby craft building at one of the prisons.

Profane, vulgar words bounce off the windows and ceiling. Hatred and anger spew from their lips. The most common prison epitaph, profaning one's mother, is shouted at the tops of their voices. Some brag about their attitudes and escapades, both inside and outside of prison. Some curse the officers and seem to dare them to do anything about it.

Some are rappers, muttering unintelligible words that mean absolutely nothing. Others scream at the one man who was selected as bus orderly and wears no cuffs. "Get me some more [blankety-blank] coffee, you [blankety-blank]." One has some kind of dope platted in his dreadlocks.

There is one guy, about forty years old, with tattoos from his finger nails to his shoulders and some even on his face; one eye is slightly cocked, and he's handcuffed with a black box, indicating maximum-security (a bad one), sitting by the window on the left side of the bus. He is a lifer, sentenced for murder, with additional charges for attempting to stab a correctional officer. He's headed for a maximum-security prison.

Evidently, he has seen very few newspapers, magazines, or television commercials in the sixteen years he has been behind the wall, for he is fascinated at the shapes of the cars passing by. The styles have changed, there are more curves; cars are aerodynamic and more streamlined, and the man is flabbergasted at the changes in designs and colors. Occasionally, he describes, in typical prison language, a female driver or passenger as he looks directly down into the passing cars, but his fascination is with the automobiles' shapes and colors. One after the other, he exclaims, "Look at that one—it looks like a bullet," or "Look at that one—it looks like a rocket." For mile after mile, this goes on, and finally he says, "I've been locked up too long. The world is changing and I'm in here." The big diesel engine roars and takes his rolling jail on down the road. As the tattooed man lays his head back, trying to find a comfortable position, he can be heard muttering, "I've been locked up too long."

I Don't Work for Rats

Wayne is a bright young man, convicted of disposing of real estate, even though he possessed a deed for it. He has served a number of years and has been at six different institutions from California to New Jersey. He has appeared before the parole commission several times, to no avail. He came to Atlanta from Eglin to appear again at a parole hearing, and again was turned down.

His current home address is Nassau, Bahamas, and he will return to Eglin when his papers are done. He spends much of his time helping other inmates in legal matters, preparing several documents every week, even every day. He has gained vast knowledge of the law.

One man wanted him to help with his case. When Wayne read his PSI, he found that this inmate had turned someone in. When confronted by Wayne he said, "It was just a blankety-blank Bahamian, and he was no good." Wayne replied, "I don't work for rats!" The man picked up his papers, and quickly walked away.

Recanted, But Too Late!

A certain man and his sons own a landscaping company in a distant state. He is a super fine man, small in stature, but giant in integrity, a Baptist with eight children and fourteen grandchildren, by five of his children.

He and his sons love to golf and keep up courses as well as far away as Atlanta, where he has men living and working in the area. They decided to build a golf course, and being prominent in his area, had no trouble getting investors, including several bankers.

A long time friend and former partner in another business, was included and brought him a check for $122,000.00 made payable to himself and endorsed over to the landscaper. Several months later (maybe a year), the FBI called. They found a brochure about the golf course in a man's brief case in California, and traced it back to the landscaper. His former partner had given it to the man. The man got the partner to take drug money and launder it through the golf course project. The developer claimed he didn't know it was drug money. The FBI kept trying to get him to confirm it. He said he couldn't, because he didn't know that it was. He claimed to be telling the truth. After five tries, the FBI convinced his lawyer that he should plead to one count. After much threatening to put him behind bars forever, the man pled.

The other two men, the drug dealer and the friend, recanted—saying they had lied, and the landscaper knew nothing about their scheme.

The judge told them, "I'm sorry, you already pled; I can't turn that around."

The landscaper reported to FPC, Atlanta, never having even had a speeding ticket.

Thousands of men are in the system because someone lied to save his own skin.

"It's too late—you've already pled guilty."

North Georgia – Militiaman or What?

A quiet time on an out of the way bench came to an abrupt halt when this bearded man from North Georgia sat down. The first words out of his mouth were profane. He cursed the United States government in general, all federal office holders, and then all law enforcement personnel. From there, he blasted the Justice Department, the Bureau of Prisons, and every correctional officer alive.

"To hell with the United States. I would not pledge allegiance or stand for the Star-Spangled Banner if my life depended on it. They can take the flag and wipe their behinds on it. They are all a bunch of SOBs—crooked as snakes. If there was a battlefield right out there (referring to the ball field), I would join the other side and fight against the United States with all my might."

As I tried to get in a word or two about bitterness and it being a terrible cancer that would eat you alive, he assured me he was not bitter.

"I'm guilty," the truck driver said, "but the government created the crime. They sure didn't work to catch me. They set it up." Then he went off on the FBI, DEA, and other government agencies.

He revisited Waco with expletives I would not dare write down or repeat. He said all the agents were dogs playing war. As I tried to assess just where this man was coming from, and endeavored to get in a positive word here and there, I began to realize that he was somehow connected with a militia group. I grew more convinced when he assured me that concentration camps were already in place, and the government would someday put good people away. Even road signs were encoded on the backside, and one day, traffic would be reversed, sending men one way and their families another.

A man walked up, and after hearing the gist of the comments, immediately went away. I prayed silently about what to say. Finally getting a few words in, I tried to show this man that the way to fight is not through violence, but through the courts. We could spend the rest of our lives trying to get justice through legal means.

"It won't do you any good. You can't win," he said.

"Maybe so, but I'll keep trying," I said. "By the way," I asked, when do you think the government will have us all in jail?"

"It could be in our lifetime," he replied.

I then told him, "I'm glad my faith is in the Lord. I refuse to be bitter. I trust him to see me through, and he will be with me, regardless of what transpires."

"That's good," said the Georgia militiaman, "but I will fight. I hate the government; I'll never change."

The expletives kept flying. How pathetic!

Thank God for Small Things

We remember big things and the prayers answered by God, but what about the answers to small things?

To urinate or not to urinate—for one who can't pass a rest room without stopping, the thoughts of being on a bus all day, handcuffed and shackled, caused cold chills to come upon me. How I dreaded the thoughts of such pressure. Cold sweat popped out on my forehead. My nerves ran away with me.

"Oh Lord, I have to have your help. You made my plumbing system and me. This is a long trip, and I cannot do a thing about it. You must take absolute control. Please let this be as comfortable as possible. Amen."

For hours, I was on the bus; and for hours, we went through processing from cell to cell. Each had a commode, but there were all these men. I wanted to go, but kept praying for the Lord to help me hold it a little bit longer. The day passed. Finally, after settling down in the Tallahassee DCU, I went to the toilet. After at least ten hours, oh yes, I was able to go! Thank God for small things!

My name, along with ten others, came over the public address system "Report to the OIC (officer in charge) station. Upon arriving, I saw the officer with the gloves and small bottles. "Oh no," I thought, "not a urine analysis test."

It was. I drank water and more water. I tried and couldn't. More water, warm water from cups, many cups, and still no success. Then the harsh words, "You will be locked up if you don't go in twenty minutes." This was about an hour and a half into the ordeal—I drank more warm water. No, by now, I was drinking hot water—more hot water.

Then another officer yelled, "Here, do something constructive while you are waiting—help me with a Breathalyzer test."

I said, "Sure, I haven't had a drink in nearly forty years."

Two officers simultaneously asked, without even thinking, "What happened?"

The first words out of my mouth were, "I turned my life over to the Lord, and he took alcohol away from me."

"That's good," one of the officers said.

Then the one with the gloves said, "You want to try again?"

Into the restroom we went, with him standing within a foot of me, so he could see what was going on. Nothing was going on—that was the problem. I was full of water and could not make a drop. I was petrified and horrified, and cried out "Oh Lord, help me—make a way out of this for me. I simply cannot urinate."

I advised the officer that it was impossible. We went back into the OIC office, and I saw the man responsible for the tests packing up his briefcase. I did not know what to expect. He looked at me with a grin on his face. I didn't know if he was about to lock me up, or what. He smiled, and said, "You are not top priority; you can go." God made a way. Again, thank God for small things.

The Broken Tooth

My mouth was already sore. A problem with a back tooth on my right lower jaw was giving me much discomfort. I had to eat ever so slowly, mostly chewing on the left side. I normally eat slowly, and it was taking even more time now. Sometimes two different groups would finish their meal before I was through.

At this particular meal, as I slowly chewed with my left side, I bit down on something and there came an excruciating pain. Something was terribly wrong.

The next day, I went to the dentist. He could not detect any cracks, or anything amiss on the left side. At the same time, he told me what to do about the right side. I went my way.

I prayed. "Lord, please do not let this be a major problem. I don't need an additional burden at this time." Pain continued; prayer continued.

Two days later, while eating, another terrible sharp pain hit me, and something came loose in my mouth. It was about a third of that left upper tooth. I retrieved it. As air hit the remaining tooth, pain shot through that side of my mouth. "Oh Lord, don't let this be as bad as it feels right now," I prayed.

The next day, I went back to the dentist. After checking, he said the nerve would become less sensitive as time went on, and I could get the repair done later. This turned out to be the case. Again, thank God for small things.

Mercy Package

When inmates are in transit, they are dressed in t-shirts, under shorts, thin tan pants, socks, and cheap blue canvas slippers. The institutions furnish very few toilet items.

Shower shoes are necessary, but not provided. "What will I do? I don't want to shower without shoes." Then I prayed, "Lord, please make a way."

Ten minutes after I arrived on the compound, a man approached me with a nice package of toilet items provided by the church community on the compound. Right there in that package was a pair of shower shoes. Again, thank God for small things.

The Strip Search

Strip naked—socks and all
Open your mouth
Wiggle your ears
Flip your private parts
Spread your cheeks
Show me the bottom of your feet
Get dressed
Hurry up!

Four times, I heard these words. Four times, I stripped. Four times, I was humiliated, some worse than others, depending on the officers. I don't know why, but all were black. Some were kind and patient with a sixty-six-year-old white man, and some arrogant and very impatient, showing their authority.

The mantra was, "Hurry up, we don't have all day," as I stood on one foot and then the other to remove my shoes and socks, or to put them back on.

"Get with it; it's time to go," some shouted, as I tried to find jump suits or tan pants that would fit a big man. In-bound inmates put on orange jump suits and out-bound men dressed in tan pants with no pockets and no belts. They were always the wrong size. White t-shirts, rejects from the manufacturer, and wrong-sized under shorts are commonplace. Time didn't permit us to look for clothing that fit, if there was such a thing.

"Get in the cell." Clank, goes the lock. A few minutes later, "Get over here." Clank, goes the lock. In a short while, it doesn't matter about the keys or the doors. By then, you've been through so many doors and are so far back in the inner guts of the detention center, so far back behind the wall, that it doesn't matter. You just pray, "Oh God, help me through this ordeal, please." And he does!

Pops

I never knew I had so many sons. The officers and the other in-mates called me "Pops." The white hair, the age, the weight, and I suppose, the grandfatherly image, labeled me. I resented it. I wasn't their pop. I have two sons, and they call me daddy. I called my father "Daddy"; these were the thoughts that went through my mind as I re-belled at someone who didn't know me from Adam calling me Pops.

Some Spanish guy, who couldn't speak English, called me Pops. Some black guy says, "Hey, Pops." Officers, whose paycheck came from my tax money, call me Pops. Backwoods, tobacco road, drug-dealing whites call me Pops. I didn't like it. I resented it all!

I knew I had to deal with this resentment. Although I tried not to let it show, on the inside, it was upsetting. What do I do? I prayed. Then a still, small voice came back to me.

"What difference does it make what they call you? Remember, blessed art thou when men shall revile you and persecute you for my name's sake."

So go ahead, call me "Pops." I'm blessed!

It was either "Pops" or "Mayor." Even some of the officers called me mayor. After transferring from the chapel job, because it was "too high profile," I was determined to go to Atlanta FPC and remain low key. That lasted at least ten minutes after I arrived at the new com-pound.

Men were there who had been at Maxwell, and word spread like wild fire over the compound. The mayor is here for a parole hearing. The mayor is here! You would have thought the only mayor in the U.S. had arrived. One by one, men came to me, calling me mayor. I tried to remain low key, but many continued to address me in this way.

When I came into the system, we were told at A&O that we should address one another simply as mister; that our positions or titles before should not be mentioned; but as was the case in Atlanta, it was even more widespread at Maxwell, because the news media had carried numerous stories about my arrival. They were looking for me, and as time went on, I became the un-official mayor of Maxwell. Even after my transfer from the chapel to custody, as I circulated around the compound, it was "Hello, Mayor"; "Good morning, Mayor"; "Good evening, Mayor" and "How are you, Mayor?"

Here I came to Atlanta FPC to remain low key, meet the parole commission officer, get good news, and return to Maxwell, but not so. I kept getting comments like, "Mayor, how is your little city today?" "Is everything in our town under control, Mayor?" "Mayor, are we safe tonight?" and so on.

I walk out of the dorm and straight into an officer who greets me with, "How are you today, Mayor?" I entered the chow hall, and an officer says, "Mayor, you don't have too long to eat." I leave, and another says, "How was the meal? Have a good day, Mayor."

Low key?—No way. A high profile was the last thing I looked for, but when even the officers call you Mayor, how can you be low key? One thing is for sure; they couldn't demote me any lower than "butt" man—a designation for the one who sweeps cigarette butts into a dustpan.

The Locked Doors

At Maxwell, there were no locks on the sleeping quarters, for two main reasons: 1. Campers are non-violent, mostly first-time offenders on an honor system. You can walk away at any time, but you will suffer the consequences. 2. The camp is located on an Air Force Base, and it is the feeling of the Air Force that if the men here have to be locked up, then they shouldn't be on the reservation.

At Atlanta, it is different. The doors are locked at night. It is not so much to keep men in, but to keep others out. In the past, women would come in while men slipped out. Some shot up to the liquor store or made a run to the fried chicken place to deliver orders back to the other inmates.

Some institutions allow an inmate to draw as much as fifteen dollars in change per week out of his commissary account, and use it to purchase merchandise from vending machines. This practice was discontinued at Atlanta, and everything is now purchased by card, even candy and snacks from the vending machines. Of course, before this policy was discontinued, inmates used the change to buy chicken, pizza, liquor, and other things.

About the same time the policy on money changed, the administration started locking the doors on all the dorms at night. Locked doors—to keep some in, and some out.

Chapter 35

Appeals:
Seeking Justice

My same bunk, Montgomery E11B, was awaiting me at Maxwell, as was my job at CO-8, the dining hall. I picked up right where I left off, attending chapel services, sharing my faith with all who would listen and trying to be a good Christian example on the compound. Some listened and some did not. I remember one real rough-looking guy who had been in some maximum-security prisons who came to us during the last few years of his incarceration. He had tattoos all over his sixty-year-old body. His hair was long and his language vulgar. He would intentionally sit near me or join my table at the chow hall. His swearing and carrying on, especially using God's name in vain, was just about more than I could stand. I tried to be nice and show the deep feelings of my heart, but I decided it was time to put an end to this obnoxious guy's ugly ways.

This particular morning, he sat down, swearing, as he began to eat. As I look back at the situation, I am surprised he didn't jump on me physically and cause us both to be shipped. He started his rampage, and I began to talk to him about Jesus. Immediately, he blew up. "I don't want to hear this God stuff."

I said, "You have been cursing God's name ever since you came here, and I have listened even when I didn't want to, so you listen to me. If you can talk about God then so can I, so you listen to me."

He settled down. I was able to share how I had put my faith in Jesus, whom God had sent as a gift—that we might be saved from our sins—and I didn't appreciate him belittling God the way he was doing. I couldn't get him to make a commitment, but I didn't have to listen to him anymore, either. He never came to my table again, nor did he ever come to a chapel service.

Things were routine again, and I was blessed, day by day, as I prayed for the decisions of the Supreme Court. Of some eight thousand petitions that year, only about eighty were docketed, mine was one of them.

I heard my name called over the public address system — "Report to the administration building." I went as quickly as I could. The warden's administrative assistant invited me into her office. "The media is calling. The Supreme Court has remanded your case to the Eleventh Circuit and the media wants to see you. If you agree, we will permit them to come in."

I was trembling. I was overjoyed. I praised the Lord, because few people ever get a favorable ruling out of the U.S. Supreme Court. I was so nervous I could hardly talk, but told the lady I would have to call my attorney to see just what the court had said.

I made my way to the phone room and made a collect call to my wife and sons. Sure enough, the court had ruled favorably, according to the media. My family had not received anything in writing, and we decided I did not need to see the press or make any comments.

The whole compound was buzzing with excitement. Someone had gotten a favorable ruling, which gave encouragement to many who had appeals pending. There were special prayer meetings, to praise God for the wonderful news.

It took a few days for it all to sink in. The warden's office expected me to be released. My family and I thought that surely I would be sent home until this all could be settled. My attorneys filed documents for bond, but to our great disappointment, the same judge that had heard my case, and who had allowed the travesty to take place, would not grant my release or bond. Our excitement was short lived.

After some time, the Eleventh Circuit ruled that the Supreme Court, in essence, didn't know what it was doing and rejected the Supreme Court's decision. The Eleventh Circuit stamped "Do not publish" on the order, making it impossible for anyone to know its thinking or reason for its decision. The ruling to our many petitions by the Eleventh Circuit Court had "Do not publish," stamped upon them, and therefore, no one can read about the case.

This court had ruled several different ways on Hobbs Act cases and on matters of quid pro quo. The same court in U.S. vs. Martinez, a case out of Florida where the mayor of Hialeah was charged with violation of the Hobbs Act, ruled that although the mayor had, in fact, received some lots in a subdivision, the government could not and did not prove that the mayor had acted in an official capacity to obtain the property. In other words, it is necessary that quid pro quo be proved to convict one of a Hobbs Act (extortion) violation.

Throughout all of our appeals, we tried to raise the quid pro quo matter and cite the Martinez case, to no avail. The Eleventh Circuit Court of Appeals has gotten by with differing rulings on the same law, and conflicts with other circuits on this issue. On all my appeals, the order always came back "do not publish."

The Eleventh Circuit has handled the Mims case differently, and maybe someday we can find out why a person was tried and convicted of violating the Hobbs Act, with no sign or evidence of quid pro quo.

Our challenge to this double standard can be seen on pages 12-15 of the "cert" petition, found in the appendix.

We went back to the Supreme Court several times for further relief of the lower court's decisions but were denied each time. My last avenue for relief was appealing to the Eleventh Circuit Court of Appeals, in the denial of a motion in the District Court, to vacate, set aside or correct, the sentence brought under 28 U.S.C. & 2255. The circuit court affirmed the lower court's denial, and again we were forced to go back to the Supreme Court. Our last petition for a writ of certiorari is included in the appendix.

After spending tens of thousands of dollars, and after some of the finest lawyers in the country had made our case, there is absolutely no evidence that I ever received anything or indicated I wanted anything from anyone for any official act or decision I made. In other words, there was no quid pro quo. The same circuit court had ruled there must be an "explicit promise" to violate the Hobbs Act, and that is not found anywhere in my case.

In spite of all the petitions and presentations to the district court, the circuit court, and the Supreme Court, in spite of all the time, effort, and money spent, we came to the end of the line as far as appeals are concerned and still had no relief.

Most attorneys agree that this case was one of the greatest travesties of justice ever. As hard as it is to be falsely accused and convicted of a crime, my contention is that all of this was just another bump on the road, which we climb to greater heights. Through it all, with God's Grace and the support of family and thousands of friends, I am glad I can say, "I am still a mayor on mission."

Chapter 36

Headed Home

U pon release, most inmates are sent to halfway houses, some of which are so poorly run that men violate rules just to be returned to the camps. They would rather spend their last three to six months there, than in an overcrowded, insect-infested, and haphazardly run place, where they get very little sleep and not much food. During my period of incarceration, I saw numerous men leave for the halfway house and soon return. I was very fortunate to be sent straight home, consequently missing the experience.

My release did not mean I was free. I spent four months with an electronic monitor on my ankle. I could not leave the property except to attend church on Sunday and Wednesday nights or go to the doctor, if need be.

It was a joyous day in July that I left Maxwell. My wife and son Dale were there, right on time, and I can remember how thrilled I was as I made my way across the compound and saw our blue Chrysler sitting in the parking lot, waiting for me.

I went to R&D a final time. All papers were in order, and my personal things were already boxed. The boxes were hand-trucked to the waiting car. I glanced one last time at the chapel where I had worked for several years. Waving goodbye to me was a number of inmates. A fine female officer escorted me to the car, where I would greet Dale and his mother

All three of us were ecstatic about me going home. It was a far different feeling than that dreadful day in January 1990, when they'd had to leave me there.

I gathered us to the side of the car, along with the female officer who had always been so kind to me, and offered a prayer of thanksgiving that I was going home, and prayed for the well-being of the inmates I was leaving behind, as well as the officer who had escorted me to the car.

Dale had placed some of the old campaign bumper stickers on the car—Mims for Mayor—, which he thought was amusing. They looked great, but brought back thoughts of that last campaign and the time the marshal came to my headquarters with the indictment that ultimately caused our family so much grief. I was so nervous about not breaking any rules, I asked him to remove the stickers before we left the parking lot.

As we made our way through the Air Force Base and onto the main streets, it seemed to me that the traffic was doing a hundred miles an hour and heading directly toward us. I had only been off the compound a couple of times to see the doctor downtown, and on a couple of occasions the chaplain had taken me with him over to the base chapel to pick up something. We stopped for a big breakfast and headed down the interstate. Dale was driving well within the limit, but all the way home, I was uneasy because it looked as if we were flying. It is amazing how things like this affect you. I had driven thousands of miles as a traveling salesman and speaker, but I was as nervous as a cat on a hot tin roof.

We were in contact, by cell phone, with Danny, who was handling things at home. At noon, we rolled onto our street, and there were yellow ribbons everywhere. I couldn't help but think of the song Tony Orlando made famous—"Tie a Yellow Ribbon 'Round the Old Oak Tree." The song was about a former inmate, heading home on a bus, after serving three years in prison. He wrote, on a paper bag, a few words that later became the song.

In his case, he'd had an affair with his secretary and when the affair turned sour, she accused him of rape. It was very ugly and embarrassing, and when arrested, he asked his wife and children not to come see him—to just forget him!

The humiliation and embarrassment was so bad, he asked his family not to come to the trial, but every day, they came and sat on the front row. He would not even look at them, because he was so ashamed. They kept coming, in support of the one they loved. He was sentenced to three years in prison, and every visiting day, his wife and children came, but he would not go meet them.

Another inmate saw what was happening and tried to get him to go see his family, but to no avail. Finally, he agreed to contact them, just before his release; he told them if they really wanted him to come home, to put a yellow ribbon around an old oak tree in the city square. That would be a sign for him to get off the bus. If he did not see it, then he would know they had not forgiven him.

When the bus approached the square in his hometown, he could not bear the thought of looking, so he asked the bus driver to watch for a yellow ribbon, while he buried his head in his hands. "Let me know if there is a yellow ribbon, I will know my wife has forgiven me, and I'll get off the bus.

"Mr. Bus Driver, what do you see? Is there a yellow ribbon for me?" The driver replied, "No! There is not one yellow ribbon, but hundreds—on every tree down the street, as far as I can see, and the square must have a yellow ribbon on every tree!"

He knew his wife had forgiven him and he got off the bus, and was met by the waiting arms of his wife and children and neighbors by the dozens.

The words of the song were later set to music. Tony Orlando and Dawn recorded, "Tie a Yellow Ribbon 'Round the Old Oak Tree," and it became a hit.

I'm coming home,
I've done my time.
I've got to know
What is and isn't mine.

If you received my letter
Telling you, I'd soon be free,
Then you know just what to do
If you still want me,
If you still want me.

Tie a Yellow Ribbon
'Round the ol' oak tree.
It's been three long years,
Do you still want me?
If I don't see a
Yellow Ribbon 'round the
Ol' oak tree,

I'll stay on the bus,
Forget about us –
Put the blame on me.
If I don't see a Yellow Ribbon
'round the ol' oak tree.

As we approached our driveway I had longed to see, I noticed a big sign made by members of our church, who had stood by my family and me through the whole ordeal, which read, "Welcome Home, Lambert."

As I looked up the driveway, I saw three television remote units with antennas raised high in the air. All were broadcasting live from our home. Then I noticed the huge number of friends in the yard waiting to welcome me. What a glorious sight; what a reception; what a welcome. I looked past the crowd and saw the river in front of the house for the first time in three and one-half years. I had prayed for this day and joy overflowed my heart.

People hugged and kissed me. Everyone was glad to see me, and I was thrilled to see everyone.

The news people got the first shot at me, because they were going live with the interviews. The newspaper reporter took notes and later talked with me.

When things settled down a bit, and the news people had gone, I joined a host of friends inside, around more delicious food than an army could consume. The church folk had brought all kinds of scrumptious food, and we had a feast. While my wife and Dale picked me up, dozens of people had been preparing for my homecoming.

It took a considerable period for everything to settle down. I had not seen our granddaughters yet, because Danny, their father, an attorney and a municipal judge, did not want them in the television shots or newspaper photos. The youngest one, Katie, would not have understood what was going on. Lindsay, the oldest, had been with her parents many times to visit me at Maxwell. I was anxious to see them and could hardly wait for things to quiet down so I could. It was one of the highlights of the day. There I was, AT HOME, with my family, especially those precious girls. It was shouting time on the river that afternoon.

Later in the afternoon, a federal officer came to equip me with the electronic monitoring device that allowed me movement around the place, but not off the property, except at scheduled times, like going to church, or doctor or dentist visits. The little square box sent signals to the main unit, which alerted headquarters if taken out of range. It was a little inconvenient, but not unbearable.

The officer was very cooperative and I was grateful for his understanding of the situation. I was assigned a probation officer, and had to file monthly reports for some time to come.

The next Sunday, our pastor asked me to speak, and to everyone's astonishment, Riverside Baptist Church was filled to capacity. We have not had such a crowd, since. People came from far and near to hear me speak on the subject, "Trouble, and how to deal with it." The essence of the message was that troubles come; it wasn't a matter of "if" they were coming, it was "when." Trouble comes in different shapes and forms and affects everyone in a different but definite way. You could deal with it in three ways: One, ADMIT you're in trouble. To deny trouble only makes matters worse. Two, ADJUST to trouble. Nothing remains the same. We have to adjust. Third, keep the right ATTITUDE. Attitude means everything. Trouble will make you bitter or better, and one must allow it to run its course and refine and re-focus one's thinking. The right attitude will see us through the darkest valleys. Someone once said, "To be strong in the Lord and his might, strength must be born in storm." The response was overwhelming. People were happy to see me and to know that the storm I had been through had not diminished my spirit.

Several hundred people wanted to greet me, but because of the ankle bracelet's timing, I had to exit through a side door and get home as quickly as possible.

A few Saturdays later, a large crowd came to our home for a welcome home reception. One Saturday afternoon was set aside, just for our neighbors on the street. What a joy it was to visit with them, all of them anxious to hear my experiences.

After several months, the electronic device was removed, and I was able to move freely about the area, but still had to make monthly reports to the probation officer.

My acceptance in the community and entire state was marvelous. Even folks who never voted for me or agreed with me politically were glad to see me, and many expressed how sad they were about the raw deal handed to me by the very system we all loved and cherished.

It is sad when the law is twisted and manipulated to accuse and convict innocent people; many have been ruined, and even put to death in murder cases, only to discover later that DNA did not match and investigators and prosecutors had sent the wrong person to jail or death.

Unfortunately, there is no DNA to prove anything in a case like mine. I have no anger or animosity toward those who are responsible for this travesty; I am thankful for the grace God gave me to hold my head up high.

Things have changed since I entered politics. Then, candidates never mentioned opponent's names. People running for public office talked about what they could do to improve conditions for its citizens.

Now, it's a dog eat dog thing. People will do anything to knock out competition or eliminate political opposition.

Those responsible for pressing this fictitious case know in their hearts that this case never should have been prosecuted. They contend that none of this was political; but the U.S. Attorney is now a U.S. senator, and the prosecutor is now a federal judge, appointed for life. I just pray that they have the same peace I enjoy.

I can hold my head up high. Being innocent of the violation, I had absolutely nothing of which to be ashamed. Most people knew I had been incarcerated for a crime I never committed and eagerly greeted me, expressing admiration for the way my family and I handled a devastating situation. To God be the glory. "What men meant for evil, God meant for good." To God be the glory.

Speaking engagements began to open up, and I was able to share some of my experiences in public meetings and local churches. I immediately returned to a place of leadership in the local Baptist Association, becoming Director of Men's Ministries, a position I had held for many years, previously.

I again became active in the Kiwanis Club, where I had been a member for more than forty years; and renewed my twenty-five year membership in the Masonic Lodge, where I became chaplain and was elected president of the Masonic Breakfast Club.

The Waterfront Rescue Mission wanted me back on the Advisory Board, and I later became its president as well as a member of the board that operates missions along the Gulf Coast. In addition, I became active in the Deep South region of the Antique Auto Club of America and later became president and enjoyed showing my antique Studebakers and presiding over monthly meetings.

I became involved in Team Jesus Ministries, an evangelistic organization that puts on bass fishing tournaments, reaching men who don't normally attend church services.

Of course, I returned to serving in my local church, Riverside Baptist, where I had taught Sunday school, and continue to serve as deacon, leading ministries at a local assisted living facility.

Overall, it was as if I had returned from a mission trip and picked up where I left off. There was no rehabilitation or any need for it. I had served the Lord and ministered during my incarceration. I was not, and am not, a criminal. I had never felt like a criminal, and was not about to act like one when I returned home.

The entire homecoming experience and picking up my community activities is one that most people are never fortunate enough to have. I am indeed grateful to all of the wonderful people for their acceptance, encouragement, and understanding. What a homecoming!

Chapter 37

Ready

The Apostle Paul, in II Timothy 4, stated that he was ready to be offered, to depart this world. He said, "I have fought a good fight; I have kept the faith."

It is a glorious thing to be able to say, "I am ready to be offered; I am ready to go; I am ready to depart this life."

I have had at least three occasions where I had to say, "I am ready." There was a near plane accident, heart surgery, and the multiple myeloma diagnosis.

I was in my forties when I faced a situation where I stared death in the face. It was a beautiful afternoon, and the flight to northwest Alabama was picture perfect. I was to speak at a Chamber of Commerce meeting in the tri-city area. I had mentioned this to a friend who had a new twin-engine plane and a retired Navy pilot as his pilot. He had an appointment in Memphis that evening and said he'd be delighted to drop me off at Tri-Cities Airport and pick me up on the way back. Everything went fine; the men who had invited me met me and took me to the hotel where the banquet was being held. I enjoyed visiting with my friend on the way up, and wished him well on his business endeavor in Memphis.

The Chamber crowd was gracious, the speech went well, and I returned to the airport for my trip back home. It was still a beautiful evening in north Alabama. The stars were bright and visibility was great. However, the pilot evidently misread a weather system that had moved into central Alabama.

As we approached the area south of Tuscaloosa, the weather closed in on us. The turbulence grew worse by the moment. The pilot kept his boss apprised of the situation and tried to locate a place to put the aircraft down. As he radioed various airports, he was told he couldn't land at Meridian and then he was advised it would not be safe to try to land at Selma. It was not wise to try to go back north. The only choice was to try to make it to Montgomery.

Although there are not many miles between Selma and Montgomery, it seemed we were in the air for an eternity. I have been in a few storms aboard commercial airlines, but had never witnessed anything like this.

The plane stood still, as far as forward progress was concerned. We pitched to and fro and up and down with violence I can't describe. The lightning was so fierce it was like broad daylight in the cabin. My friend, sitting across the aisle was as white as the proverbial sheet.

The pilot fought with all his might to control the plane. We saw him through the cockpit door as he wrestled with the controls. We were dropping with such tremendous force that it seemed the wings would come off at any minute. At one point, the fall was so sudden that the New Testament I carry in my shirt pocket fell out. It was an awesome ride.

Somewhere between Selma and Montgomery, the pilot stuck his head out of the cockpit door and told his boss, "I don't think we are going to make it."

I remember thinking we were going to wind up in one of the cow pastures below, at any time. The owner of the plane was horrified. No one said much, although I am positive that all three of us were praying hard.

I stared death squarely in the face. Any second could have been my last on earth. I said, "Lord, I'm ready. Thank you for your salvation and the many blessing you have bestowed upon me. It's been a great life." At forty-something, I had accomplished much more than most people ever thought about. "I've been active in your kingdom's work; you allowed me to serve as mayor of Mobile. You have given me a good family. I'm grateful.

"If this is the end, then I look forward to seeing you in a few moments. I am ready." The greatest peace came over me, and I could have floated right out of my body and on to glory that moment. This, indeed, was the most exhilarating peace I had ever experienced. It was total and complete surrender to Almighty God, and he gave me peace that passes all understanding.

The second time dealt with my heart surgery, when I underwent five bypasses. I will go into that experience and saying, "I am ready," in the next chapter.

The third time I said, "I'm ready" dealt with a rare type of cancer known as multiple mylenoma. I want to talk about how I knew I was ready on one hand, as well as not having any fear, because I had received word from the Lord that "I will not die, but live and declare the works of the Lord" (Ps 118:17). I shared my thoughts in this e-mail, sent to friends:

> I pen these comments, not as a cry for sympathy, but as words of encouragement.
>
> For more then twenty years, I have been an iron-deficient anemic. After several bypasses in 2002, my cardiologist prescribed iron capsules, which I took until recently, when I went for a check-up. He found everything positive: low cholesterol, low triglycerides. He discontinued the iron, but instructed me to go to the laboratory to have blood drawn.
>
> Three days later, I received a call from the cardiologist's office, stating that he had made an appointment for me with a hematologist to ascertain what caused my red blood count to remain low. As I drove up to the building for my appointment, the first thing I saw was "CANCER CENTER" in big, bold letters. Although I was not afraid, because "God has not given us a spirit of fear" (2 Tim. 1:7), my feet and legs were a little weak as I made my way into the building.
>
> I registered to see the new doctor. After several vials of blood were drawn and preliminary tests were made, the doctor explained that the tests pointed to something called multiple myeloma, a rare type of cancer that causes the white corpuscles to generate too many proteins in the blood. That forces the red corpuscle's count down and causes one's blood count to be off balance.
>
> I immediately rejected the thought of cancer; I was convinced that cancer would not be what took me out of this world. The next morning, during my "quiet time," the Lord gave me word that "I shall not die, but live, and declare the works of the Lord" (Ps. 118:17). That word gave me peace.

Two more tests were ordered—a bone marrow biopsy and a bone density scan. The doctor gave me three options: 1) to see the nation's foremost expert in the field of bone marrow transplants, a very expensive procedure, and because of my age, not recommended; 2) Do nothing, and take the chance of kidney failure and dialysis for the rest of my life; 3) Undertake a medication routine involving Thalidomide by capsule. This twenty-eight-day routine was supposed to bring the protein counts down and the blood count back into balance.

I chose the third option, experiencing unwavering faith as I remembered God's word to me. We praise God for doctors, nurses, and all who minister to our needs, however, I am reminded often that God said, "I am the God that heals thee" (Ex 15:26) and "By his stripes ye are healed" (1 Pet 2:24).

I trust these good doctors, but I trust God more. He is love, and "perfect love casts out fear" (1 John 4:18). Fear and faith don't abide in the same place. I remember the promises of God and anchor my faith on his word; however, there was one step more, and that was to obey his word as recorded in James 5:14-16. "Is any sick among you? Let him call for the elders of the church; and let them pray over him, anointing him with oil in the name of the Lord: and the prayer of faith shall save the sick..."

I called for the elders, the deacons at Riverside Baptist Church, and our pastor, the ordained leaders of our local congregation, in an open Sunday morning worship service to obey that portion of God's word. The men and the pastor, Eddie Holmes, gathered around me on the platform, laid hands on me and anointed me with oil, and prayed for me.

The conclusion is that I have heard the word of God, and have observed it. "His word is truth" (John 17:17). We can stand on it. I am healed, and positive, that when I return to the doctor for my check-up, my blood count will be in balance.

Be encouraged! "The word of the Lord endures forever" (1 Pet 1:25) "I shall not die, but live and declare the works of the Lord" (Ps. 118:17).

As the apostle said, I am ready, but I am still here, and I am thankful that, over the years, I've learned to obey God and grow in the grace and knowledge of Jesus Christ. In Ps. 23:4, we read, "Yea, though I walk through the valley of the shadow of death, I will fear no evil: for thou art with me; thy rod and thy staff they comfort me."

Thank God for the assurance that he walks with us through the valleys. "I am ready"—yes, but praise him, he is walking with me, and he will walk with anyone who trusts and obeys him.

I had great peace about the situation, and I am pleased to report that my blood is back to normal. Prayers have been answered, yes; but I am convinced that we must come to that place of surrender, be "ready to be offered."

Chapter 38

No More Jokes

There is one more experience in being ready that I want to share. My clothes size had increased over the years from 42 to over 48 at the waist, and 44 to 52, in my jacket. My weight jumped from 185 to 280. Sizes and weights inched up over the years while those who cared for me kept pushing me to back away from the table. Backing away from the table is hard for me, since I love country cooking—hot biscuits, pork sausage, bacon, ribs—you name it.

I have never seen a food I didn't like. I have never sat down to a meal I didn't enjoy. Home cooking, which I have been blessed with, over the years, through the good cooking of Mama and Reecie, is my favorite.

Over the years, we have dined at fancy places, here and around the country. Being active in politics and national organizations gave us the opportunity to enjoy the handiwork of some of the finest chefs in the most lavish restaurants in the country.

One of the joys of life for me was having lunch nearly every day with our two sons. Our favorite places were the down-home, country-cooking, soul food establishments like Saucy Q, Dreamland, Dew Drop, Tiny Diny, and Mattie's. The pounds and the sizes kept going up, and my agility went the other way. I couldn't do the things that had been so easy to do for so many years. A morning person for most of my years, I felt that I could attack the world everyday, as soon as I awoke. If ever there were a person that hit the floor going every morning, it was I. I knew I could not live forever, but I always felt that with those Lambert genes, I would make it to a ripe old age.

My mother lived to be ninety-five, and just played out. Her siblings all lived long lives. Their father, my grandfather, lived to be a hundred and one years old, and I thought I would, also. I have no fear of dying; that is how God arranged things. We live and die, but we can live forever. Thankfully, I took care of that when I was twenty-seven years old, on March 2, 1957.

With my history of strong genes and tremendous guts and confidence, still from time to time, the devil's subtle voice reminded me that two of my brothers had had open-heart surgery.

There were six of us—three older brothers and then three more, with me being the oldest. The oldest died at twenty-five, in an accident. The next oldest died from a stroke in his eighties. Feeling strongly about living my life out, as momma had done, that little voice of the devil reminded me constantly, "Remember, your brothers had heart surgery." I would rebuke him, and move on.

One of my favorite jokes to my wife, when she was on me about my weight, was, "Just get two more pallbearers when I die." Another of my favorite comebacks was, "There are more skinny people laid out at funeral homes than fat people; what does that tell you?"

I declare unto you that there will be NO MORE JOKES about death.

I had my wakeup call. It was real, and I hope others might learn from my experience, and extend their time and quality of life on earth.

December 12, 2002 was a normal night. What a meal! Hot biscuits, pork sausage, soupy, southern style grits, and three scrambled eggs, topped off with country syrup and biscuits. We ate, watched a little TV, and then I nodded off while Reecie perused a new cookbook put together by our church.

She was reviewing the pecan pie recipes. The more she talked about those luscious ingredients, the more I thought about the caramel pecan candies in the cabinet just above my head. I made my way to the candy jar and inhaled two of them. That was not unusual. We went to bed, snug under my electric blanket, and slept like babies until four a.m.

I woke up, and it seemed all the wheels were running off. On my stomach, I was freezing. I was jerking so bad it was amazing I hadn't fallen off the bed. I turned the blanket up, to no avail. More covers were placed on the bed, but I became colder and colder. Two hours later, I had a fever of a hundred and two degrees.

I was sick at my stomach. The past several hours had taken their toll. I was weak. My chest was tight. Tightness ran down my left arm. I was as sick as I have ever been in my life. My wife, who didn't believe in going to doctors said, "You need to get to the doctor." I argued with her. "I'll be alright. It's okay. It will pass soon." I took an antacid. I didn't get better; I felt so bad I couldn't shave.

My regular doctor was not in, so I had to see the walk-in doctor. She was a jewel, my kind of person, and a straight shooter. After the routine check, she discovered the EKG report didn't look like the last one made within the year. She said it indicated a mild heart attack and needed further evaluation by the cardiologist at the Medical Center. This stunned me.

I explained my problem. "My brother Maston is dying up in Monroe County, and I need to go to the services, which could be any day now." The doctor reared her small frame back, looked me straight in the eye, and said, "You wouldn't want to beat him to the graveyard, would you? This is serious. It could be minor, or it could carry you out. I can't let you leave without a promise that you'll go to the Heart Group, and at least get an echogram to see what is going on."

She got my attention. We went to the infirmary, where arrangements had been made. Admission details had already been handled. The nurse wheeled me to a room and a heart doctor visited me. During the process, my sciatic nerve kicked up and really gave me fits, but I endured.

The doctor took pictures of my heart and showed them to my family, deacons, friends, and me. I argued for permission to go to my brother's funeral service, while everyone told me not to go—that the delay in surgery could be fatal.

My brother did pass away and was buried while I underwent surgery. I wanted so badly to be there; he and I were only two years apart, and had many things in common. I fretted over not being able to go to his memorial service with the rest of our family, but first things were first. His wife and sons and my other brothers understood; there was nothing I could do for him, anyway. I had told him goodbye the last time I saw him, a few weeks earlier.

"Okay, let's do the heart catheter." The test took less time than the preparation, and was painless. In a few minutes, the doctor was finished and the photos printed. The surgeon and his assistant came in to explain what the photos showed, as well as each step of the procedure.

Afterwards, I looked him right in the eyes, and said, "Doc, you may be the greatest, you may have done five thousand of these, but I am a believer in Jesus Christ; I don't want anyone cutting on me who is not. Are you a believer?" "Indeed I am," he replied. With his answer, I was satisfied. We would determine what was needed, and then we would go further.

Another consultation revealed four or five blockages, some that needed immediate attention. The doctor was given the high sign, the consent forms signed, and the hair on the front part of my body began to fly.

I was carried from my family and friends, who had gathered around me, and committed to the surgeons, technicians, and all the others who now ministered to my needs. Absolute trust in God was declared, and away I went, through long corridors into a cold prep area. Blood pressure, heart rate, temperature, and every other vital sign you could imagine was checked and rechecked. They explained every step of the procedure in full detail.

The anesthesiologist explained how much gas he would administer and assured me he would be there every moment throughout the surgery.

Wheeled down another long cold corridor, I was brought into the operating room. It was awesome, with lights, equipment, tools, towels, medicine, and plenty of people.

They transferred me to the operating table, which to my surprise, was very warm. I mentioned my sciatic nerve problem and the pain I was experiencing. They told me the pain would soon be gone, and it was. The doctor told me he was ready to put me to sleep. I wanted to make sure the heart surgeon was there, and he said he was.

The last thing I remember saying was, "Dear Lord, I've confessed all my sins, and they are under the blood of Jesus Christ. If I wake up here, or with you, it will be alright." The purest peace came upon me. I had no fear whatsoever, only the glory of God. "I am ready." I added a postscript. "Lord, if possible, I would like to see my granddaughters grow up." Total peace came over me. Blessed be the name of the Lord.

In my many years as a Christian, and through many deeply spiritual encounters, this was the most blessed, the most serene, and the most holy thing I had ever experienced. It was truly from God, and his servant tasted his glory.

My family was advised at intervals as to how the surgery was progressing, and eventually the surgeon reported that five bypasses had been successfully completed. After about four hours, I was transported to room #12 SICU, where I saw Dale and his mother standing by my bedside, along with several nurses and technicians.

I remember trying to get Dale to understand that my left hand was numb. He had the left hand and Reecie had my right hand, which felt normal. I remember the hoses being removed from my throat and nostrils, which was a great relief. Those were blessed moments.

I remember seeing and conversing with my family during the eight o'clock visitation. Everyone said how well I had done, and how great the surgery had gone. The doctors, head nurses, and personnel gave me their utmost attention.

As the visiting hours ended, I grasped Dale and Reecie's hands and led a brief prayer, giving God the glory, credit, and honor for all that had been accomplished.

For the next three nights and four days, the SICU was my home. Doctors and nurses ministered with the greatest of care. I cannot express, with my limited vocabulary, my gratitude for their expertise or my appreciation to the Mobile infirmary's surgical, recovery, and nursing staffs for their good and kind attention. Everyone, from the floor, department managers, nurses, aids, and technicians, to those who cleaned the rooms were not only efficient in the administration of their duties, but exercised them with the greatest desire to make me well and see that I was comfortable.

On Friday afternoon, late, I was assigned a room. I had visitors waiting for me. Reecie stayed with me and helped me maneuver to the bathroom a few times. By now, only a few wires were connected to me, and getting up and down and walking was easier. Having been gotten up, to sit in a chair the morning after surgery, was very helpful when I arrived in my room.

On Saturday morning, I was able to get a long-awaited shower and go home. What a beautiful day; Dog River had never looked so good. The sky was blue, the river rippled, the birds sang—what a glorious day! I had said, "I am ready to be offered," but I was thankful that God had allowed this second great homecoming.

There would be no more jokes about getting more pallbearers when I die. Those days are over. Praise the Lord!

Chapter 39

Regrets Overshadowed
By Pride

It has been a long and exciting journey; it has taken me a long way from the cotton patch, but it's been an example of survival of the many bumps along life's highway. It has been a journey of storms and troubled seas, but I have learned to do what Ralph Cushman put forth in his very beautiful poem "In the Morning."

I met God in the morning,
When my day was at its best
And His presence came like sunshine
Like a glory in my breast.

All day long the Presence lingered,
All day long He stayed with me.
And we sailed with perfect calmness
O'er a very troubled sea.

Other ships were blown and battered
Other ships were sore distressed.
But the winds that seemed to drive them
Brought to us a peace and rest,
Then I thought of other mornings,
With a keen remorse of mind,
When I, too, had loosed the moorings
With the Presence left behind.

So I think I know the secret
Learned from many a troubled way.
You must seek God in the morning
If you want him through the day.

His presence sees us through, and by his grace, we are able to use the bumps along life's highway as stepping-stones to a better and more productive life.

The cotton rows of my youth were long; plowing with the mules up one side of the row and down the other sometimes became tedious. The journey back and forth, all day long, was tiring, yet exciting, as I observed nature and God's wonderful creations, like the blue sky, green trees, plants, and growing crops, the cattle and wild animals, the sunrises and sunsets, the rainbows and much more.

Life, in its entirety, has been exciting, even with its vicissitudes, disappointments, and even disasters, as well as the stress connected with being a public official and in the spotlight much of my adult life.

Some have asked about regrets. "What are your deepest regrets?" Although my early years involved things I am not proud of, such as drinking, smoking, carousing, fast cars, partying, and playing, they brought me to a point where my life changed to a more purposeful and useful existence, I do have deep regrets.

One of my regrets is the wasted years as a young adult. If I could change anything, I would remake some of those decisions. There's no telling what I might have been able to do for my fellow man, and God, if I had not wasted those ten years. If only I had begun my mission earlier.

Another is that I didn't spend more time with my family. When our sons were growing up, I was so busy serving the public that I lost out on many blessings of being with them. Early risings and late night meetings, just passing, in coming and going, cheated me out of so much. If I had it to do over, it would be different. Instead of depending on their mother, the teachers, the Sunday school leaders, the little league, and high school coaches, I would try to be there, involved with them.

I went to lots of games. They both played basketball, football, and baseball. Their coaches did great jobs, for which I am most grateful, but Daddy was not there. They both like to fish and hunt, but Daddy didn't teach them. This I regret very deeply. They both turned out to be good men, and I am proud of them, but look what Daddy missed. Their mother did a tremendous job raising them while Daddy was busy working, traveling, speaking, and leading in civic and community affairs.

I remember one day, near Danny's high school graduation, I was to go to the honors ceremony at his school. Just as I was leaving my office at city hall, someone walked in. "Can I have just a minute?" Minutes multiplied, and then it was too late to get to the program. When I got home that night, Danny showed me several plaques he had received and asked why I wasn't at the awards ceremony. I dropped my head and cried like a baby. I had failed my own son while trying to help others.

I regret not spending more time with my sons, and I regret not taking more time for family. Although I spent time with my parents in their declining years and had some precious moments with them, I regret not respecting and honoring them more when I was younger. Young reader, listen to me—you will not know how much your parents mean to you until they are gone, so show your love, honor, and respect while you can, while they are with you.

Another of my regrets is feeling that I have not reached my full potential as a parent, a public official, a businessman, or a churchman. My gifts are numerous, my talents vast; yet I feel that I have just tapped into what I could have been. On the other hand, regardless of our age, accomplishments, or failures, I am convinced that the best is yet to come.

The regret of all regrets, I suppose, has to do with my legacy. I hope that my incarceration doesn't overshadow all the good I tried to do, or all the hard work and concern for my community over the years.

It's a shame that a few people can take the law that is supposed to protect us, and twist it with falsehoods and innuendos, and destroy good reputations and careers. It's done every day. They will answer to a higher court, someday.

Regardless of what some might think or say, God knows the truth, I know the truth, and in the end, he gets the glory. "What they meant for evil, God meant for good."

Others ask, "Of what are you most proud?" It is a good question, and it could take volumes to record my response. First, I am proud of my heritage, of being from a family who, on both sides, helped forge our great country, in some cases, giving their lives. I am proud of being brought up on the farm, taught to work hard, do a good day's work for a good day's pay, and to be honest and treat others as I would want to be treated.

There is nothing like waking up to roosters crowing, cows mooing, birds singing, and the smell of fresh-plowed ground and the fragrance of spring flowers. There is nothing like looking out of the window, across fields of growing, blooming, cotton plants and seeing the sun come up in the morning, or the smoke softy settling on the farm houses in the evening, the aroma of biscuits baking and pork frying, as the sun settles into the west. That's country living, something all boys and girls should be able to experience.

I am proud to have owned a business at a young age and come to the big city and been elected commissioner/mayor, against all odds, in my first try for political office. I am extremely proud of twenty years of continuous service and my accomplishments in community progress, public improvement projects, and programs too numerous to mention. Much of the infrastructure put in place during those years have been the foundation for the great growth of the city today.

I am proud of a beautiful park in the western part of the city that bears my name, and the street that leads to it, Dandale Drive, named for our sons.

I am proud—a better word would be grateful—for the opportunities to serve in the local church, denominational, and interdenominational groups. To be ordained a deacon and serve as Sunday school teacher, men's director and just about every other place of leadership in the local church, has been a great privilege.

To have opportunity to speak in many laymen-led revivals and weekend retreats, to be a part of mission trips to California and Northern Ohio, are unforgettable experiences.

Prison gave me many opportunities to serve the Lord, for which I am deeply grateful.

I am proud of my achievements, such as winning sales contests, obtaining trophies, awards, and accolades. I am proud to have had the opportunity to meet presidents, governors, ambassadors, and leaders from other countries along with the privilege to serve as president of numerous national and state organizations.

It is hard to believe a timid farm boy from the cotton patch was afforded the privilege and opportunity to address conventions, churches, crusades, rallies, governor's prayer breakfast meetings, and so on, across the country. For this, I am both proud and humbled.

It's been a long, bumpy road from that cotton patch, but with God's grace, a lot of grit and determination, and a lot of guts, I am proud to say it has been an honor to serve God, country, family, and my fellow man.

I am reminded of a story I heard of a little boy and his sister, who were climbing an unusually rocky path up a mountainside. The sister began to complain about the rocks and the bumps and the hard time she was having keeping up with her brother. She kept complaining, until her brother said, "Aw, come on, sis; bumps are what people climb on."

The bumps along my road have, at times, been tough. There have been troubles, trials, and temptations. There were times when it seemed I was on a fence or a wall, facing temptations that have taken many mighty leaders down, but thanks be to God, I was able to come down on the side of right. Those bumps could have thrown me for a loop, but I have learned that they truly do serve as stepping-stones, and opportunities for personal and professional growth.

From plowboy, to peddler, to politician, to president of prestigious organizations, to prison, I am convinced that "all things work together for good to those that love the Lord and who are called according to his purpose" (Rom 8:28). I can say with Andre Crouch, as he put it so meaningfully in his song, "Through it All" —

I thank God for the mountains
And I thank Him for the valleys;
I thank Him for the storms He brought me through;
For if I'd never had a problem,
I wouldn't know that He could solve them;
I'd never know what faith in God could do.

I've had many tears and sorrows;
I've had questions for tomorrow;
There've been times I didn't know right from wrong.
But in ev'ry situation
God gave blessed consolation
That my trials come to only make me strong.
Through it all, through it all,
(Oh,) I've learned to trust in Jesus; I've learned to trust in God.
Through it all, through it all,
I've learned to depend upon His word.

Mama and Daddy are gone, but I remember, and have never forgotten, the line uttered on television the night of my very first campaign victory. "I'm a long way from the cotton patch." Thank God, I am still a MAYOR ON MISSION.

Whatever your path may be, whatever your mission, whatever your goal, so long as it is honorable and God honoring, keep the faith, let the bumps be what you climb on. Keep on climbing, and stay on mission.

God will never leave nor forsake you! STAY ON MISSION.

Appendix

[DO NOT PUBLISH]

IN THE UNITED STATES COURT OF APPEALS

FOR THE ELEVENTH CIRCUIT

No. 90-7436

D. C. Docket No. CR89-00105-B

UNITED STATES OF AMERICA,

Plaintiff-Appellee,

versus

LAMBERT C. MIMS,

Defendant-Appellant.

Appeal from the United States District Court
for the Southern District of Alabama

(February 26, 1996)
ON REMAND FROM THE SUPREME COURT
OF THE UNITED STATES

Before BIRCH, DUBINA and BLACK, Circuit Judges.

PER CURIAM:

No.

IN THE

Supreme Court of the United States

OCTOBER TERM, 2001

LAMBERT C. MIMS,
Petitioner,

--against--

UNITED STATES OF AMERICA,
Respondent.

ON PETITION FOR A WRIT OF CERTIORARI
TO THE UNITED STATES COURT OF
APPEALS FOR THE ELEVENTH CIRCUIT

PETITION FOR A WRIT OF CERTIORARI

NATHAN Z. DERSHOWITZ
DERSHOWITZ, EIGER &
ADELSON, P.C.
350 Fifth Avenue, Suite 7912
NEW YORK, NY 10118
(212) 967-0667
COUNSEL OF RECORD

AMY ADELSON
Of Counsel

Attorneys for Petitioner
LAMBERT C. MIMS

QUESTIONS PRESENTED FOR REVIEW

I.   Whether, under the Hobbs Act, a "quid pro quo" is a requirement of extortion "under color of official right" in cases that do not involve campaign contributions, and, if so, whether the jury must be charged that, to convict, it must find that payments have been made in return for an explicit promise or undertaking by the official to perform or not to perform an official act.

II.   Whether a Local Rule of the federal Court of Appeals that provides that unpublished opinions have no precedential effect violates Article III of the United States Constitution.

· i

TABLE OF CONTENTS

ii

APPENDIX

TABLE OF AUTHORITIES

CASES

CONSTITUTION, STATUTES AND RULES

v

OTHER AUTHORITIES

.

OPINIONS BELOW

The opinion of the United States Court of Appeals for the Eleventh Circuit is unpublished, and is set forth in the appendix at App. 1.

JURISDICTION OF THIS COURT

The judgment of the Court of Appeals for the Eleventh Circuit was entered on April 30, 2001. (App. 1) A petition for rehearing and suggestion for rehearing en banc was denied by order entered on July 27, 2001. (App. 3) This Court has jurisdiction to review the judgment of the Court of Appeals pursuant to 28 U.S.C. § 1284.

CONSTITUTIONAL PROVISIONS AND STATUTES INVOLVED

Article III, § 1, cl. 1, of the United States Constitution, provides:

> The judicial Power of the United States, shall be vested in one supreme Court, and in such inferior Courts as the Congress may from time to time ordain and establish.

The Hobbs Act, 18 U.S.C. § 1951, provides in pertinent part:

> (a) Whoever in any way or degree obstructs, delays, or affects commerce or the movement of any article or commodity in commerce, by robbery or extortion or attempts or conspires so to do, or commits or threatens physical violence to any person or property in furtherance of a plan or purpose to do anything in violation of this section shall be fined not more than $10,000 or

1

imprisoned not more than twenty years, or both.

(b) As used in this section . . .

(2) The term "extortion" means the obtaining of property from another, with his consent, induced by wrongful use of actual or threatened force, violence, or fear, or under color of official right.

Local Rule 36-2 of the Rules of the Eleventh Circuit provides:

An opinion shall be unpublished unless a majority of the panel decides to publish it. Unpublished opinions are not considered binding precedent. They may be cited as persuasive authority, provided that a copy of the unpublished opinion is attached to or incorporated within the brief, petition, motion or response in which such citation is made.

STATEMENT OF THE CASE

Petitioner Lambert Mims is a former Mayor of the City of Mobile, Alabama, who for twenty years served as a member of the City Commission and as the Public Works Commissioner. In 1989, Mims, who was in the midst of a mayoral election campaign, was charged in three counts of a thirty-five count superseding indictment. In 1990, he was convicted of two counts of violating the Hobbs Act, 18 U.S.C. § 1951. Mims was sentenced (pre-Guidelines) to two ten years terms of imprisonment to be served concurrently.

The relevant facts are as follows:

In the late 1970s and early 1980s, because of skyrocketing oil prices, the City of Mobile was contemplating a

2

steam generator plant that would convert garbage into steam energy. To be economically feasible, there had to be a purchaser for the steam generated by the plant, and the City and County of Mobile had to provide sufficient solid wastes for use as fuel. (R10-82-85)[1]

In October, 1983, the City publicly announced that it would accept proposals for building and operating a steam plant. (R10-164-65) Gerald Godwin, who had been pursuing a garbage-to-steam proposal for some time, formed Area Services, Inc. ("ASI"), and submitted a proposal that set forth his plan to use Degussa Corporation as the steam purchaser.[2] ASI was a shell corporation – no stock was issued, and it had no bank accounts and no assets other than a non-exclusive, contingent contract to supply steam to Degussa. (R11-422, 454; R12-320-21, 796-97; R13-900-01)

The City received a number of proposals, which were opened on November 7, 1983. Although ASI was the apparent low bidder, an independent professional engineering firm the City had hired to evaluate the steam plant proposals reported that an even better proposal had been submitted by a company called Alabama Energy Recovery, Inc. ("AER") (R15-1633, 1685) AER was owned by a co-defendant in this case, Charles Shaw, a local businessman who had been friends with Commissioner Mims for years and had been awarded other City contracts. (R30-6143)

---

[1] The references to "R" are to the record in the earlier appeal of Mims's conviction, which was made part of the record on appeal in this case.

[2] Godwin had sought and obtained an introduction to Commissioner Mims, and the two men began an acquaintance that lasted many years.

3

The AER proposal set forth a plan to locate a steam plant at Stone Container Corp., which was financially attractive because, unlike Degussa, Stone Container was centrally located within the City of Mobile. As a result, transport costs would be much lower. (R12-890-92; R13-1093-97; R15-1164-67)

In their proposals, both Shaw and Godwin had named the construction company of another co-defendant, Ellis McDonald, as the company that would build the plant. (R12-780)

According to the government, the alleged extortion took place at a meeting on December 8, 1983. At that meeting, according to Godwin, McDonald introduced Godwin to Shaw, and allegedly told both men that if a steam plant was going to be built, he was going to build it. McDonald then advised the two men that they should work out the arrangements. After this "introduction," according to Godwin, Shaw insisted that Godwin transfer to him 50% of ASI. (R11-430-31; R12-791-95) Mims was not present at this meeting and there was no evidence that he was aware of it. As Godwin readily admitted, his name was not even mentioned. (R11-432-35; R14-1238)

Over the next few weeks, Godwin attempted to convince both Shaw and Mims that AER's proposal was not feasible. Mims allowed AER until February 1, 1984 to put the project together. In the meantime, in January, 1984, Godwin transferred an interest in ASI to Shaw. (R11-452-457; R12-632-33)

The crux of the case against Mims rested on Godwin's testimony about a second lunch meeting that took place on either January 30, 1984 or February 2, 1984. Godwin testified that at this luncheon Mims asked both him and Shaw if their business was worked out. Both said that it was. Mims then asked Shaw to send a letter advising the City that Stone Container would not be the steam purchaser and that the contract should go to ASI. (R11-460-61)

4

Godwin did not testify that Mims ever told him he had to do business with Shaw in order to obtain the contract with the City, or that Shaw ever told him that he had to transfer an interest in ASI in order to secure Mims's approval. Nor did Godwin testify that Mims explicitly promised him anything or that Mims personally obtained anything from Godwin or from anyone else in connection with the steam plant proposal.

On March 2, 1984, the City gave Godwin a letter of intent. (R10-168-69; R11-47) Ultimately, however, the City of Mobile never awarded a contract to any company because oil prices dropped and the proposal for a steam plant was no longer economically desirable. (R10-106-08; R12-629)

In 1993, the Court of Appeals for the Eleventh Circuit, in an unpublished opinion, affirmed Mims's conviction. United States v. McDonald, 12 F.3d 217 (11th Cir. 1993) (sub nom.) (Table, No. 90-7436). Shortly thereafter, the Eleventh Circuit decided United States v. Martinez, 14 F.3d 543 (11th Cir. 1994), holding that a "quid pro quo" is a requirement in all Hobbs Act cases involving extortion "under color of official right." Mims promptly alerted the Court to the importance of that decision to his conviction, but his petition for rehearing and rehearing en banc was denied.

This Court granted a petition for a writ of certiorari on another issue, vacating the judgment and conviction, and remanding for further consideration. Mims v. United States, 513 U.S. 1107 (1995). On remand, Mims again raised the conflict between the decision in his case and the Eleventh Circuit's decision in Martinez, and in United States v. Davis, 30 F.3d 108 (11th Cir. 1994), which reaffirmed that a jury must be instructed on the "quid pro quo" requirement. The Eleventh Circuit again affirmed the conviction, in an unpublished opinion. United States v. McDonald, 79 F.3d 1158 (11th Cir. 1996) (sub nom.) (Table, No. 90-7436). Certiorari was denied. Mims v. United States, 517 U.S. 1246 (1996).

5

On June 6, 1997, Mims commenced an action, pursuant to 18 U.S.C. § 2255, to vacate and set aside his conviction. On September, 9, 1997, the District Court denied the petition; on December 12, 1997, the District Court denied a motion for reconsideration.

On April 30, 2001, the Eleventh Circuit, again by unpublished opinion, affirmed. Mims sought rehearing, once again specifically raising the conflict between the unpublished opinion in his case and the Eleventh Circuit's published opinions in <u>Martinez</u> and <u>Davis</u>. Mims also challenged the constitutionality of the Eleventh Circuit's rule providing that unpublished opinions have no precedential effect.

On July 27, 2001, Mims's petition for rehearing and rehearing en banc was denied.

<u>REASONS FOR GRANTING THE WRIT</u>

I.   CERTIORARI SHOULD BE GRANTED TO RESOLVE A CONFLICT IN THE CIRCUITS OVER WHAT CONSTITUTES EXTORTION "UNDER COLOR OF OFFICIAL RIGHT"

The jury in this case was never told that to convict Mims of extortion "under color of official right" it had to find a "quid pro quo," or, more particularly, that it had to find that Mims obtained property in return for a promise to take or not to take official action. In essence, Mims, who did not ask for or receive any payments from Godwin or anyone else, was convicted of extortion because, according to the government's theory of the case, he helped steer a potential government contract to a friend.

While this case is extreme, the proper reach of the Hobbs Act has plagued the federal courts since the early 1970s, when

6

the government first began aggressively using the Hobbs Act to attack public corruption at the state and local levels. <u>See</u> <u>generally</u> Ruff, <u>Federal Prosecution of Local Corruption: A Case</u> <u>Study in the Making of Law Enforcement Policy</u>, 65 Geo. L. J. 1171 (1977). This Court has twice addressed the scope of the "official right" prong of the Hobbs Act, but many questions remain unanswered and the Circuit Courts, and, as this case demonstrates, even different Panels within a single Circuit, have decided these questions in conflicting ways.

In <u>McCormick v. United States</u>, 500 U.S. 257 (1991), this Court held that a public official does not commit extortion "under color of official right" when he accepts a campaign contribution unless the government proves an explicit quid pro quo. Receiving a contribution is a crime only **"if the payments are made in return for an explicit promise or undertaking by the official to perform or not to perform an official act."** <u>Id</u>. at 272. (Emphasis added)

The following year, in <u>Evans v. United States</u>, 504 U.S. 255 (1992), the Court held that "inducement" is not an element of the crime of extortion "under color of official right." The Court then affirmed the defendant's conviction despite jury instructions that did not incorporate the "explicit promise" language of <u>McCormick</u>, explaining that, "the Government need only show that a public official has obtained a payment to which he was not entitled, knowing that the payment was made in return for official acts." <u>Id.</u> at 268.

<u>McCormick</u> and <u>Evans</u> did not resolve whether the "quid pro quo" requirement is an element of "official right" extortion in cases, such as this one, that do not involve campaign contributions. Moreover, <u>Evans</u> raised questions about what the Court meant by the "explicit promise" language employed in

7

McCormick, and it left open whether the "quid pro quo" requirement is satisfied, even absent an "explicit promise" to perform or refrain from performing an official act, if the jury finds the defendant "knew" a benefit was being extended in exchange for official action. See Yarbrough, The Hobbs Act in the Nineties: Confusion or Clarification of the Quid Pro Quo Standard in Extortion Cases Involving Public Officials, 31 Tulsa L.J. 781 (Summer 1996).

After McCormick and Evans, the lower courts have grappled with how to treat "official right" Hobbs Act cases, particularly those, like Petitioner's, that do not involve campaign contributions. A conflict in the Circuits has developed, and, as this case vividly illustrates, even within a Circuit there is no consistent approach to what a jury must find before it convicts of "official right" extortion.

The Eleventh Circuit, at least until the unpublished decision in this case, has required that, in all "official right" cases the jury be told that it must find an "explicit promise" by the public official. United States v. Martinez 14 F.3d 543 (11th Cir. 1994); United States v. Davis, 967 F.2d 516 (11th Cir. 1992), on rehearing, 30 F.3d 108 (11th Cir. 1994). Indeed, in Davis, decided after Evans, the Court held that **"an explicit promise by a public official to act or not act is an essential element of Hobbs Act extortion, and the defendant is entitled to a reasonably clear jury instruction to that effect."** 30 F.3d at 108. (Emphasis added)

Other Circuits have disagreed, holding that, at least in non-campaign contribution cases, a "quid pro quo," to the extent it is required, may be implicit – that the jury need not be instructed that it must find an "explicit promise" by the public official. United States v. Giles, 246 F.3d 966 (7th Cir. 2001);

8

United States v. Bradley, 173 F.3d 225, 231 (3d Cir.), corrected by, 188 F.3d 98 (3d Cir.), cert. denied, 528 U.S. 963 (1999); United States v. Tucker, 133 F.3d 1208 (9th Cir. 1998); United States v. Delano, 55 F.3d 720 (2d Cir. 1991); Hairston v. United States, 46 F.3d 361 (4th Cir.), cert. denied, 516 U.S. 840 (1995). And the Sixth Circuit has held that, even in campaign contribution cases, Evans modifies McCormick, and that the "explicit promise" seemingly required by McCormick can be satisfied by a mere showing of "knowledge." United States v. Blandford, 33 F.3d 685, 696-97 (6th Cir. 1994), cert. denied, 514 U.S. 1095 (1995). See also United States v. Collins, 78 F.3d 1021 (6th Cir.), cert. denied, 519 U.S. 872 (1996) (extending this rule to non-campaign contribution cases).

The confusion over just what is required to convict a defendant of "official act" extortion has created conflict, not only among the Circuits, but within individual Circuits as well. This case makes that clear. In Martinez, the Eleventh Circuit, construing Evans as adopting the "explicit promise" requirement of McCormick, reversed the defendant's conviction because the jury charge did not adequately convey the "quid pro quo" requirement. Id. at 553.[3]

---

[3] In Martinez, the jury was instructed:

Extortion also includes the wrongful acquisition of property from someone else under color of official right.

Extortion under color of official right is the wrongful taking by a public official of money or property not due to him or his office, whether or not the taking was accomplished by force, threats or use of fear. In other words, the wrongful use

9

The charge in this case was virtually identical to the charge given to the jury in <u>Martinez</u>,[4] as the government frankly

---

> of otherwise valid official power, may convert lawful action into extortion.
>
> So, if a public official threatens or agrees to take or withhold official action for the wrongful purpose of inducing a victim to part with property, such action would constitute extortion even though the official was already duty bound to take or withhold the action in question.
>
> Acceptance by an elected official of economic benefits does not in itself constitute a violation of federal law, even though the giver of the benefit has business pending before the official.
>
> However, passive acceptance of a benefit by a public official is sufficient to form the basis of an extortion violation, if the official knows he had been offered the payment in exchange for the exercise of his office power, or that such payment is motivated by hope of influence.

14 F.3d at 552.

> [4] Here, the jury was instructed:
>
> "Extortion" also includes the wrongful acquisition of property from someone else under color of official right.
>
> Extortion "under color of official right" is the wrongful taking by a public officer of money or property not due him or his office, whether or not

10

acknowledged in its Brief in Opposition to Mims's Petition for a Writ of Certiorari during the direct appeal process, arguing to this Court that "any tension between the Eleventh Circuit's unpublished decision in this case and its later decision in Martinez is for that court to resolve." (Brief in Opposition at 12, n. 5) Yet, in this case, the Eleventh Circuit, without any explanation, and without citation to Martinez, ruled that the instruction in this case "adequately charged the 'Quid Pro Quo' element of the Hobbs Act offense." (Add. 2) Consequently, what is required now in the Eleventh Circuit, in light of this conflict, is far from clear.

Undoubtedly, there will continue to be inconsistent rulings on what is required to prove extortion "under color of official right." Whether McCormick/Evans apply to non-campaign contribution cases, whether the "explicit promise" requirement of McCormick is limited to campaign contribution cases, or whether that requirement, even in campaign contribution cases, survived Evans remain open questions.

---

the taking was accomplished by force, threats, or use of fear. The wrongful use of otherwise valid official power may convert lawful action into unlawful extortion. So, if a public official misuses his office by threatening to take or withhold official action for the wrongful purpose of inducing a victim to part with property, such a threat would constitute extortion even through [sic] the official was already duty bound to take or withhold the action in questions.

"Wrongful" means to obtain property unfairly and unjustly by one having no lawful claim to it.

11

The elements of this extraordinarily important and far-reaching federal criminal statute should not depend on the jurisdiction or on the particular Panel that hears a particular appeal within a jurisdiction. This Court should grant review in this case to resolve the conflict and finally decide what the government must prove in "official right" Hobbs Act cases.

II.   CERTIORARI SHOULD BE GRANTED TO DECIDE THE IMPORTANT QUESTION OF WHETHER CIRCUIT COURT RULES THAT LIMIT THE PRECEDENTIAL EFFECT OF UNPUBLISHED OPINIONS VIOLATE ARTICLE III OF THE CONSTITUTION

Virtually every federal Court of Appeals has some rule addressing unpublished opinions. The rules vary, although most, in one form or another, deprive unpublished opinions of precedential effect, or, at a minimum, afford them "disfavored" status. See D.C. Cir. LR 28(c); First Circuit LR 36.2(6); Third Circuit IOP 5.3; Fourth Circuit LR 36(c); Fifth Circuit LR 47.5.3 et seq.; Sixth Circuit LR 28(g); Seventh Circuit LR 53(b); Eighth Circuit LR 28A(i); Ninth Circuit LR 36-1 et seq.; Tenth Circuit LR 36-3(A); Eleventh Circuit LR 36-2; Fed. Cir. LR 47.6(b).

A rule that deprives unpublished opinions of precedential effect encourages opinions that contain little or no reasoning, and that may be, or may appear to be, in conflict with published opinions. This, in turn, creates the appearance, if not the reality, of a dual system of laws: published opinions that supposedly have precedential effect and purport to provide a governing body of law, and unpublished opinions, an "underground" and often "secret" body of laws, that apply only to the litigants involved in the unpublished opinion. Litigants seeking appellate review may

12

well question which set of laws will apply to them.

Moreover, a rule that deprives unpublished opinions of precedential effect may also create a "shadow body of law." Unpublished opinions, as a practical matter, are unavailable to many litigants. Some litigants and some judges, however, will have access to those opinions and they may become a powerful indicator of how a Court, in practical terms, is treating a particular precedent, and may influence future decisions of the Court. Yet some litigants before the Court may be unaware of the existence of this anonymous body of law. See, e g., Carpenter, The No-Citation Rule for Unpublished Opinions: Do the Ends of Expediency for Overloaded Appellate Courts Justify the Means of Secrecy?, 50 S.C.L. Rev. 235 (1998).

This case illustrates this problem. The opinion of the Eleventh Circuit in this case (and, in all of the prior opinions rendered in this case) is stamped with the directive, "Do Not Publish."[5] As a result, the decision in the case, upholding a jury instruction virtually identical to the instruction struck down in Martinez, is technically unavailable to litigants. Nevertheless, some prosecutors and some District Court judges will know of

---

[5] Local Rule 36-2 of the Rules of the Eleventh Circuit provides:

> An opinion shall be unpublished unless a majority of the panel decides to publish it. Unpublished opinions are not considered binding precedent. They may be cited as persuasive authority, provided that a copy of the unpublished opinion is attached to or incorporated within the brief, petition, motion or response in which such citation is made.

13

the decision and may rely on it in formulating jury instructions under the Hobbs Act. Others may not be aware of the decision. Consequently, it is unclear whether the rule announced in Martinez and Davis requiring that a jury be instructed that it must find an "explicit promise" will be followed by some judges, or whether some judges will view the unpublished decision in this case as modifying the Martinez/Davis rule, or whether, for some reason, Mims alone will not be entitled to the benefit of the Martinez/Davis rule.

Recently, a panel of the Eighth Circuit, in an opinion written by Justice Richard Arnold, after conducting a searching examination of its own similar "not for publication" rule, and of the history of the "doctrine of precedent," concluded that requiring adherence to precedent was essential to the separation of legislative and judicial power, and that a rule that limits the precedential effect of judicial opinions violates Article III of the Constitution. Anastasoff v. United States, 223 F.3d 898 (8th Cir.), vacated on rehearing en banc on other grounds, 235 F.3d 1054 (8th Cir. 2000). Rehearing en banc was granted to address the continuing validity of the unpublished opinion that was involved in the merits of the case. Although the decision was vacated as moot, with a note that the constitutionality of the Eighth Circuit Local Rule remained an open question, 235 F.3d at 1056, Judge Arnold's scholarly opinion remains persuasive. See Williams v. Dallas Area Rapid Transit, 256 F.3d 260 (5th Cir. 2001) (Smith, J., Jones, J., and DeMoss, J., dissenting from denial of petition for rehearing en banc) (arguing for en banc consideration of constitutionality of no citation rule). See also Price, Precedent and Judicial Power After the Founding, 42 B.C.L. Rev. 81 (2000); Merritt & Brudney, Stalking Secret Law: What Predicts Publication in the United States Courts of Appeals, 54 Vand. L. Rev. 71 (2001) But see Hart v. Massanari, 2001 WL 1111647 (9th Cir. 2001) (rejecting reasoning of

14

Anastasoff).

Unpublished opinions now account for nearly 80% of all dispositions on the merits in the Courts of Appeals, with wide variations in publication rates among the Circuits, and even among different Judges. Merritt & Brudney, supra, at 72, 112-113. The proliferation of unpublished opinions may well be an unavoidable consequence of an overburdened judiciary. But, as Justice Arnold observed in the panel decision in Anastasoff, whether or not an opinion is published should not be determinative of whether or not it is to be given precedential effect.

We urge this Court to take this opportunity to grant review to address the very important and much debated question of whether local rules that limit the precedential effect of unpublished opinions comport with the doctrine of separation of powers and with Article III of the Constitution.

CONCLUSION

For the foregoing reasons, the Petition for a Writ of Certiorari should be granted.

Respectfully submitted,

Nathan Z. Dershowitz
Dershowitz, Eiger & Adelson, P.C.
350 Fifth Avenue, Suite 7912
New York, NY 10118
Counsel of Record

Amy Adelson
Of Counsel

15

[DO NOT PUBLISH]

IN THE UNITED STATES COURT OF APPEALS
FOR THE ELEVENTH CIRCUIT

No. 98-6092

D.C. Docket No. 97-00515-CV-CB-M

Filed
U.S. Court of Appeals
Eleventh Circuit
APR 30, 2001
Thomas K. Kahn
Clerk

LAMBERT C. MIMS,

versus   Petitioner-Appellant,

UNITED STATES OF AMERICA,

Respondent-Appellee.

No. 98-6932

D.C. Docket No. 97-00515-CV-CB-M

UNITED STATES OF AMERICA,

versus   Respondent-Appellee,

LAMBERT C. MIMS,

Petitioner-Appellant.

App. 1

Appeals from the United States District Court
for the Southern District of Alabama

(April 30, 2001)

Before DUBINA and KRAVITCH, Circuit Judges and
DUPLANTIER*, District Judge.

PER CURIAM:

This is an appeal from the district court's order denying
appellant Lambert C. Mims's ("Mims") motion to vacate, set
aside, or correct sentence brought under 28 U.S.C. § 2255. We
granted a certificate of appealability on one issue only: did the
district court's instructions to the jury sufficiently charge the
"Quid Pro Quo" element of the Hobbs Act offense, and if not,
was any resulting error harmless?

After reviewing the record, and specifically after
reviewing the district court's jury instructions pertaining to
extortion, we conclude that the instructions adequately charged
the "Quid Pro Quo" element of the Hobbs Act offense. *See
generally McCormick v. U.S.*, 500 U.S. 257 (1991); *United
States v. Evans*, 504 U.S. 255 (1992); *United States v. Davis*, 30
F.3d 108 (11th Cir. 1994).

Accordingly, we affirm the district court's judgment
denying Mims's § 2255 motion.

AFFIRMED.

---

* Honorable Adrian G. Duplantier, U.S. District Judge
for the Eastern District of Louisiana, sitting by designation.

App. 2

IN THE UNITED STATES COURT OF APPEALS
FOR THE ELEVENTH CIRCUIT

NO. 98-6092-CC & 98-6932-CC

Filed
U.S. Court of Appeals
Eleventh Circuit
Jul 27 2001
Thomas K. Kahn
Clerk

LAMBERT C. MIMS,

                    Petitioner-Appellant,

versus

UNITED STATES OF AMERICA,

                    Respondent-Appellee.

On Appeal from the United States District Court for the
Southern District of Alabama

ON PETITION(S) FOR REHEARING AND PETITION(S) FOR
REHEARING EN BANC
(Opinion _____, 11th Cir., 19___, ___ F.2d ___).

Before: DUBINA and KRAVITCH, Circuit Judges and
DUPLANTIER*, District Judge.

PER CURIAM:

The Petition(s) for Rehearing are DENIED and no member of
this panel nor other Judge in regular active service on the Court
having requested that the Court be polled on rehearing en banc

App. 3

(Rule 35, Federal Rules of Appellate Procedure; Eleventh Circuit Rule 35-5), the Petition(s) for Rehearing En Banc are DENIED.

ENTERED FOR THE COURT:

_____/S/_____
UNITED STATES DISTRICT JUDGE

ORD-42
(6/95)

*Honorable Adrian G. Duplantier, U.S. District Judge for the Eastern District of Louisiana, sitting by designation.

App. 4